The Politics of Modern Central America

This book analyzes the origins and consequences of civil war in Central America. Fabrice Lehoucq argues that the inability of autocracies to reform themselves led to protest and rebellion throughout the twentieth century and that civil war triggered unexpected transitions to nonmilitary rule by the 1990s. He explains how armed conflict led to economic stagnation and why weak states limit democratization – outcomes that unaccountable party systems have done little to change. This book also uses comparisons among Central American cases – and between them and other parts of the developing world – to shed light on core debates in comparative politics and comparative political economy. It suggests that the most progress has been made in understanding the persistence of inequality and the nature of political market failures; it draws lessons from the Central American cases to improve explanations of regime change and the outbreak of civil war.

Fabrice Lehoucq is Associate Professor in the Department of Political Science at the University of North Carolina, Greensboro. He is the author of articles that have appeared in *Comparative Political Studies*, *Comparative Politics*, and the *Journal of Democracy*, among others, and he has published several books, including (with Iván Molina) *Stuffing the Ballot Box: Fraud, Democratization, and Electoral Reform in Costa Rica*.

D1613531

The Politics of Modern Central America

Civil War, Democratization, and Underdevelopment

FABRICE LEHOUCQ
University of North Carolina, Greensboro

CAMBRIDGE UNIVERSITY PRESS
Cambridge, New York, Melbourne, Madrid, Cape Town,
Singapore, São Paulo, Delhi, Mexico City

Cambridge University Press
32 Avenue of the Americas, New York, NY 10013-2473, USA

www.cambridge.org
Information on this title: www.cambridge.org/9780521730792

First published 2012

Printed in the United States of America

A catalog record for this publication is available from the British Library.

Library of Congress Cataloging in Publication data
Lehoucq, Fabrice Edouard, 1963–
  The politics of modern Central America : civil war, democratization, and
  underdevelopment / Fabrice Lehoucq.
    pages cm
  Includes bibliographical references and index.
  ISBN 978-0-521-51506-1 – ISBN 978-0-521-73079-2 (pbk.)
  1. Central America – Politics and government – 1979–   2. Central America – Economic
  conditions – 1979–   3. Civil war – Central America – History – 20th century.   I. Title.
  F1439.5.L45   2012
  972.805'3–dc23   2011048652

ISBN 978-0-521-51506-1 Hardback
ISBN 978-0-521-73079-2 Paperback

To Mariana and Aida

Contents

Figures

Tables

Introduction

When I started graduate school in 1984, interest in Central America was at a post–World War II high. A region whose politics and economics generated little interest had become, by the late 1970s, an area making daily international headlines. A civil conflict in Nicaragua ended with the overthrow of President (and dictator) Anastasio Somoza in 1979. In neighboring El Salvador and Guatemala, left-wing guerrillas fought military regimes backed by the United States. A conservative administration in Washington led by Ronald Reagan interpreted these events as part of a Soviet and Cuban conspiracy to gain control of the isthmus, one that it chose to battle in what became the cold war's last decade.

More than three decades later, these events seem both distant and surreal. Interest in Central America has evaporated. It seems odd, perhaps even bizarre in retrospect, that both the left and the right spilled so much blood about the horrors or benefits of political change and social revolution. I wonder how many of these protagonists would agree with former Nicaraguan Vice-President Sergio Ramírez (1985–90) that the Sandinistas should have reached a compromise with the Reagan administration to end the bloodshed (Kinzer, 2001b). The U.S. decision, one spearheaded by the Barack Obama administration, to support or at least not oppose the Arab Spring (2011–present) reminds us how the Cold War put us on the wrong side of political change in so much of the Third World. I also wonder what participants and observers from the 1980s would say if we could transport them to the present, one that has seen an eviscerated Sandinista movement led by an aging Daniel Ortega be reelected president in 2006, in part by colluding with his erstwhile opponents, and obtaining supreme court backing to run for consecutive reelection to the presidency in 2012, which he won by a landslide, with 62.5 percent of the vote.

One objective of this book is to analyze political and economic developments since the 1970s in the countries of Central America. It is an effort that draws on more than three decades of research, travel to, and observation about the region. I first started thinking about Central America when I was an adolescent, when U.S. "allies" in the Third World, such as Somoza of Nicaragua and the Shah of Iran, fell and became the subject of intense debate about the motivations and consequences of U.S. foreign policy decision-making. Articles in the *New York Times* about El Salvador by Raymond Bonner, Clifford Krauss, Stephen Kinzer, and others described how a reformist junta, which had come to power in a coup d'état in October 1979, was steadily drifting to the right. U.S. foreign policy makers ignored the shift; the Reagan administration defended the return of hardline governments – judging by their slaughter of thousands of civilians – as necessary to fight communism. I kept reading and turned to the pages of *Estudios Centroamericanos*, the journal published by the Universidad Centroamericana in San Salvador. It was the material in these pages and elsewhere that sparked my interest in speculating how inequality becomes the basis of political protest.

A more central objective is to marshal this experience to shed light on three central debates of comparative politics and political economy: why civil wars happen; why political systems democratize, especially in the aftermath of civil wars; and, finally, the impact of economic development on democratic consolidation. A key way to engage the fascinating cross-national literature on these issues is by asking whether its arguments are useful for making sense of macro change in specific societies. It is a necessary step, one that obligates us to identify the mechanisms that link macro characteristics with outcomes, and whether these are consistent with statistically based generalizations. My book therefore marries "old-style" comparative politics, and its concern with context, with the theoretical ambition of "modern" comparative politics, one that concentrates on generating cause and effect generalizations possessing cross-national validity. I hope the reader, whether a novice about the region or a sophisticated social science consumer, finds my creation to his or her liking.

The first of three literatures this study draws on is the origins and outcomes of civil war and revolution. Why some regimes fall and set the stage for major social revolution was a central concern of the comparative politics of development until the 1980s. Curiously, just as Theda Skocpol published her *States and Social Revolutions* (1979), interest in the study of revolution began to wane. By the late 1990s, however, interest in revolution resurfaced under a new rubric, the study of civil war, in large part because multilateral institutions such as the World Bank funded research on what Paul Collier insightfully calls *The Bottom Billion* (2007). With the important exceptions of the mid-level developing countries of Costa Rica and Panama, the other countries of the isthmus belong to a group of approximately 100 developing countries with gross domestic product (GDP) per capita rates of less than $U.S. 10,000 (2009, purchasing power parity [PPP]). Like half the Central American isthmus, more than half the countries of the bottom 100 have experienced civil war or bad governance (or both).

Debate in what is an empirically rich and increasingly sophisticated field of study revolves around whether civil war is a product of greed, grievance, or closed political systems (Kalyvas, 2007). Central America offers a great opportunity to scrutinize the central predictions of this literature. This book suggests that inconsistently authoritarian regimes – ones afflicted by factionalism and unable to incorporate or eradicate their adversaries – gave rise to guerrilla movements on the isthmus. It was the inability to forge institutions regulating access to state power that led to a decade of civil war and conflict in much of Central America.

The second area of research this book draws on is democratization. The dramatic increase in the number of democracies during the 1980s, which Samuel P. Huntington (1991) dubbed the third wave, produced an outpouring of research on why political systems change. With the exception of Costa Rica, Central American political systems were authoritarian well into the 1980s and 1990s (Bowman, Lehoucq, and Mahoney, 2005), regimes aptly described as reactionary despotisms by Enrique Baloyra-Herp (1983). Nicaragua democratized by 1990, when political forces of the left and right began to compete in regularly scheduled and honest elections. El Salvador and Honduras completed their transitions from authoritarian rule by the mid-1990s. Military rulers in Guatemala gradually turned power over to elected politicians after trouncing their opponents in a brutal counterinsurgency.

Discussion is about whether authoritarian regime legacies shape transitions to democracy (Geddes, 2007) and how economic growth changes societies so democracy endures (Robinson, 2006). Central Americanist controversies revolve around whether the eclipse of traditional oligarchies was a product of the shift from landed to financial wealth (Paige, 1997) or the result of civil war, as I heard Rubén Zamora, a leader of the Salvadoran social democratic left, explain at the meetings of the Latin American Studies Association in the early 1990s (Zamora, 1997; also, see Rouquié, 1994; Wood, 2000). This is an argument consistent with the point that old orders rarely give up without a fight, without a sustained threat to their interests (Markoff, 1996; Tilly, 2004). This region-specific debate invokes another pioneered by international relations scholars, about the consequences of civil war (Gurses and Mason, 2008; Toft, 2010; Walter, 2010), one where the balance of evidence suggests that war improves the quality of political systems – perhaps because new regimes cannot but improve upon the old.

By examining why autocracy fell in Central America, this book shows that it was the struggle of peasants, workers, and guerrillas that forced despotic regimes – typically backed by the United States – to reform themselves. It was, in other words, the actions of thousands of ordinary people that, at enormous cost, changed Central America in a pattern that, one historian (Acuña Ortega, 1995) suggests, holds for other periods of political reform on the isthmus. The resiliency of reactionary despotism meant that violence was (unfortunately) the only way to make regimes more accountable, even if my analysis suggests that centrist compromises could have modernized political systems more peacefully; yet, at key points – Guatemala in 1954 and El Salvador (at least) in 1979, spring to mind – elites and the United States refused to endorse compromises that would surely have led to the spilling of less, perhaps significantly less, blood. It is a sobering conclusion, but one that strikes me as a central lesson of a fair reading of the evidence. Social reform never comes easy, especially in unequal societies where autocrats are unwilling to share power.

Civil war and revolution, if they generate benefits at all, do so in the long term. In the short and medium term, they are costly, perhaps expensive enough to wonder why, ex ante, key actors do not compromise to maximize benefits and minimize costs. A look at macroeconomic indicators over the past three decades makes this point. Only in Costa Rica and Panama are economies, in per capita terms, richer than they were in 1980. In 2006, both have GDP per capita rates approximately 50-percent larger than they were on the eve of the revolutionary decade. Economic growth in Guatemala and Honduras, however, has stagnated. Both had the same GDP per capita by 2006 that each had in 1980. Although El Salvador's GDP per capita rate has slightly increased, Nicaragua's has declined by almost a fourth since 1980 (Maddison, 2010).

The gap between Central America and the developed world therefore has widened: Although Costa Rica and Panama had GDP per capita rates slightly more than a third of the average of Western Europe's twelve largest economies in 1980, this ratio fell to slightly less than a third by 2008. Lack of development not only has worsened international comparisons, but also has increased disparities on the isthmus itself. Whereas the richest Central American states had GDP per capita rates twice as large as their poorer neighbors in 1980, this ratio is now three or four times as large. Understanding why development continues to stagnate in much of the region and why some economies have prospered are questions worth asking in light of the cataclysmic events of the 1980s.

The third area of research this book examines is the political economy of democratic consolidation. My discussion uses the six Central America cases to determine whether economic decline leads to political decay, a long-standing claim in comparative political economy. It analyzes the operation of electoral governance, executive-legislative relations, party systems, and state revenues to explain why democratization has produced disappointing results and even been reversed in Honduras and Nicaragua. This book shows why, contrary to standard economic models (Meltzer and Richard, 1981; Romer, 1975), pressure for social reform does not (easily) translate into public policies that reduce the differences between the rich and the poor. After a decade or more of electoral competition, rates of inequality have hardly budged, even if rates of poverty have fallen in some countries of the isthmus. This is a particularly depressing finding because so many revolutionaries demanded that dictatorships reform themselves and address pressing social needs. I point out that the war-induced lack of economic growth has contributed to political market failures, ones that do little to foment the political accountability necessary to deepen democracy and promote development in most countries on the isthmus.

Analysis of all three issues will show that politics – its conflicts, dynamics, and institutions – is driving the core political economic trends on the isthmus. The persistence of reactionary despotism led to the bloodbaths of Central America, outcomes that point to the importance of modeling regime dynamics to account for the outbreak of violent conflict. Civil war led to the transitions from authoritarian rule; it was politics, through violent means, that reordered the Central American political landscape. It was the destruction of war that led to a permanent decline in rates of economic growth in El Salvador, Guatemala, and especially Nicaragua. It was a long history of political competition that helped Costa Ricans minimize the social dislocations of a negative shift in the terms of trade in the late 1970s and 1982 foreign debt crisis. It is deficient party systems, along with resource poor states, that lead to political market failures, to the inability of refashioned political systems to create the basis for sustained growth and to reduce the distance separating the rich from the poor.

Approaches and Sources in the Study of Central America

Writing a book about the political economy of Central America is not easy. The canonical texts, from those authored by Edelberto Torres-Rivas (1993; first published, in Spanish, in 1961) to Jeffrey Paige (1997), neglect the study of politics, in part because dictatorship and open-economy policies did lead to rather primitive states in most countries of the region. The Marxist or materialist social science that inspired so many of these accounts also led analysts to see states as little more than instruments of local elites, foreign companies, and of the U.S. government. Most studies thus focused on the economic and social constraints on political as well as economic development (Smith and Boyer, 1987; Smith, Boyer, and Diskin, 1988).

Dana Munro's much earlier study, first published in 1918, is an exception. This is a curious result because his *The Five Republics of Central America* is an outgrowth of his Ph.D. dissertation for the Department of Economics at the University of Pennsylvania. Munro argued that dictatorship and the often violent exchange of state power retarded development in Central America. Although poverty and the lack of economic growth contributed to authoritarianism and economic underdevelopment, Munro argued that political traditions and geostrategic factors also contributed to the region's backwardness. Unfortunately, Central Americanists largely ignored Munro's pioneering analysis, even as it anticipates contemporary political economic discussions about the origins of civil conflict, regime types, and lack of economic growth (Lehoucq, 2003).

Although this book looks to the comparative research on political economy for inspiration, it also takes cues from Munro's pioneering work. It builds, in particular, on Victor Bulmer-Thomas (1987) and Carlos Vilas's (1995) fine political economies on the region to analyze how economic policies and the material organization of society, respectively, shape the struggle for power. My book relies on the periodic reports on the *Estado de la Región* (State of the Region; e.g., PENR, 2008; 2011), which has commissioned a plethora of working papers on social science and public policy topics on the isthmus. The book incorporates findings of the newer research on the region that concentrates on electoral laws, party systems, public opinion, and executive-legislative relations, which makes it possible to write a modern political economy of the region: one that explains how the nature and dynamics of the political system affect the economy as well as how economic interests and structures shape public policy. This book is part of a dialogue with friends and colleagues – past, present, and future – about the origins of the civil wars of the 1970s and 1980s and their political and economic consequences. It is to the conversations among Central Americanists that I bring to bear my reading of central debates in comparative politics and political economy, a combination that I hope benefits region-specific researchers as well as comparativists, more generally.

Civil War, Democratization, and Underdevelopment in Central America uses controlled comparisons among five cases over a forty-year period and what John Gerring (2007) calls "cross-case" analysis to examine central themes of comparative politics and political economy. I pursue cross-case analysis by drawing on the findings of social science research about three sets of cases: the universe of all nation-states; the population of developing countries, especially of politically fragile societies; and the set of eighteen Latin American countries. Having chapters revolve around core topics – and not countries – maximizes the opportunities for fruitful comparisons between the countries of the isthmus and the rest of the world. With the exception of Héctor Pérez-Brignoli's (1989) impressive synthesis or Salvador Martí i Puig's (2004) more recent tome, books on Central America typically assign chapters to each country of the isthmus (e.g., Bethell, 1991; Booth, Wade, and Walker, 2010; Dunkerley, 1988; Parker, 1964; Woodward, 1999), which hinders identifying commonalities and dis-similarities among Costa Rica, El Salvador, Guatemala, Honduras, Nicaragua, and Panama and, most importantly, how these experiences shed light on central themes in comparative politics and political economy.

Overview of Chapters

The first chapter depicts the political and economic setting of Central America in the 1970s. It analyzes the impact of an economic model, one based on export-ing coffee and bananas (and, after World War II, cattle, cotton, and sugar), in unequal societies on growth rates and on social well-being. States were highly responsive to export interests not only because they were well-organized and vocal about their demands, but also because the prosperity of these socie-ties – and of state revenues, in particular – depended on international trade. It scrutinizes classic arguments about the development of dictatorships in most countries and democracy in Costa Rica, suggesting that it was the structure of political competition that led to divergent regime trajectories on the isthmus. Where it produced partisan stalemates, as in Costa Rica, democracy emerged – a system that gave politicians an interest in compensating the losers as well as the winners in international trade. Where political struggle ended because one faction monopolized violence, tyrannies proliferated, ones that had little interest in improving social conditions for the majority. This chapter ends with an eval-uation of the region's post–World War II boom: Although most economies grew and social conditions (marginally) improved, the gains from trade were concentrated among agro-exporters; domestic industrialists; and, to a lesser extent, the urban labor force.

Chapter 2 concentrates on explaining why, in the 1970s and 1980s, civil wars erupted in El Salvador, Guatemala, and Nicaragua, but not in Costa Rica, Honduras, and Panama. Most quantitative, cross-national research emphasizes the impact of economic underdevelopment, poverty, and inequality. This chapter emphasizes the role of political factors, presenting the results of a new political system classification to explain how, what I call inconsistently authoritarian regimes, ignited the civil wars on the isthmus. This chapter analyzes why revolutionary forces only triumphed in Nicaragua, lost in Guatemala, and forced the government into a stalemate in El Salvador. It assesses the consequences of the cold war on political developments, demonstrating how the Carter administration's human rights policy weakened dictatorships (but hardly caused their collapse) before changing its policy – a stance the Reagan administration pursued and hardened – to prevent the overthrow of hardline governments in the region.

Chapter 3 analyzes the shift to semi-democratic and democratic forms of government during the last decades of the twentieth century. This chapter determines whether these transitions are consistent with cross-national models of democratization that highlight the impact of economic development on political change. It identifies the reasons civil war and peace negotiations paved the way for political and economic reforms, paying particular attention to the role foreign governments and multilateral institutions play in Central America. This chapter explores why, with the partial exception of El Salvador, post-conflict governments have done little to hold human rights violators of the past accountable for their actions.

The fourth chapter examines economic growth and development over the long run. It assesses the impact of more than a decade of civil war on development, an outcome that coincided with the dramatic fall in the region's terms of trade (and debt crisis in Costa Rica, Nicaragua, and Panama). It analyzes the consequences of neoliberal reforms and why these have been unable to reignite economic growth outside Costa Rica and Panama. It shows how the absence of viable states, ones that collect revenue and invest it in infrastructure, public security, health, and education, undermines development on the isthmus. This chapter ends by analyzing continuities and changes in the region's production profile, one in which light manufactures and especially labor increasingly vie for dominance as the isthmus's key exports.

Chapter 5 examines the nature and consequences of democratization and war-induced economic decline. The most important accomplishment of the civil wars has been to incorporate the left into the political system. This chapter analyzes the interaction of voter turnout rates, public opinion, party system dynamics, and government expenditures to explain why most political systems have experienced market failure: Their structural characteristics undermine accountability, their ability to meet public demands to narrow the differences between the rich and the poor and otherwise create the conditions for sustained growth. Several democracies have regressed, even if no Central American country has witnessed the return of civil war, an outcome all too common in postwar civil war settings.

The conclusion summarizes the findings of this book and identifies their implications for debates on comparative politics and political economy. It argues that the cross-national, statistical research on the political economy of income distribution generates the most useful findings, ones that help explain why the results of democracy have been meager on the isthmus. It suggests that the large-N research on democratization and the origins of civil wars is less useful, with much research on civil wars being the least useful. Politics, by which I mean the structure of political competition, the nature of regimes and of political institutions more narrowly, turns out to explain the outbreak of civil war, democratization, and the economic and political consequences of social policy. This chapter also identifies what has and has not changed since the civil wars of the 1970s and 1980 and, more broadly, how the past two and a half decades fit into broader patterns of development since the beginning of the twentieth century.

This book is as much a reflection on comparative political economy as it is an homage to teachers and friends. The person who introduced me to the region was Harold Sims, a historian at the University of Pittsburgh who helped me understand U.S. foreign policy toward the isthmus when I was an undergraduate. Another influential teacher was Richard Cottam, whose course on the Middle East, and how U.S. foreign policy makers struggled to fashion policy to an aging dictator, the Shah of Iran, and to its revolutionary replacement, I remember well almost three decades later. The parallels with U.S. foreign policy making toward Central America are striking, as his book on *Iran and the US* (Cottam, 1988) reveals. John Markoff's graduate course on historical sociology and revolutions introduced me to state-of-the-art thinking on rapid social change, one that sparked my interest in quantitative social science and to the systematic study of revolutions. Both his own award-winning works on the French Revolution (Markoff, 1996a) and on the role of social movements on democratization (Markoff, 1996b) mark my book. In graduate school, I was fortunate to take coursework with several gifted faculty. Arturo Valenzuela taught me to take political institutions in Latin America seriously. Judging from Chapter 5, Peter Lange's course on the political economy of advanced, industrial societies left an imprint, one that gradually got me to think hard about income inequality. Robert Bates ignited my interest in the political economy of development, and I have learned a great deal from his work.

Many individuals helped shape my thinking about the region. Héctor Pérez-Brignoli shared his systematic understanding of the isthmus's history with me. His writings on economic history (Pérez-Brignoli, 1994; 2011) and, with Carolyn Hall (Hall and Pérez-Brignoli, 2003), on economic geography continually forced me to rethink my more politically centered arguments. My

trips to Central America often overlapped with those of Marc Edelman and
Steven Palmer, two North American researchers with whom I shared notes and
observations, especially on Costa Rica (Lehoucq, 1998b). Marc's admonish-
ment to take social protest seriously not only dovetailed with a central point
of John Markoff's research, but also led to a central theme of this book. Steve
was a constant source of insight on Central American history. Victor Hugo
Acuña's friendship and intellect both inspired me and got me to reflect about so
many things, especially long-term developments and comparisons among the
countries of the isthmus. More recently, the researchers at the *Programa del
Estado de la Nación* reignited my interest in the isthmus. Without its research,
this book would have been much harder to write. I thank Miguel Gutiérrez and
Jorge Vargas Cullell for their friendship and interest in my work.

I thank Kirk Bowman and Jim Mahoney for their collaboration on a regime
classification index (Bowman, Lehoucq, and Mahoney, 2005). David Wall is a
generous friend who helped me understand how geographers think. I am grateful for the map (Figure 1.4) that he requested Mounica Kondamur make as
well as his collaboration on the institutional and sociological determinants of
voter turnout rates across the 330 municipalities of Guatemala (Lehoucq and
Wall, 2004). Clark Gibson helped me understand rural political economy in a
research project on local governance (Andersson, Gibson, and Lehoucq, 2006;
Gibson and Lehoucq, 2003).

Several other individuals shared their data and expertise with me. Charles
Brockett sent spreadsheet files on social protest in El Salvador and Guatemala,
shared insights, and produced several key works whose findings I happily recognize here and in the text. Manuel Orozco supplied me with his data on remittances
in Central America. Evelyne Huber and John Stephens shared data from their
project on social policy and inequality. Matt Kocher gave me pointers on the civil
war literature in international relations. Juan Carlos Rodríguez-Cordero supplied
data about Costa Rica at key moments and taught me about judicial politics in
his country (Wilson and Rodríguez-Cordero, 2006; Wilson, Rodríguez-Cordero,
and Handberg, 2004). David Close and David Dye answered questions about
Nicaragua; Salvador Martí i Puig gave me comments on a preliminary outline of
the book. Juan Diego Trejos, Natalia Morales, and Rafael Segura answered questions about measuring inequality in Central America. Ken Snowden corrected
my calculations in Table 5.1. Marc Dixon helped me produce Figures 1.3, 3.1,
and 5.1, which required roundabout maneuvers in Excel.

The Center for Inter-American Policy and Research at Tulane University
kindly invited me to present an early version of Chapter 5 in San José, Costa
Rica in June 2010. I thank a 2010 Summer Fellowship from UNC-Duke
University Consortium on Latin American studies. In April 2011, the members
of the social policy working group at Duke and UNC provided comments useful to revise this chapter of the book. Erik Wibbels, Ceci Martínez de Gallardo,
and Guillermo Trejo offered comments that made me recast Chapter 5. I am
grateful to Ken Klasse and Ruth DeHoog for providing several MPA students
to serve as my research assistants. Steve Elliot, Jana Raczkowski, Seth Steele,

and Philip Freeman provided indispensable help. Philip double checked many facts for me, supplied me with key time series data, and largely assembled the bibliography for this book. Jana helped me proofread the manuscript and helped me with the production of the index.

The five anonymous reviewers deployed by Cambridge University Press to read the précis and draft of the manuscript made important suggestions on this book. Jorge Vargas went beyond the duty of either collegiality or friendship when he provided pages of comments on every chapter. Jorge's keen intellect forced me to sharpen all my arguments and think hard about key issues in political economy. I must share responsibility of the book's virtues with him, although none of its remaining vices. Bill Keech gave me comments on the penultimate version of this book, which helped me emphasize the comparative implications of my findings. Kirk Bowman offered keen insights on the manuscript, ones that I hope he recognizes in the book. Sarita Jackson provided comments on the introduction, and Aníbal Pérez-Liñán made important remarks on Chapter 2 (and insights for Chapter 5), which I presented as a paper at the 2011 meetings of the American Political Science Association in Seattle, Washington. Robert Williams gave me feedback on Chapter 4, and Juliana Martínez helped me see several issues more clearly in Chapter 5. Eric Crahan was a supportive editor.

My wife and daughter helped me finish this book. They created databases. They gave me comments on the figures. They listened to plenty of monologues about the book or the music (mostly Mozart's piano sonatas and concertos) I listened to locked away in my office. They motivated me to complete this book (while teaching a full courseload). The book is dedicated to them, with gratitude and love.

I

Central America on the Eve of the 1980s

Introduction

The six economies of Central America, sandwiched between Mexico and South America (Hall and Pérez-Brignoli, 2003), are prototypical of the smaller economies of the developing world. Each depends on the export of agricultural commodities, which generates the foreign exchange necessary for development. The price of coffee and bananas, the region's dominant exports during the twentieth century, remained subject to the whims of international supply and demand, because both crops are grown throughout the tropics (Bates, 1997). This production feature, which made these economies price-takers in global markets, had profound effects on Central American societies, ones that would shape relations between landlords and peasants, the nature of their states, and their economic and social well-being.

Inequality in land distribution, coupled with demands of the international market for coffee and bananas, led to a predictable social structure. The spectacular returns of export agriculture enriched landowners, coffee processors, and banana producers. Most of the population, which remained predominately rural until the 1970s, either grew crops for domestic consumption or worked for wages on large estates. For many observers, dictatorship was inevitable in Central America, for only military despots could ensure the conditions needed for the docile labor force required to plant and harvest coffee and pick bananas.

Identifying the central political economic features of the isthmus on the eve of civil war is the central goal of this chapter. I discuss the reasons to be skeptical of the claim that inequality and export agriculture explain the rise of reactionary despotism on the isthmus. As the development of democracy in Costa Rica demonstrates, open as well as closed regimes fomented the specialization in agro-exports. It was this country – the one with the longest history of democratic government – that achieved the region's highest growth rates and best social outcomes. Only an account that takes the power struggle seriously can explain this outcome, one consistent with the cross-national, statistical findings

TABLE 1.1. *Populations of Central America, 1960–80*

Country	Population (in Millions)			Rural Population (as a Share of Total)			Population Density (per Km²)		
	1960	1970	1980	1960	1970	1980	1960	1970	1980
Costa Rica	1.3	1.9	2.4	66%	59%	56%	26	37	48
El Salvador	2.5	3.6	4.8	61%	60%	56%	121	172	229
Guatemala	4.3	5.2	6.1	66%	64%	67%	40	48	56
Honduras	2.0	3.0	4.6	70%	63%	61%	18	27	41
Nicaragua	1.5	1.9	2.7	59%	52%	56%	13	16	23
Panama	1.1	1.4	1.8	59%	52%	50%	14	19	24
Averages									
Central America	2.6	3.4	4.5	61%	57%	56%	25	33	44
Latin America	10.2	13.4	17.4	56%	42%	36%	10	13	17
Developing	20.5	25.3	31.3	76%	72%	67%	85	108	132

Sources: PENR (2008: 583); data to calculate the Latin American average stem from SALA (1984: 139, 116); data for the developing-world averages are from World Bank (1983).

about the survival and performance of different regimes (Bueno de Mesquita et al., 2003).

Demographic Characteristics

Data in Table 1.1 indicate that, with the partial exception of El Salvador, populations were small. Guatemala, with the second largest land mass on the isthmus, had the largest population – 6.1 million in 1980. At the other extreme, Panama had 1.8 million inhabitants in 1980. Comparison with Latin America reveals that the average Central American society had a population less than a third the size of the Latin American average. Central American societies were especially small in the context of the developing world, as averages in Table 1.1 show.

With one exception, population density figures in Table 1.1 confirm that the region did not have unusually large populations for its equally small territories. With a population density of forty-four per square kilometer, the region was, by 1980, only a third as densely populated as the developing world, even if its average was more than twice as large as Latin America. Only El Salvador was an exception, with a population density rate of 229 by 1980, making it almost twice as populated as the developing-world average.

That so many people lived in the region's smallest republic made international press headlines in 1969, in the so-called soccer war between El Salvador and Honduras that the great Polish journalist, Ryszard Kapuściński (1991) later made famous. At the time of the war, neo-Malthusians blamed overpopulation in El Salvador for the war with its neighbor because the war was ignited by the Honduran government expelling Salvadoran immigrants from its territory. Yet, it was the poor distribution of resources – not an excessively large population – that had forced many Salvadorans to migrate to Honduras in search of land to grow subsistence crops. By 1971, nearly half of all farms were smaller than 1 hectare each and held less than 5 percent of the country's farmland. In contrast, farms of 200 hectares or more held 28.2 percent of the country's farmland but accounted for only 0.3 percent of all farms (Durham, 1979: 38). At most, overpopulation did lead to the virtual disappearance of forests by the end of the 1970s (Browning, 1971). It was the growth in the numbers of rural poor in a country with high levels of economic inequality, one where the best land produced coffee, cattle, and sugar for export, that had decimated forests.

Most Central Americans still lived in rural areas by 1980. The most rural country was Guatemala. More than two-thirds of the population lived in hamlets and other small settlements, a large portion of which belonged to one of two dozen Maya ethnic groups. Belize, Panama, and Nicaragua were the least rural, but still had nearly half of their populations residing outside of cities. For most of the region's people, life was dominated by agriculture, the key activity in rural areas: the planting and harvesting of crops for subsistence or for sale and, for many poorer families, travel to large-scale *fincas* to harvest bananas, coffee, sugar, and other export products. The rhythms of rural life – the alternation of wet and dry seasons in isolated hamlets or small towns and the difficulty of moving around – shaped the lives of millions of individuals. It was a world that had not changed substantially in several generations.

Outside of Guatemala, most Central Americans were *mestizos* or people of mixed ancestry. Although statistics using racial classifications are fraught with difficulties, data from 1978 suggest that only 6.8 percent of the population of Panama was indigenous and less than 5 percent were Native American in Costa Rica, El Salvador, Honduras, and Nicaragua. Population censuses often do not make it clear whether the enumerator is classifying a person's race or whether, as is now the practice, he or she lets individuals classify themselves. Only in Guatemala were indigenous peoples a majority, one that comprised nearly 60 percent of the population, a classification based on physical features, dress, and, most importantly, language (Inter-American Indian Institute, 1979: 4; also see Adams, 1993). These figures reflect the decline of Indian cultures, ones that in El Salvador and Nicaragua, for example, were larger as recently as the early twentieth century (Gould, 1998).

Economic Characteristics and Trends

Data in Figure 1.1 show that the Central American economies were heavily agricultural. At mid-century, the agricultural sector comprised a bit less than 40 percent of the value of the region's production. Thirty years later, the value of agriculture had fallen by a fourth, to 28 percent of the isthmus's production. Figure 1.1 displays the most agricultural economy of the region – Honduras – and the least – Panama, which had less than 10 percent of its economy revolving around cultivating and selling crops. Until 1970, more than half of

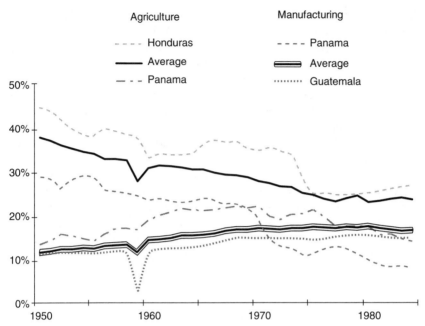

FIGURE 1.1. Value added by agriculture and manufacturing to GDP.
Note: Only lowest and highest values around the average are displayed.
Sources: Bulmer-Thomas (1987: 308, 314–315, 322–323); data for Panama are from
CEPAL (2001).

the economically active population worked in agriculture. Panama had the
least agricultural labor force, and Honduras had the largest share of workers
growing crops. Even by 1980, when the civil wars in the region were underway,
almost half of the region's labor force worked in agriculture.

Figure 1.1 indicates that the industrial sector has been a historically small
but increasingly important sector of Central American economies. In 1950,
manufacturing generated 11 percent of national production. Thirty years
later, it grew to 17 percent, indicating that two decades of import substitution
industrialization had created a vibrant and protected manufacturing sector in
Central America. Under the aegis of the Central American Common Market
(CACM), industrial policy lowered barriers to trade among countries of the
isthmus, even as it erected them to stimulate regional industrial production.
The benefits of the CACM were mixed: Although it raised GDP growth rates
largely through the economies of scale that increasing market size allows, it
was biased toward producing consumer goods and did little to build backward
linkages with the rest of the economy (Cline and Delgado, 1978) or to improve
the distribution of income (Reynolds, 1978). The growth of manufacturing and
of the service sector (which is not shown here) is the corollary to the urbaniza-
tion of Central American societies.

Even with large numbers of Central Americans producing for subsistence and
a protected manufacturing sector, trade statistics in Figure 1.2 highlight how

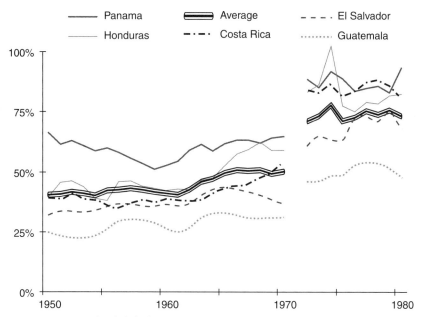

FIGURE 1.2. Levels of globalization, 1950–80 (imports and exports as a share of GDP). *Note*: Series uses 1970 constant prices until 1980, when it uses 1980 constant prices. *Source*: CEPAL (2001).

open the Central American economies were. With the exception of Guatemala, the value of exports and imports exceeded 40 percent of each country's GDP. This is a figure comparable to the twelve small European social democracies (along with Australia and New Zealand) that have had historically open and successful economies. Guatemala's economy is the least open, reminding us that the country's large and predominately indigenous population is mainly producing for domestic consumption.

For most of the twentieth century, coffee and bananas were the region's most important exports. Coffee was first cultivated in Costa Rica in the 1840s and, by the late nineteenth century, spread throughout the isthmus. By 1929, coffee accounted for more than two-thirds of export earnings from Costa Rica, more than nine-tenths of export earnings from El Salvador, more than three-quarters of export earnings from Guatemala, and more than half of Nicaragua's export earnings. Only in Honduras were these exports insignificant (less than 3 percent). In 1970, only El Salvador still mostly exported coffee (72 percent). Although still important, coffee export earnings became less essential in terms of overall exports in the other republics. They accounted for nearly 40 percent of export earnings from Costa Rica, 54 percent in Guatemala, 17 percent in Honduras, and 24 percent in Nicaragua (Bulmer-Thomas, 1987: 34, 188).

Coffee production was mostly in national hands, but bananas were not. Costa Rica did have a fairly large number of small property holders, although their share in the population was less significant than it had been. Even if

42 percent of Costa Rican coffee was produced on farms of 6.8 hectares (or 9.9 *manzanas*, as coffee land measures go) or less in 1955, the average size of coffee farms was 145 hectares (or 210 *manzanas*). The average size of coffee *fincas* in Nicaragua and El Salvador was 134.6 and 157.3 hectares (or 195 and 228 *manzanas*), respectively. The average size of coffee farms in Guatemala was a whopping 236 hectares (or 342 *manzanas*). Less than 14 percent of coffee was produced on parcels smaller than 10 *manzanas* in these three countries, according to the 1940 agricultural census in El Salvador, the 1947–58 agricultural census in Nicaragua, and the 1966–7 agricultural census in Guatemala (Paige, 1997: 61–62, 66; also see Weeks, 1985).

Foreign-based companies began to grow bananas on the Atlantic coast by the end of the nineteenth century. Three banana corporations – the United Fruit Company, the Cuyamel Fruit Company, and the Standard Fruit Company – came to dominate the production and export of bananas in Costa Rica, Guatemala, Honduras, and Panama. In their heyday, these companies enjoyed numerous tax privileges that, other than labor contracts, provided economies and societies with few benefits. Banana enclaves remained isolated geographically and economically on the Caribbean coast. At their worst, the banana companies left environmental minefields and unemployed workers in the wake of their departure from Costa Rica with the spread of the Panama disease by the 1930s (Viales Hurtado, 1998), worked with dictators (Dosal, 1993), or participated in the overthrow of governments in Guatemala (Gleijeses, 1991) and Honduras (Euraque, 1996). By 1929, they accounted for a quarter of Costa Rica's export earnings, 13 percent of Guatemala's, and almost a fifth of Nicaragua's. Bananas were not exported from El Salvador, but they comprised 85 percent of Honduras's export earnings. By 1970, only Costa Rica and Honduras still exported bananas in appreciable amounts, accounting for 36 percent and 47 percent of each country's export earnings, respectively (Bulmer-Thomas, 1987: 34, 188; also see Ellis, 1983 and López, 1986).

Beef, cotton, and sugar became key exports in the post–World War II period (Williams, 1986). The production of beef, cotton, and light industrial goods was more integrated into the region's economies than bananas were. The capital requirements of cattle-ranching, cotton production, and light manufacturing restricted investments in these areas to established businessmen, bankers, and well-connected politicians in perennially capital-starved economies. Even in Costa Rica, all but the largest investors did not participate in these new activities (Edelman, 1992). Often benefiting from tax subsidies and other preferential public policies, these sectors did generate foreign exchange, improved local technical capacities, and employed workers in job-scarce economies, even if they produced few new jobs.

By 1970, cotton was more than 14 percent of export earnings in El Salvador and Guatemala and comprised a quarter of Nicaragua's. Beef exports reached almost 10 percent of Costa Rica's export earnings by that time, were more than double this figure for Nicaragua, and were slightly less than 7 percent for Guatemala and Honduras. The value of sugar exports stayed below 6 percent in Costa Rica, El Salvador, and Guatemala and reached 7.4 percent in Nicaragua. Only in Nicaragua did these new exports generate nearly half of export earnings, which is precisely why coffee or bananas never became as important there as they did for the other Central American republics (Bulmer-Thomas, 1987: 188).

Panama is a partial exception to these generalizations. Its economy revolved around the fortunes of its canal, and the international trade and banking it brought (Maurer and Yu, 2010). Even at mid-century, more than half its labor force was in neither agriculture nor industry, but in the service sector. By 1980, services generated more than two-thirds of the value of its economy. Little coffee was grown in the region's smallest country. Bananas generated 38 percent of the value of its export of goods and services in 1970, a figure that continued to fall in subsequent years (Zimbalist and Weeks, 1991).

Political Economy and Regime Types

The unequal distribution of land in small, open economies generated two important consequences, as the economic sociologists from Edelberto Torres-Rivas (1993 [1961]) to Carlos Vilas (1995) have noted. First, being price-takers in global markets meant exporters had incentives to minimize costs to reap the largest gains from trade. In economies with an abundance of labor, landowners offered low wages, even if exporters required large numbers of field hands during planting and harvesting. To reduce the demand for labor, they invested in technology to increase the productivity of their farms. Economic calculations, in fact, reveal that gains in productivity during the 1960s were largely the result of technological changes that reduced the demand for labor in societies already experiencing fast population growth (Reynolds, 1978). This research shows that both capital (money invested in productive activities) and rents (income derived from the ownership of property) reaped increasing shares of the national income at the expense of labor or wages. Despite more than a decade of economic expansion, population growth had succeeded in flooding labor markets and therefore reducing labor's share of national income, especially in El Salvador and Guatemala.

Second, the concentration of land and related assets meant agro-exporters retained a preference for small states, especially in autocracies. As a percentage of GDP, the revenues of central governments were less than 12 percent of GDP in every country, except Costa Rica and Panama. In Guatemala and Nicaragua, taxes were approximately 9 percent of GDP in 1970 (IICA-FLACSO, 1991: 109). In El Salvador and Honduras, they were 11.1 percent and 12.7 percent, respectively. In comparison, states in the developed world in 1970 were collecting almost a third of GDP to invest in infrastructure, education, health, public security, and military defense (OECD, 2007: 74). Of course, the absolute amounts governments in advanced industrial societies had to spend on each citizen were significantly higher because their GDPs were much larger.

In Costa Rica and Panama, revenues had reached 14 percent and 15.7 percent of GDP, respectively, in 1970. If the revenues of the decentralized agencies are included – social security (health care and pensions), telephones, electricity, and water, to name a few – the state's reach in Costa Rica more than doubled (Wilkie, 1974). A much larger state in Costa Rica has been part of a social democratic bargain whereby left parties – principally the Party of National Liberation (PLN) – outbid their rivals on the right in quadrennial elections, ones that included establishing taxes on coffee exports (Winson, 1989). It was the necessity of winning the support of voters interested in health, pension, and education that encouraged all parties to expand social services prevented by dictatorships in the other countries of the isthmus. The existence of the canal and affiliated services provided the Panamanian state with a more predictable source of revenue than its counterparts in the region.

The revenues to fund small states came from indirect taxes, especially in the most autocratic systems on the isthmus. In the first analysis of its kind, Michael H. Best (1976) demonstrated that state income was raised disproportionately from indirect taxes, especially those on imports and consumption. More than three-quarters of central government revenue came from these taxes during the 1960s. Overall revenues could have been greater through the effective collection of direct taxes; income and property taxes could have generated at least 10 percent more income for states. This pattern stems, in part, from the political power of landowners and industrialists in nondemocratic systems in which the preferences of median voters could be largely ignored, as Best (1976) contends. That the Costa Rican state had much the same tax system (although its overall share of taxation with respect to GDP was greater), however, suggests that the grim logic of exporting agricultural commodities helped exporters convince states to keep income and property taxes low.

State policies favored large and established producers, which did little, outside of Costa Rica, to spread the gains from trade. In perhaps the only effort of its kind, Carlos Vilas (1995: 50–51) compiled the results of several technical studies to trace the distributional impact of state policies. Per capita public investment in Guatemala's predominantly agro-export departments was 55 percent higher than the national average in the early 1980s. It was an astounding 350 percent higher in these departments than in the departments of the western highlands, where the Maya lived, as either peasants or urban-based artisans. These studies update the detailed empirical work by a research team led by Richard Adams (1970), which demonstrated how concentrated the gains from development were in Guatemala. Per capita public spending in Honduras's northern banana-growing regions was almost double the national average in the early 1980s. Bank credit was also channeled to agro-exporters in El Salvador. Only 10 percent was loaned to basic grain producers during the 1960s and 1970s. More than 90 percent of all bank credit during the first half of the 1960s went to agro-exporters in Nicaragua, despite the fact that they cultivated less than half of all farmland. Public policies, in other words, were highly responsive to export interests.

Historians and sociologists argue that democracy in Costa Rica – and dictatorship in the rest of Central America – was the result of a more egalitarian distribution of resources in this country. It was the scarcity of labor in the nineteenth century that allowed peasants to find land on an expanding frontier (Gudmundson, 1989; Samper, 1990) and that forced landlords to pay laborers decent wages to harvest coffee – the exact opposite of what prevailed in El Salvador and Guatemala (Pérez-Brignoli, 1994). The gradual privatization of Indian lands in late-nineteenth-century El Salvador created a growing rural workforce that kept wages low (Lauria-Santiago, 1999). The unwillingness of the Maya to leave their high-altitude communities to work on coffee plantations led large landowners to pressure the state to force Indian communities to supply laborers to coffee *fincas* (McCreery, 1994). Democracy or listening to demands of the majority was the result of a series of bargains between upper and lower classes in Costa Rica. States, in contrast, militarized to promote the interests of large coffee producers in El Salvador and Guatemala, echoing Barrington Moore's (1966) influential treatise about the development of dictatorship in nineteenth-century Germany (Gudmundson, 1995). Autocracy, in other words, emerged to protect commercial agriculture. This is the argument of the classics of Central American sociology (Paige, 1997; Torres-Rivas, 1993) and of economic history (Cardoso, 1975; Samper, 1998; Williams, 1994), and is implicit in works of political economy (Bulmer-Thomas, 1987; Weaver, 1994; Weeks, 1985) and other influential accounts (Baloyra-Herp, 1983; Brockett, 1998; Dunkerley, 1988; Pérez-Brignoli, 1989; Robinson, 2003; Vilas, 1995). It is the argument that has informed much of the social science about Central America and that finds echoes in central works in comparative political economy (Acemoglu and Robinson, 2006; Boix, 2003; Rueschemeyer, Stephens, and Stephens, 1992).

Even if dictatorship protected the interests of agro-exporters, it is unclear that autocracy was necessarily the product of a highly stratified class structure. The construction of states in Central America was spearheaded by ambitious dictators, who did not monopolize the use of violence until well into the twentieth century (Holden, 2004). James Mahoney (2001) contends that liberal dictators allied with coffee exporters to finance their efforts to vanquish conservative strongmen, which led them to agree to build the roads, ports, and other elements of market economies sought by agricultural producers. Only by promoting exports could ambitious autocrats levy the taxes to build the armed forces to defend themselves from overthrow. It was the dictates of political survival that drove rulers to protect coffee producers and banana companies. With time, this partnership congealed into militarized regimes in much of the region. Where coffee producers were unable to form stable alliances with a strong man, as in Honduras and Nicaragua, political instability persisted well into the twentieth century.

That political ambition also fueled civil war was a conclusion reached by Dana Munro (1918), in his classic analysis of the region's political economy. Civil war and coups were common in the central republics of the isthmus for geostrategic reasons. Nicaragua, in particular, was in the path of the great powers searching for interoceanic canals. The presidents of El Salvador, Guatemala, and Honduras often gave refuge to each other's opponents. Attempts to overthrow a president typically involved an invasion by exiles from a neighboring country, with at least tacit support of nearby dictators (Taracena Arriola, 1993). Instability was the result of power vacuums, ones that caused governments to remain or become autocratic – all of which followed policies favored by coffee exporters and banana companies. To argue that the Central American economies required the existence of dictatorships confuses a cause with a consequence of the struggle for power.

The key to understanding democracy's development in Costa Rica stems less from the structure of its coffee economy, in part because a competitive political system was perfectly compatible with the dramatic increase in the productivity of coffee farms (Raventós, 1986) and the concentration of land after the 1948 civil war (Winson, 1989). Democratization, in fact, was the product of a long-term and simmering political stalemate – one that could, if any party became politically marginalized, turn violent – that prompted parties to channel their disputes about state control in the electoral arena by the end of the nineteenth century (Lehoucq, 1996; 1998a). Unsuccessful in repeated attempts to use the military to eradicate their opponents, incumbents compromised and gradually reduced the powers of the presidency, especially their ability to rig elections in their favor. By the end of the nineteenth century, government and opposition parties fielded candidates in elections in which suffrage rights were extensive. Although the 1871 constitution did create a gender as well as a property restriction on the franchise, all adult males had been registered to vote since the late nineteenth century, in large part because many met what was an ambiguously worded wealth requirement and competitive political races encouraged parties to enfranchise all adult males. Women got the right to vote in 1949. Since 1901, turnout has been 71 percent of the eligible adult population (Lehoucq, 2010: 51).

The regime classification displayed in Figure 1.3 makes the point that, until the 1980s, there were two types of political trajectories – ways of selecting chief executives – in Central America. In different ways, the politicians and citizens of Costa Rica and Panama relied largely on elections to select their chief executives and legislatures. In Costa Rica, they constructed a democratic system that became known for its stability and openness, one that we label semi-democratic for much of the twentieth century because franchise rights were restricted to men until 1949. We date full democracy, that is, a political system in which virtually all political forces can compete for elected offices and the entire adult population is entitled to vote, from the late 1950s, when the losers of the 1948 civil war returned from exile and began to compete for elected offices once again. The exception was the ban on antidemocratic parties that kept the Popular Vanguard Party (PVP), the Costa Rican Communist Party, out of politics until 1975, when the supreme court declared this ban unconstitutional. Since 1958, when the incumbent Party of National Liberation (PLN) reluctantly conceded defeat in the presidential

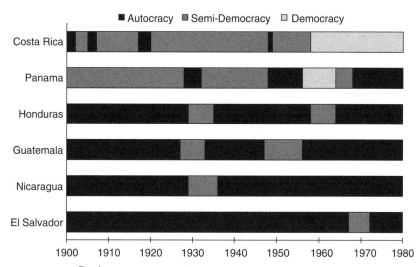

FIGURE 1.3. Regime types, 1900–80.
Sources: Bowman, Lehoucq, and Mahoney (2005); Brinks, Mainwaring, and Pérez-Liñán (2011) for Panama.

elections of this year (Bowman, 2001a), executives and legislators have come to power in concurrent and quadrennial elections renowned for their openness and fairness. In Panama, politicians competed for power in regularly scheduled, if not infrequently fraudulent, elections ending with the 1968 military coup that brought General Omar Torrijos to power.

Figure 1.3 shows that autocracy dominated the other four political systems of the isthmus, which were only briefly interrupted by reformist or semi-democratic interludes. Judging by the low number of coups and insurrections (see Table 1.2), the political systems in Nicaragua and Panama evolved into stable autocracies with their counterpart in El Salvador slightly more unstable than they were. In different ways, the political systems of Guatemala and Honduras were chronically unstable. The high number of coups in Honduras reveals that politicians could not develop or stick with rules governing political succession. An above average number of coups and repeated insurrections also made Guatemala into an unstable autocracy.

Dictatorship was the form of government in 72 percent of the country-years (the share of years a country had a certain regime type) in the six largest countries of Central America between 1900 and 1980. Semi-democratic governments existed in 22 percent of the country-years, political systems that limited political competition, suffrage rights, or civil rights in a significant way. In Central America 6 percent of the total country-years were democratic, that is, political systems that hold fair and competitive elections, institutionalize widespread suffrage rights, and possess an ample system of civil rights. Democracies existed in Costa Rica and Panama 30 and 10 percent of the time, respectively, during the first 80 years of the twentieth century.

The Politics of Modern Central America

TABLE 1.2. *Dictatorship and Instability, 1900–80*

Country	Percentage of Years under Autocracy	Number of Coups	Date of Last Coup	Years of Revolt	Date of Last Revolt
Costa Rica	10%	2	1917	3	1955
El Salvador	94%	6	1979	5	1980
Guatemala	83%	9	1963	15	1980
Honduras	84%	13	1980	0	n/a
Nicaragua	90%	4	1947	12	1979
Panama	33%	4	1968	1	1931
Averages					
Central America	72%	7.8		6	
Latin America	55%	10.2		n/a	

Sources: Bowman, Lehoucq, and Mahoney (2005); data about Panama and the Latin American regime's average stem from Mainwaring, Brinks, and Pérez-Liñán (2008); data about Latin American coup average are from Lehoucq and Pérez-Liñán (2009); data on revolts are from Collier, Hoeffler, and Söderbom (2008: 475).

This information, along with other politically relevant facts, is summarized in Table 1.2, and is the result of an effort I conducted with two colleagues to correct the errors made by Polity IV and other regime classification indices (Bowman, Lehoucq, and Mahoney, 2005).

Autocracies came in two types. Most consisted of personalist tyrannies. In El Salvador, Maxmiliano Hernández Martínez ruled the country between 1931 and 1944. In Guatemala, Manuel Estrada Cabrera (1898–1920) and Jorge Ubico (1930–44) continued the tradition begun by Rafael Carrera (1839–65). In Honduras, Tiburcio Carias (1933–48) organized a dictatorship that lasted more than a dozen years. One-man rule flourished in Nicaragua, where Anastasio Somoza García (1937–47, 1950–6) consolidated an autocracy that, on his assassination in 1956, his eldest son, Luis Somoza Debayle (1956–63), inherited before himself turning power over to his brother, Anastasio Somoza Debayle (1967–72, 1974–9). The other type of dictatorship was more institutional in character, one whereby a military junta governed the country until new elections could be convened or until a new strong man formed an alliance that consolidated his hold on the presidency. Prominent examples of these include the 1944 and 1954 military juntas that came to power in the wake of Jorge Ubico and Jacobo Arbenz's overthrow, respectively, in Guatemala as well as the 1948–50, the 1960–2, and 1979 juntas that ended the governments of Salvador Castañeda Castro, José María Lemus, and Carlos Humberto Romero, respectively, in El Salvador.

The majority of autocratic presidents ruled with a constitution and the formal trappings of democracy. Virtually all held elections regularly, even if little doubt existed about their outcomes. There were ninety-six presidential elections or one every 4.2 years between 1900 and 1980. The average share of votes obtained by presidents was a whopping 67.5 percent, suggesting that many presidents ran unopposed and obtained most of the votes (allegedly) cast in elections. Why did autocrats hold elections? Holding elections revealed the strengths and weaknesses of regime factions (Cox, 2010), allowing incumbents to identify real from spurious opponents. Elections allowed dictators to co-opt members of the opposition and keep track of their activities. The Somozas of Nicaragua, for example, nominally members of the Liberal Party, allowed the opposition Conservative Party to obtain one-third of the legislative seats in elections governed by the incomplete list version of plurality rule. Holding elections made it easier to obtain diplomatic recognition from foreign powers, which was indispensable for securing loans and credits on international bond markets.

Despotic regimes responsible for large numbers of human rights abuses were not unknown. General Hernández Martínez came to power in a 1931 coup that, in the following year, organized the repression of an Indian uprising (*la matanza*) at the cost of more than 20,000 lives (Gould and Lauria-Santiago, 2008). The quasi-totalitarian Estrada Cabrera dictatorship so dominated Guatemalan society that congress ceased to exist and public opinion was forced underground. In the letters he wrote his parents, the young Munro (1983: 39–40) described this "cruel, unprogressive despotism:"

Estrada Cabrera, a civilian lawyer who was *designado*, or vice-president, had taken over the executive power when President Reyna Barrios was murdered in 1898, and for eighteen years had successfully resisted the efforts of other leaders to displace him. He killed or exiled his rivals and permitted no criticism or even discussion of his policies. This sort of thing was not uncommon in Central America, but Estrada Cabrera carried it farther than most dictators did. His treatment of potential opponents, and of people who were merely suspected of disaffection, became more and more barbarous as time went on, and there were many executions after the failure of each of the two or three attempts to kill him.

Decades later, military governments recreated the terror of these years. Both the Carlos Arana (1970–4) and Lucas García's (1978–82) dictatorships systematically exterminated domestic opponents until political dissent and guerrillas were eliminated (Brockett, 2005). Between the early 1960s and early 1990s, the security forces killed or disappeared an astounding 200,000 Guatemalans.

Dictators survived if they eliminated rivals, both in the opposition and especially in the armed forces, and reached agreements with key economic interests. It was important for autocrats to create macroeconomic stability and respect property rights so coffee and banana producers would continue to invest and make the economy grow. Lack of growth endangered these regimes because it was easier for dissident officers to depose incumbents if they capitalized on social discontent to mobilize workers, students, and opposition movements. Between 1930 and 1985, Marc Lindenberg (1990: 409) finds that economic crises generated a 57 percent probability of what he calls "non-programmed changes of presidents." During periods of economic growth, there was a 37.5 percent probability of a non-programmed change in military rulers. Coups and countercoups made up the political cycle in much of the isthmus, even if economic downturns aggravated the instability of Central American tyrannies, an outcome consistent with the finding that recession shortens all regimes, including narrowly based ones (Bueno de Mesquita et al., 2003: 307).

The data contained in Table 1.2, which displays the number of coups and years of insurrection in Central America between 1900 and 1980, reflect attempts to change the status quo. As unstable as our overviews suggest they were, regimes were more stable than unstable. On average, each Central American country had slightly less than eight coups during this period or one coup per decade. Comparable figures for Latin America as a whole were 20 percent higher, as the last row in this table reveals. Only Guatemala and Honduras were more unstable than the Central American norm. Costa Rica and Honduras are the societies with the least number of insurrections. It is Guatemala and Nicaragua that had the most experience with guerrilla activity until the 1980s.

Agro-Export-Led Growth and Social Conditions

Economic growth did improve average incomes in most of Central America in the decades after World War II. GDP per capita grew by an average annual rate of 2.8 and 3.1 percent in Costa Rica and Panama between 1950 and 1980, the golden age of economic growth in the post–World War II era. Stated differently, the economies of these countries would double their GDP per capita in 24.8 and 22.8 years at these growth rates. The economy grew by 2.1 percent in Guatemala and 1.5 percent in El Salvador, allowing these countries to double the GDP per capita rates in 33.1 and 47.8 years, respectively. It grew by 1.5 in both Honduras and Nicaragua. At this rate of growth, GDP per capita would double every 46 years. The GDP per capita rates would have been almost twice as high – 3.0 percent – in Nicaragua in this thirty-year period if it had grown at the average annual rate registered between 1950 and 1975, meaning that GDP per capita would have doubled in 23 years (Maddison, 2010). Armed conflict sent the growth rate into a nosedive by 1977 (a pattern we analyze in the second and fourth chapters of this book). Two years of civil war cost the Nicaraguan economy dearly, a contrast that illustrates the power of compound interest or, put differently, of why even minor changes in average annual growth rates have long-term and dramatic consequences.

Was this an impressive or lackluster performance? On the one hand, many criticized these results, especially during the 1970s and 1980s, because they concentrated the gains from trade in a few households (e.g., Torres-Rivas, 1993; Vilas, 1995; Weeks, 1985; Williams, 1986). Data on the distributional impact of tax and agricultural policies and of economic growth suggest that states did little, outside of Costa Rica and Panama (and perhaps Honduras), to alter highly unequal societies. The grim logic of being small, agro-exporting economies with an unequal distribution of land and other resources meant that median rural households most likely saw their incomes stagnate over a thirty-year period, even if per capita incomes were steadily increasing in most republics. This led to the decision to flee to urban areas, which fueled the growth of the informal sector in Central American cities, or to join the ranks of migratory wage labor, a trend especially notable in El Salvador and Guatemala.

Only in Costa Rica did social policy compensate these households so economic growth was accompanied by a rapid decline in the number of households living in poverty. As a result, the population living in poverty fell by half, from 50 to 25 percent between 1950 and 1980 in Costa Rica (PEN, 2003: 398). Although the absence of comparable figures for the rest of the isthmus prevents calculating the trends in poverty levels since mid-century, available data suggest that the social costs of authoritarianism were high. In 1980, the first date for which comparable data exist, an average of 62.8 percent of Central Americans lived in poverty (IICA-FLACSO, 1991: 121), a rate almost twice as high as the Latin American mean. Even Panama, the other country that experienced strong growth since World War II, had half of its population living in poverty in 1980.

These figures no doubt exaggerate the depth of poverty, and perhaps even the differences between Costa Rica and her neighbors. By 1980, incomes had fallen dramatically from the mid-1970s, the post–World War II high because of civil war and the collapse of the international price of coffee and bananas (and the rise of international interest rates by the end of this decade). In the form of a map, Figure 1.4 displays the 1980 poverty rates as well as each country's GDP per capita as a share of the Western European average in 1975, the high point in post–World War II levels of economic development.

On the other hand, related indicators suggest that social conditions were getting (slightly) better or (marginally) less intolerable. By 1980, a majority of each country's population – an average of 70 percent – had learned to read and write, an improvement of nearly 10 percent since 1960. By 1980, nearly 8.3 and just about 15.2 percent of Costa Ricans and Panamanians, respectively, could not read or write. High literacy rates in Costa Rica were, in part, the result of state efforts, starting in the last quarter of the nineteenth century, to send all citizens to school (Molina and Palmer, 2004). By 1980, average life expectancy in Central America was 66.5 years, an improvement of 10 years, with these rates in Costa Rica and Panama approximating the rates of developed countries. These results are summarized in Table 1.3.

Infant mortality rates provide perhaps the best single measure of development because they are a product of a mother's nutrition (which largely depends on her income and educational level) and how her society organizes health care provision (which is a function of the amount of public sector funds available and how effectively its bureaucracy is organized). Although the regional average infant mortality rate fell by half – from 82.6 to 40.9 deaths per thousand live births – between 1960 and 1980, it remained above the regional average in El Salvador, Guatemala, Honduras, and Nicaragua even by 1980. It fell most dramatically in Costa Rica because public pressure, in the context of a

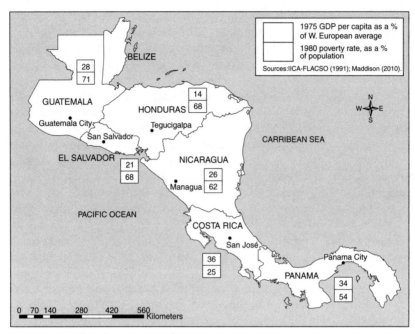

FIGURE 1.4. Development Levels, circa 1975.

TABLE 1.3. *Leading Social Indicators, 1960–80*

Country	Illiteracy Rate (as a Share of Adult Population)			Life Expectancy at Birth (in Years)			Infant Mortality (per 1,000 Live Births)		
	1960	1970	1980	1960	1970	1980	1960	1970	1980
Costa Rica	17%	12%	8%	66	71	75	68	30	17
El Salvador	52%	42%	34%	56	57	64	110	95	54
Guatemala	65%	55%	47%	50	56	61	116	91	67
Honduras	56%	47%	39%	51	58	65	119	81	53
Nicaragua	53%	43%	39%	52	58	62	113	90	65
Panama	27%	21%	15%	64	69	72	52	36	30
Averages									
Central America	40%	33%	30%	57	61	67	83	60	41
Latin America	37%	29%	23%	55	60	64	68	60	54
Developing	61%	55%	46%	44	53	59	153	112	94

Sources: Illiteracy rates are from Bergés, FitzGerald, and Thorp (2007); all other data are from PENR (2008: 583).

competitive political system, empowered bureaucratic agencies to improve the quality and access to public health (McGuire, 2010).

Comparisons suggest that illiteracy rates were lower in Central America than in the average developing country. Even in 1960, illiteracy never affected a majority of Central Americans, although it did afflict slightly more than 60 percent of the inhabitants of the developing world. By 1980, 30 percent of Central Americans remained illiterate while 46 percent of the developing-world population was unable to read and write. Average illiteracy rates in Central America were always higher than in Latin America as a whole, where less than a fifth of the population could not read or write. Again, global comparisons suggest that individuals in many other developing countries faced even worse conditions. Data in Table 1.3 indicate that infant mortality rates were twice as high in the average developing country.

We can say much the same about growth rates themselves. It is hard to say that results between 1950 and 1980 were remarkable because most Central American countries were growing at a rate below the world average. During these three decades, the world's average economic growth rate per capita was 2.6, a rate that allows a doubling of average incomes every 27 years. Only Costa Rica and Panama's rate of economic growth surpassed the global growth rate. The average annual growth rate in GDP per capita of fifty-seven African countries, many of which belong to the bottom billion, was 1.8 percent during this period, a rate that El Salvador, Honduras, and Nicaragua fail to match. So, by the standards of their past and of comparable countries, a barometer Bulmer-Thomas (1988: 43) finds useful, economic growth was varied and mediocre.

Exporting coffee, bananas, and a handful of other commodities did not – and perhaps – could not transform these economies. This development model created powerful incentives for states to concentrate on improving the conditions for agro-export growth, especially in a region dominated by nondemocratic political systems. This situation not only limited economic diversification, but also did little to shield the isthmus from downturns in the world economy. The slump of 1978, for example, reduced three decades of GDP per capita increases in El Salvador and Nicaragua, two decades in Honduras, one decade in Costa Rica, and one-half decade of per capita increases in Guatemala (Bulmer-Thomas, 1987: 269). This is why, over the course of three decades, Central America did not decrease the breach separating the region with that of the developed world. As the data in Figure 1.4 show, only Costa Rica was a third of the way to the Western European average, with Honduras just below 15 percent of this mean.

Conclusions

This chapter has sketched a model of a developing country that matches many central features of Central American societies. It suggests that capital-scarce economies in the tropics will specialize in products for which international demand exists. This explains why these economies exported coffee and bananas and, after World War II, also began to export cattle, cotton, and sugar. In markets with a nearly infinite supply of these commodities, Central Americans could not set the prices for these exports, which put a premium on keeping the costs of production – especially labor and tax rates – low. This model explains why the economies of Central America did grow during the three decades after World War II, but why the gains from trade, outside of Costa Rica, remained concentrated in a relatively small number of households. These are the central economic and distributional facts of development on the isthmus on the eve of the 1970s.

The received wisdom does less well in accounting for the establishment of reactionary despotism, which assumes that the development of the coffee economy required dictatorship to keep the costs of production low. Yet, developments in Costa Rica suggest that democracy would have been perfectly compatible with export-led growth. The production of coffee (and bananas) thrived with regularly held elections in what became the region's most vibrant agro-export economy.

The origins of divergent regime trajectories instead reside in the nature of political competition itself. Where the struggle for hegemony led to ongoing stalemates, as in Costa Rica, contending political forces learned to share state power, an arrangement that gradually reduced the powers of the executive and enfranchised increasing numbers of voters. Where strongmen managed to impose themselves, as in the rest of the isthmus, the military became the arbiter of state power. The chaos that engulfed Central America – so well analyzed by Munro (1918) and later by Mahoney (2001) – typically ended when a strong man vanquished his rivals and institutionalized his rule in the personalist dictatorships once so commonplace on the isthmus. Whether elected or imposed, executives nurtured the burgeoning export economy because state revenues largely hinged on taxing the imports and commerce made possible by the international trade in coffee and bananas. And it was preferential access to the executive, along with the familiarity with ways of protecting privileges, that led exporters to back democracy in Costa Rica and autocracy everywhere else on the isthmus.

Reactionary despotism was stubbornly resistant to change because oligarchs could easily defend their privileges. Even if democratic leaders enact policies that lead to more growth (and better social indicators), the diffuse nature of these benefits makes it harder to mobilize support among the much larger constituency – the electorate – to which such leaders are accountable. A narrow set of interests, in contrast, does not face the collective action problems that democratically elected officials do. Small size facilitates reaching decisions about which executives oligarchs chose to support – and which to oppose. Interest in maintaining the status quo bred a preference for captive governments, ones whose benefits always appeared larger than the uncertain results of political change.

The long-term costs of manifestly political decisions were vast, which are perhaps best comprehended by imagining a world of what democracy might have wrought. Competitive party politics would have made public officials responsive to electoral majorities, not principally to oligarchs and officers. It would have generated incentives to provide physical infrastructure, education, health care, and pensions that, as the case of Costa Rica demonstrates, would have increased growth rates and the livelihoods of millions. That a political standoff developed in this country – one that dispersed power and the gains from international trade – therefore had enormous benefits for development and the welfare of its citizens, ones that their Central American counterparts can only rue that they did not obtain.

2

Civil War, Revolution, and Economic Collapse

Introduction

Civil war raged in Central America throughout the 1980s and into the 1990s. It led to the killing of at least 300,000 people, the vast majority of whom were civilians. It produced between 1.8 million and 2.8 million refugees.[1] War also devastated the economies of El Salvador, Guatemala, and Nicaragua. It was not until the first decade of the twenty-first century, as we will see in Chapter 4, that GDP per capita rates regained prewar levels.

These were surprising outcomes because civil wars rarely happen. There was less than a 2 percent probability that a country, in any given year, experienced an ongoing attempt to overthrow the government (and in which at least 1,000 soldiers and insurgents lost their lives) between 1945 and 2000 (Fearon and Laitin, 2003; Sambanis, 2004). Revolutions – or rebellions that toppled governments and tried to transform their societies – are rarer still. Since the French Revolution of 1789, there have been only seventeen social revolutions, a number that increases by half if we include the "velvet" revolutions of Eastern Europe after the fall of the Berlin Wall (Goodwin, 2001: 4).

The same methods suggest that civil war was a lot more common in Central America. Sixteen percent of the country-years in Central America involved violent conflict between governments and insurgents – eight times more than in the rest of the world. What made civil war so much more likely on the isthmus? One popular response to this question, especially common during the 1970s and 1980s, is that poverty and underdevelopment made conflict "inevitable," to cite the title of one diplomatic historian's account of these years (LaFeber, 1983). It is very much this account that quantitative, cross-national studies champion. Another reply emphasizes political dynamics, one that suggests that the closed nature of most political systems left the deployment of violence a viable (unfortunately) option to end tyranny in Central America.

---

[1] The penultimate section of Chapter 3 contains the sources for this estimate. The source for refugees is Dunkerley (1994: 47).

This chapter synthesizes more than three decades' worth of research – especially those by Brockett (2005), Goodwin (2001), and Wickham-Crowley (1992) – to argue that it was a political crisis of enormous proportions that destabilized the ancien regimes of the isthmus, not a crisis that can be attributed to increasing poverty or inequality. While war did not break out in the wealthier countries – Costa Rica and Panama – it also did not occur in the region's poorest country – Honduras. Although some social indicators took a turn for the worse in several countries during the 1970s and everywhere in the 1980s, they were still better than in prior decades, when the region remained largely quiescent. As it turns out, violent conflict preceded the decline in economic growth – a situation that became much worse in 1979, when the price for the region's exports dropped precipitously, although the dramatic fall in growth and incomes, once underway, no doubt intensified political struggle.

My analysis builds on the insights of the previous chapter, where I explained why reactionary despotism was simultaneously resilient and faction-ridden. While the beneficiaries of dictatorship could easily mobilize to veto political change, their behavior only added to the factional instability of regimes where generals and colonels were jockeying for power and privilege. These were what I now call inconsistently authoritarian regimes, ones unable to exterminate the opposition and establish stable rules governing political succession. State weakness and executive instability furnished the openings for reformers, street protesters, and insurgents to contest brutal dictatorships. Where guerrillas exploited a crisis of succession – one accelerated by Somoza's August 1977 heart attack – to isolate the dictatorship from its (upper-class) allies, as in Nicaragua, they helped defeat the regime in a bloody civil war and lead a social revolution. Where they did not, as in El Salvador – and, moreover, provoked the opposition of U.S. foreign policy makers – insurrection split the old order and forced it to fight a prolonged civil war. Where dominant factions regrouped, as in Guatemala, they used the military to deploy unparalleled brutality to defeat the insurgency.

This chapter analyzes the impact of foreign powers, especially the United States, on the balance of power between right-wing governments and left-wing insurgents because it so often shaped political outcomes on the region. Since the nineteenth century, U.S. interventionism in Latin America has occurred largely in Central America and the Caribbean (Blasier, 1985; Black, 1998; Leonard, 1991; and, on the Soviet Union's limited role, see Blasier, 1987). From occupying Cuba (1898–1902), the Dominican Republic (1915–24), Haiti (1915–34), and Nicaragua (1912–33), it has sponsored coups against governments in Guatemala (1954), sent military and intelligence assistance to El Salvador and Guatemala, and funded insurgents in Nicaragua (1981–90) – actions that American conservatives have defended as necessary to rid the region of communists and thus to protect the national interest (Kirkpatrick, 1979). U.S. foreign policy makers, as a result, typically sided with the military and against democracy until well into the 1980s. Only in Costa Rica did Washington support democracy, even as it pressured governments in San José to get embroiled in its war against the Sandinistas (Honey, 1994).

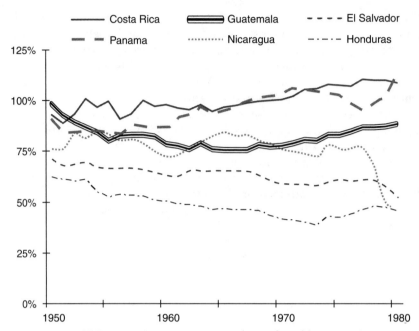

FIGURE 2.1. GDP per capita, 1950–80 (as a share of world average GDP per capita). *Source*: Maddison (2010).

The Social and Economic Prerequisites of Civil War

The cross-national, statistical literature on civil war identifies several conditions that increase the likelihood of massive civil conflict (Fearon, 2010, and Sambanis, 2004 contain a review of the key papers). The first condition is poverty: Countries with lower GDP per capita levels are more prone to civil war. The second is, oddly enough, population size: Countries with larger populations are more likely to witness civil wars. These two conditions are the ones over which there is the most confidence: Their coefficients are statistically significant in the dozen or so papers on civil war.

Poverty, as proxied by GDP per capita rates, accounts for the ranking among most cases on the isthmus. Civil war did afflict the poorer countries (El Salvador, Guatemala, and Nicaragua) but not the wealthier ones (Costa Rica and Panama). Honduras, however, defies expectations: Its GDP per capita was the lowest on the isthmus, but it did not experience violent conflict. Yet, with two exceptions, all countries had GDP per capita rates of 75 percent of the global mean, as trends in Figure 2.1 reveal. El Salvador and Honduras had GDP per capita rates hovering around half the international average. So, in the cross-national regressions about civil war, most of Central America was not in an economic zone likely to lead to civil war.

Population size also is not a factor distinguishing countries that went to war from those that did not. Although the most populous country, Guatemala (6.1 million in 1980), experienced a civil war, El Salvador's population (4.8 million) is just above the regional mean of 4.5 million, and Nicaragua's (2.7 million) is substantially below it. The isthmus had an average population size just above a quarter of the Latin American mean and slightly more than an eighth of the developing world's average in 1980 (see Table 1.1). Civil war still engulfed three of the societies on the isthmus, despite their small populations.

There are some surprises on this list. Lack of economic growth is rarely associated with the onset of civil war. Recessions turn voters against incumbents in democratic systems, but they seem to have no effect on the outbreak of civil war. Civil war, however, does undermine economic growth: It took more than a decade to recover prewar GDP per capita levels in El Salvador, Guatemala, and Nicaragua. The maintenance of political peace since the 1980s on the isthmus also suggests that lack of growth does not reignite armed conflict, a finding at odds with the cross-national literature. I caution to add that this is a less robust finding than others, because not all studies agree on this point.

Ethnic diversity rarely leads to civil war. Although the Western imagination might be fixated on the handful of cases of primordial hatreds leading to massacres and wars (Rwanda comes to mind), the research is unambiguous in failing to unearth a relationship between ethnic complexity and civil war. Indeed, with the exception of Guatemala, the cultural homogeneity of Central American societies illustrates the point that ethnic complexity has little to do with civil war. Although violence can break out because of ethnically based conflict, it does not develop any more frequently in ethnically complex than in culturally homogeneous societies.

Perhaps the biggest surprise is that inequality does not contribute to civil war, even if most analysts agree that inequality should be fueling political conflict. The absence of systematic data on income distribution is an important reason cross-national statistical research is mostly silent about the impact of inequality on civil war. With the exception of the two dozen or so rich societies (Atkinson and Piketty, 2007), we can only speculate about inequality levels before the 1980s, because household surveys – the basic building block of Gini coefficients and related measures – simply do not exist for many countries until the last decades of the twentieth century. Similarly, inspection of landholding patterns in Costa Rica and Guatemala indicates that agricultural censuses – the standard source for measures of land redistribution – underestimate the weight of big farms, because large landholders will register their properties with cadastral authorities but not with census enumerators (Edelman and Seligson, 1994; Seligson and Kelley, 1986). As a result, most cross-national statistical studies on civil war simply do not assess the impact of this factor, although several studies using available data on income and land inequality find that countries with larger levels of inequality are slightly more likely to experience violent conflict (Boix, 2008; Mueller and Seligson, 1987).

The Central American cases do not provide a lot of evidence for the argument that inequality leads to civil war. First, the shares of national income received by the bottom and top 20 percent did not really change between 1970 and 1980, as Figure 2.2 shows. The bottom 20 percent received less than 5 percent of national income in Central America at the beginning and end of this decade. The bottom 20 percent in Guatemala received slightly more than 5 percent. The top 20 percent obtained more than half of all income, with Costa Rica

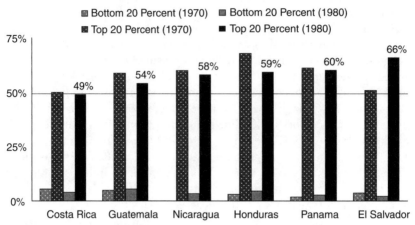

FIGURE 2.2. Income distribution, 1970–80.
Source: IICA-FLACSO (1991: 117).

registering a rate of 49 percent in 1980. Everywhere but in El Salvador, the top 20 percent witnessed a slight decline in their share of national income. Indeed, only in El Salvador did income distribution worsen during this decade – and this country did undergo a major civil war. In Guatemala and Nicaragua, the two other societies to experience violent conflict, income distribution slightly improved, although missing data for the bottom 20 percent makes it hard to know for sure in Nicaragua.

Second, the countries with the most inequality did not become the most violent. Income becomes noticeably more concentrated only in El Salvador, which distinguishes this case from the others. The share of national income going to the richest 20 percent of the population is similar in Honduras, Nicaragua, and Panama, but only Nicaragua saw its government battling insurgents. Costa Rica is again the least inequitable country, and Guatemala is less inequitable than its neighbors. Data on land distribution in the mid-1970s tells a similar story (Brockett, 1992: 171). For example, the percentage of rural families without land is roughly a quarter of the rural population. At one extreme, 36 percent of rural families are landless in El Salvador. Both Guatemala and Honduras have similar rates of landlessness: 32 percent. Landless families are 20 percent of rural families in Costa Rica and 27 percent in Nicaragua. Other measures of land or rural inequality, including the average size of smallholder farms and the Gini index of land concentration, Brockett reminds us, reveal that the countries that remained peaceful do not look that different from the countries that exploded.

An index of real working-class wages in Figure 2.3 provides evidence that the condition of laborers declined more swiftly in the countries that experienced civil war than in those that did not. The wages of urban and rural workers shrank the most in El Salvador, Guatemala, and Nicaragua.

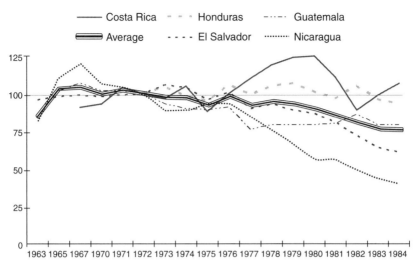

FIGURE 2.3. Index of real working-class wages, 1963–84.
Note: 100 = 1963.
Source: Booth (1991: 42).

In Costa Rica and Honduras, in contrast, wages increased until 1980 and 1979, respectively, when badly managed balance-of-payments crises led to economic collapse in Costa Rica and decline in Honduras (but even then, wages returned to their historical average in both countries). This divergence between the countries that had civil wars and those that did not, in fact, leads Bulmer-Thomas (1987: 219–224) to emphasize the importance of a broader difference between these sets of cases, between the ones in which employers negotiated differences with labor unions and the ones in which they deployed the state to crush organized workers. These trends, it bears emphasizing, are consistent not only with data on labor's declining share of national income in El Salvador, Guatemala, and Nicaragua noted by Reynolds (1978), which I discuss in Chapter 1, but also with the stagnation of GDP per capita rates in these countries (see Figure 2.1).

More microlevel studies echo the finding about the dwindling purchasing power of working-class wages. A comparison of the cases emphasizes that increasing numbers of peasants were pushed below subsistence in Central America (Vilas, 1995). In Nicaragua, Wickham-Crowley (1992) relies on Jeffery Gould's (1990) research to argue that declining rural conditions, along with a tradition of rural rebellion, helped ignite insurgency. Manus Midlarsky and Kenneth Roberts (1985) argue that greater land scarcity and inequality (Burke, 1976; Colindres, 1976) led to rebellion in El Salvador. Jeffrey Paige (1983) argues that in Guatemala, increasing numbers of rural Maya had become landless or owned plots of land insufficient for survival. It was the widespread development of a landless wage proletariat, he argues, that sparked revolution in the countryside. By 1980, an average of 69 percent of the population in El Salvador, Guatemala, and Honduras lived in poverty. The poverty rate was slightly lower in Nicaragua (62 percent), even lower in Panama (54 percent), and substantially lower in Costa Rica (25 percent; IICA-FLACSO, 1991: 121).

Yet, inspection of trends in working-class wages, the strongest evidence in favor of the inequality thesis, suggests that violent conflict preceded – not followed – the economic spiral downward. Inspection of the trends in Figure 2.3 indicates that the index for each country remained tightly around the regional average until 1976, when it started to fall swiftly for Guatemala and Nicaragua. As we shall see, it was in the early 1970s when urban protesters and rural guerrillas began to organize against dictatorship in these countries. The intensification of protest led investors to reduce their exposure in El Salvador, Guatemala, and Honduras, which, in the short term, combined with the increase in import prices since 1973 (mitigated, in part, by high international prices for coffee in the mid-1970s) to worsen inflation (Bulmer-Thomas, 1987: 212). The boom turned to bust by 1978, which reduced incomes throughout the region and thus aggravated a political crisis that was years in the making (López, 1986).

There is also the broader point that inequality in Central America, with the partial exception of Costa Rica, has always been high, with large percentages of the population living in poverty. Such facts help explain why there have always been opponents of dictatorship on the isthmus and why social movements or guerrillas found recruits for their causes. If social conditions have consistently been ripe for social revolution, then the real puzzle is why political conflict remained nonviolent in El Salvador and Nicaragua until the 1970s. Only in Guatemala did insurgents and governments fight each other between 1960 and 1996, with temporary lulls in the warfare. A related puzzle is why nothing of the sort happened in Honduras, which was just as unequal as its violent neighbors, even if working-class wages did not experience the (war-induced) decline of these cases.

Critics nevertheless could claim that the underlying weaknesses of the region's export-led development were ultimately the cause of the descent into violence in the late 1970s (Pérez-Brignoli, 2011; also, see Rouquié, 1994; Williams, 1986). Sooner or later, they argue, an explosion was going to occur. Such an argument, however, is immune to falsification because either the absence or presence of revolt is interpreted as confirmation of its key theoretical claims. It ignores the argument that explaining *when* a civil war begins is as important as speculating *why* it will occur. At any rate, there is not much comparative evidence that wages always decline before major political upheavals. In a comprehensive test of the impact of social and economic factors on civil war, Jack A. Goldstone and his colleagues (2010) find that economic decline (which tends to lead to a fall in wages) does not determine when countries will experience violent political conflict. This article, along with a handful of other papers, suggests that certain regime types are prone to armed confrontations between incumbents and opposition movements.

Inconsistently Authoritarian Regimes

The claim that the causes of civil war and revolution could be political in origin is one associated with Theda Skocpol's monumental *States and Social Revolutions* (1979; also, see Skocpol, 1994). In a comparison of the French, Russian, and Chinese revolutions, Skocpol finds that states must be financially troubled and militarily weakened before they lose an armed struggle. The existence of social grievances is not enough, although it may well set the stage for widespread popular support of the overthrow of the ancien regime.

A branch of the cross-national statistical research assesses the impact of regime variables, an effort made possible by the existence of systematic classifications of political systems such as the Polity IV project. The key claim is that mixed regimes – which are also known as partial democracies, semi-democracies, or even partial autocracies – are more likely to come under attack because they are not strong enough to exterminate dissent, even if they control or repress it. Holding elections for high and even legislative office may, in fact, be a device to identify the opposition's strength (Cox, 2010), but one that does not threaten the monopolization of state power. Although such regimes do not permit, as democracies do, genuine competition, nor do they respect an ample set of civil rights, they are not outright dictatorships – that is, political systems whose leaders inherit or conquer high office (and where elections, at most, ratify a predetermined choice) and that do not respect individual rights. They are an unstable mix of democratic and authoritarian characteristics, ones that opponents believe they can fragment and defeat.

There is cross-national statistical evidence for the claim that civil wars are most likely to afflict mixed systems. A reformulation of the first generation of civil war models suggests that measures of good governance (drawn from the World Bank's Worldwide Governance Indicators) help explain why governments and opponents fight civil wars in some poor countries but not in others (Fearon, 2010). A Norwegian group of researchers, in an analysis of regimes and civil onset between 1816 and 1992 (Hegre et al., 2001) argue that semi-democratic regimes, using the standard Polity IV measures, are most at risk of experiencing a civil war. A far-reaching effort to forecast the outbreak of civil war, using an ingenious case-control method (one that matches cases of civil war with a random sample of unaffected cases similar in background conditions), finds that different types of mixed regimes are, by far, the best predictor of civil war onset in a sample of all countries between 1955 and 2003 (Goldstone et al., 2010). The research indicates that partial democracies with factionalism are 28.5 times more likely to experience a civil war than full autocracies; partial autocracies are seven times more likely to descend into violent dictatorships. The only social or economic indicator that remains statistically significant is infant mortality, which indicates that high rates of child death make a country 4.19 times more likely to have a civil war than a country with low rates.

None of the Central American cases that experienced civil war, however, were mixed regimes. Polity IV (specifically, the POLITY2 variable) mistakenly refers to the existence of semi-democracies in El Salvador and Guatemala in the 1960s and 1970s – regimes that were unambiguously authoritarian – although correctly labels the political system of Nicaragua – the case that underwent a civil war and ended with a revolution – an outright autocracy. With the exception of Costa Rica, all regimes on the isthmus were dictatorships, especially those that waged bloody wars against their adversaries. This is the conclusion of a comprehensive classification of these systems during the twentieth century, which, along with two colleagues, I produced. It focuses on five dimensions of political democracy: broad political liberties, competitive elections, inclusive participation, civilian supremacy, and national sovereignty. We treat each of these five dimensions as a necessary condition for political democracy, based on a reading of all English- and Spanish-language sources and fuzzy-set rules for coding and aggregating necessary conditions (Bowman, Lehoucq, and Mahoney, 2005). A revised classification of the Polity IV data, based on its executive recruitment and levels of participation variables, in fact recognizes the troublesome nature of the standard classification. It depicts the Guatemalan political system as a "full autocracy" while still labeling El Salvador as having what it calls a "partial autocracy" (PITF, 2010).

A related measure of instability – large-scale protest – does reveal that the politically mobilized societies did experience civil war. As the following analysis demonstrates, Central Americans had been organizing against dictatorships for decades. Peasants and workers formed unions to fight for higher wages and better working conditions and against violations of their rights. Citizens formed parties and, where possible, organized campaigns for elected office. Others organized guerrilla movements (Kruijt, 2008), ones that permitted them to hide in the mountains covering much of Central America (Fearon and Laitin, 2003). The ability to contest autocracies tells us something vital about authoritarianism in Central America – and about the nature of anti-regime activities in repressive dictatorships.

In the paragraphs that follow, I analyze how regimes responded to the rise of opposition collective action. My aim is to show that there were numerous efforts to challenge dictatorship in the decades before 1980, because reactionary despotism was, paradoxically enough, both a durable and an unstable political arrangement. It persisted because its beneficiaries could swiftly organize to protect their interests and maintain the closed character of this regime. Although ambitious officers occasionally sought alliances with labor unions or even opposition politicians to outflank regime hardliners, the escalation of social demands that would accompany such efforts usually led to repression – and often by regime moderates themselves, largely because their hold on power was so tenuous. Regime hardliners, egged on by spokespersons of the economic right, typically overthrew these governments. This is why it was so rare for these experiments to lead to democracy. Countercoups by the right prevented liberalization from turning into democracy, which served to reinforce the equilibrium in favor of the status quo (Przeworski, 1991: 62–63).

Having no clear rules of political succession, however, made these regimes unstable: Their cliques and cabals incessantly jockeyed for position and a share of the spoils. Although failure kept reformers within the fold, ambition and rivalry repeatedly led factions to challenge incumbents. The result was regimes that were, to modify a term about the instability of mixed regimes (Gates et al., 2006), "inconsistently authoritarian." As their successful authoritarian counterparts, these regimes monopolized power and put clear limits on the activities they would tolerate. Unlike effective autocracies, however, inconsistently authoritarian regimes relaxed some of these boundaries, which fomented development of political movements that autocrats would never allow to obtain state power.

The Rise and Fall of Dictatorship in Nicaragua

It was a nearly fatal blow at the heart of the regime in August 1977 – when Somoza suffered a massive coronary attack – that accelerated the struggle over political succession, one that reignited the factionalism a dynastic autocracy had learned to quell. Businessmen had begun to defect from the regime in the aftermath of the 1972 earthquake, when Somoza appropriated much of the foreign aid coming to the country and made a drive to control larger sectors of the country's economy. The deployment of large-scale violence against his opponents and Nicaraguan society, more generally, accelerated the formation of a broad-based coalition against the regime, one that included businessmen, petty tradesmen, students, and unemployed young men. International isolation also deprived the regime of support when it needed the arms and financial resources to confront a rebellion. It was the dramatic increase in opposition activity – protests, street assaults, and guerrilla attacks – that brought down the Somoza dictatorship by 1979, despite the appalling repression the regime unleashed. To understand why the regime fell requires analyzing how the Somozas gradually undermined the coalition they had carefully assembled since 1933, when the first Somoza began his bid to consolidate power.

Opposition to Somoza started soon after the 1934 assassination of Augusto Sandino, the nationalist guerrilla leader whose name would adorn the 1979 revolution. Although Sandino had become a legendary guerrilla leader battling U.S. occupation of his country, Anastasio Somoza was consolidating his power over the U.S.-trained National Guard. U.S. Marines had arrived in 1910 to stabilize a conservative regime, one under attack by the Liberal Party, which itself had lost control of the presidency to a conservative-led insurrection in 1909. Two and a half decades later, Somoza, a member of the Liberal Party, was the latest warlord attempting to create a long-lasting regime in Nicaragua, despite U.S. efforts to create a competitive democracy bridging the divide between conservatives and liberals (Dodd, 1992). Killing Sandino, who was also a liberal, was part of a broader strategy to pacify the country under Somoza's domination.

Analysis of political dynamics suggests that Somoza almost failed to consolidate his regime (Walter, 1993), even if retrospection mistakenly suggests that creating a long-term family dynasty was inevitable. Protest and opposition greeted Somoza. Labor unions organized strikes against his government. Peasants continued to evade efforts by national governments to tax them and restrict their activities. Conservatives, who had been battling liberals for decades, were plotting their return to power, even as they witnessed Somoza send his uncle (his wife's father), President Juan Sacasa (1932–6), out of the country. They saw him resign his post as Commander of the National Guard and win the 1936 elections, in part because the governing liberals had exiled their own candidate. After his inauguration, Somoza resumed his command of the Guard and held elections in 1938 for a Constituent Assembly, one in which his followers easily controlled a majority in the body that produced the 1939 Constitution. Somoza accepted that his "transitory" regime would last until 1947, in part to forestall the unification of his adversaries around an anti-regime platform.

Somoza quashed a tentative political opening in the late 1940s. He turned against his handpicked successor, Leonardo Argüello, once the new president swiftly moved to defy Somoza and realign the complex alliances between parties and caudillos, interest-groups and voters after winning the 1947 elections unopposed. Within a year, Somoza overthrew Argüello's effort to liberalize the regime. Although Argüello had begun to use the presidential power to oppose Somoza, he had failed to replace somocista officers with his supporters. Somoza had remained in control of the National Guard, the force able to suppress dissent and maintain order (Walter, 1993: 155–160).

The dictator managed to fashion a system of domination – somocismo – that would endure until the 1970s. It was built on using spies and the National Guard, which learned to identify dissent and neutralize it (Millet, 1977). It hinged on a series of alliances that co-opted key sectors of Nicaraguan society and politics. Labor unions got recognition from the regime and negotiated collective agreements with their employers, in exchange for not backing efforts to topple the regime. Conservatives won the right to send representatives to congress as a result of several pacts and an electoral reform that awarded the most successful opposition party with one-third of a district's legislative seats (the most voted party, always the Liberal Party, got two-thirds of the legislative seats – a system known as the "incomplete list"). As the opposition was emptied of its core members, acquiescence to Somoza's rule became widespread. Efforts to overthrow the regime declined as fewer groups were willing to risk detection and punishment by the regime's security forces. In 1959, the dictatorship imprisoned Pedro Joaquín Chamorro and Enrique Lecayo, two prominent conservatives, after easily defeating their invasion from Costa Rican territory.

Remaining opposition to the Somoza dictatorship became both quixotic and violent. Although conservatives and leftists plotted against the dictator, their efforts proved fruitless against a regime with an efficient security apparatus and the complicity of major economic interests. In 1956, Rigoberto López Pérez, a young poet known for his anti-regime proclivities, shot Somoza (before being killed by the dictator's bodyguards) after managing to slip into a dance in the city of León attended by Somoza himself. In the days and weeks after the assassination, the regime rounded on more than 3,000 opponents for interrogation. Congress quickly selected its president, Luis Somoza, one of the dictator's sons, to finish his father's term before himself being elected president in 1957.

It was an act of nature – an earthquake – not a downturn in the economy or increasing levels of inequality that dislodged a pillar of support for the regime. The 1972 earthquake of a magnitude of 7.5 on the Richter scale killed 5,000, injured 20,000, left more than 250,000 homeless, and destroyed central Managua. The earthquake frayed Anastasio Somoza's relationships with the country's business class (Luis's brother, Anastasio, previously the Commander of the National Guard, had become president in 1967, after his brother had died of a massive heart attack in this year). Disaster relief was siphoned off by Somoza and members of his regime. A disproportionate share of the public works construction contracts went to Somoza's cronies. It was from this date that crucial members of the upper class – businessmen, bankers, prominent families – began to withdraw support for the regime. Leading members of the Conservative Party became openly critical of the regime; Chamorro, editor of *La Prensa*, the country's newspaper of record, began publicizing the regime's excesses and human rights violations, especially after 1977. The Chamber of Industries; of Commerce; and cotton, cattle, and coffee producers formed the Superior Council of Private Initiative (COSEP) and began to contest the regime's economic policies. Many Nicaraguans, especially the natural disaster victims, soured on an increasingly corrupt regime, although the absence of public opinion polls makes it hard to determine the magnitude and nature of ordinary opposition to the dictatorship.

The Sandinistas resurfaced in the wake of the earthquake, although the National Guard had just about exterminated them in several skirmishes by the early 1970s. The Sandinista National Liberation Front (FSLN) had been created in 1961 by Carlos Fonseca Amador and Tomás Borge (who had just quit the pro-Moscow Nicaraguan Socialist Party), Edén Pastora's Sandino Revolutionary Front, and other left-wing groups. During Christmas 1974, Borge led a small band of Sandinistas to the home of José María Castillo, where prominent members of the Somoza family were celebrating. Although U.S. Ambassador Thomas Shelton had left the party, the Sandinistas managed to capture more than two dozen dignitaries. After killing Castillo, they negotiated a ransom of fourteen imprisoned Sandinistas, including Daniel Ortega; $U.S. 1 million in cash; and the publication of their 12,000-word communiqué lambasting the dictatorship and U.S. imperialism and asking the Nicaraguan people to overthrow the Somozas. The success of this action began to shift the balance in favor of the third-force (*tercerista*) faction within the FSLN, led by

Daniel Ortega and his brother, Humberto, which favored military actions that would spark the rapid development of widespread protest against the regime. The terceristas had forsaken the long-term construction of an alliance with peasants, known as the "Prolonged Popular War" tendency, championed by Borge and Henry Ruíz, or the mobilization of urban workers favored by the "Proletarian Tendency," led by Jaime Wheelock Román.

The regime hardened its stance in the aftermath of the 1974 Christmas party ransom. It declared a state of siege. It curtailed already limited press freedoms and increased its surveillance of the population. It also went after the Sandinistas. Within a year, the National Guard had killed dozens of Sandinistas. By 1975, the U.S. State Department reported that only fifty guerrillas were left in the country (cited in Pastor, 2002: 41).

Two subsequent events shook the regime. First, U.S. President Jimmy Carter's January 1977 announcement that the promotion of human rights would become a cornerstone of U.S. foreign policy unsettled Somoza. Even if the United States did not turn against the dictator, Somoza interpreted the change in policy as a withdrawal of support, according to Robert Pastor (2002: 44–45), the Latin American specialist on Carter's National Security Council. To placate international critics of his regime, Somoza lifted the state of siege in September 1977 (imposed after the 1974 Christmas party kidnapping) and began to address questions about the future of his presidency.

Changes in Washington's policy therefore unsettled the dictatorship. On the one hand, civilian opponents interpreted President Carter's human rights policy to mean that Washington would listen to Somoza's opponents. Although the Sandinistas made opposition to U.S. imperialism a cornerstone of their policy, moderate groups were interested in gaining the backing of the United States for a transitional government, one that did not include Somoza or even the FSLN. U.S. backing for Somoza had not been universal; since the 1930s, the State Department did not hesitate to find political alternatives for Nicaragua. Its efforts had been stymied by Somoza's power consolidation. With the onset of the Cold War, U.S. presidential administrations lost interest in upsetting a seemingly permanent regime, especially if the alternative was to permit a Marxist movement to replace a pro-U.S. government in Managua. Reminding the United States that the choices were between a seemingly stable, but friendly autocratic government and communist guerrillas was, in fact, a central objective of Somoza's foreign policy, one that included cultivating the anti-communism of Republican congressmen and senators.

On the other hand, the Carter administration's foreign policy fueled opposition activities. Regardless of how important U.S. backing for the regime was, many Nicaraguans believed that Somoza remained in power because of U.S. support. Both Sandinistas and Somoza, curiously enough, benefitted from this perception. It helped the FSLN turn the fight against Somoza into an epic struggle between the nation and imperialism, one in which it would lead the people into liberation from capitalist oppression (Black, 1981). For Somoza, the perception of U.S. omnipotence was a way of discouraging Nicaraguans from challenging the regime. That the Carter administration was sending mixed messages, potentially even withholding support of the dictator (and of the Shah of Iran, halfway around the world), made it easier to collect funds, plan meetings, and recruit followers. Both opposition hardliners (the FSLN) and moderates (business groups) began to communicate and thus overcome their mutual suspicion. Although each wished to bring down Somoza, neither the Sandinistas nor upper-class Nicaraguans wished to leave the other side in charge of the struggle against the regime.

Second, Somoza – and, by implication, his regime – suffered a major coronary attack in August 1977. Although he returned from emergency surgery in Florida months later, Somoza's health became a political issue, one that galvanized his opponents that the end was near. Because the dictatorship revolved around his persona, his mortality raised troubling questions about the longevity of somocismo. Although control of the National Guard safeguarded the regime, the speculation that accompanies such events further undermined the sense of permanence vital for such narrowly based regimes.

Street protests and armed confrontation intensified after January 1978, when conservative opponent Chamorro was assassinated. Much of Nicaragua and the world, blamed him for what many considered the opposition leader's death. In response, 50,000 mourners joined Chamorro's funeral. The Chamber of Commerce and UDEL called for a national strike within days of the assassination. In less than a month, the FSLN attacked military garrisons in the cities of Granada and Rivas. Predominately Indian communities in Monimbó (a suburb of Masaya), Subtiava (a suburb of León), and Diriamba also revolted.

The dictatorship responded ferociously. It unleashed the National Guard, which bombed opposition strongholds and exterminated armed opponents. This only inflamed public opinion, both domestic and global, against the regime. In a pattern repeated almost monthly, the Sandinistas took the battle to the regime while street protesters braved the bullets of the National Guard. In August 1978, Commander Cero, as Pastora was dubbed, and twenty-five Sandinistas captured the National Palace (García Márquez, 1978). Holding more than 1,500 people, the palace contained members of the Chamber of Deputies and other key figures. In two days of tense negotiations, Pastora got the dictator to release 59 political prisoners (including Borge), give the movement US$500,000 in cash (although he demanded US$10 million), and permit publication of another communiqué calling on the Guard and the Nicaraguan people to revolt. Although not much more than a publicity stunt, the FSLN's action both demonstrated its ability to challenge the regime and revealed the dictatorship's vulnerability. The action suggested that the regime could be toppled, which encouraged bystanders to join a fight that government repression was taking into increasing numbers of Nicaraguan neighborhoods.

Armed confrontation, along with the alienation of the country's business class, led a severe contraction in economic activity. Although an economic free fall added to political polarization, severe recession was largely the product of Somoza's inability to contain protest and the gradual unification of Nicaraguan

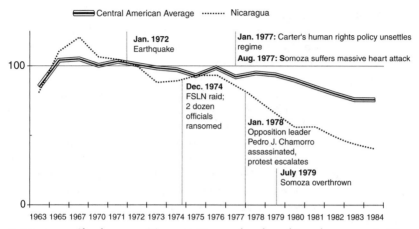

FIGURE 2.4. Shocks, opposition activities, and real working-class wages in Nicaragua, 1963–84.

Note: 100 = 1963.

Source: Booth (1991: 42).

society against the dictator, as Figure 2.4 suggests. GDP per capita contracted in 1978, when it fell by almost 10 percent with respect to 1977 (while it had grown in the previous two years). The fall in real working-class wages accelerated. Economic decline, especially when Somoza needed to spend more money on internal security, led to austerity measures. In 1977, the regime cut expenditures to deal with a blossoming budget deficit, which saw the price of many consumer items increase just when many workers and peasants were least able to afford them.

Repression widened the war. The often indiscriminate violence the National Guard practiced left many Nicaraguans, especially young males, with few options but to fight the regime to stay alive (Vilas, 1986). It was the actions of an increasingly repressive state that led peasants to join the uprising (Anderson, 1994). The civil war is estimated to have killed 10,000 to 35,000 Nicaraguans (with some estimates going as high as 50,000) between 1975 and 1979 (Seligson and McElhinny, 1996: 218) out of a population of approximately 2.7 million in 1980. All estimates agree that the monthly death rate increased with time. By mid-1979, the daily toll was 300–400; between June and July 1979, an estimated 15,000 Nicaraguans were killed in the fighting, many of them civilians. Nearly 600,000 people were left homeless or with a severely damaged home (Booth, 1982: 181). The dramatic free fall in economic activity – GDP per capita fell by almost 29 percent in 1979 or to levels not seen since the 1960s – also left many citizens unemployed. Economic desperation fed the fear of being killed.

The regime's brutality did not end street protest and guerrilla attacks in part because the regime began to waver. Virtually all of Somoza's domestic critics formed a Broad Front in 1978, including the Sandinistas and their private sector rivals. If domestic opponents were not fighting the regime, they were in exile and procuring funds, weapons, and support for the anti-Somoza struggle. Presidents Carlos Andrés Pérez of Venezuela and General Omar Torrijos of Panama led regional efforts to isolate the regime and collect money and even weapons for the FSLN. Former President José María Figueres of Costa Rica gave the FSLN the weapons he had buried on his farm after he had successfully led a rebellion against his government in 1948.

The Carter administration negotiated behind the scenes for Somoza to commit to a timetable to relinquish power, even if critics argued that Washington was one step behind events in Nicaragua (LeoGrande, 1979). When there was the possibility of forming a transitional government between Somocistas and opposition moderates, the United States did not pressure Somoza to resign, once the dictator insisted that he finish his term until the end of his presidential mandate in 1981. Once the civil war had progressed so that the FSLN would be a key member of any new government, the United States insisted on Somoza's resignation and the formation of a national unity government that included elements of the hated National Guard.

With Managua surrounded and the Guard's barracks in the city of Estelí in Sandinista hands, Somoza resigned and fled to Miami on July 17, 1979. Congress selected Francisco Urcuyo as interim president. The FSLN prepared for its final offensive. The interim government formally surrendered. On July 19, 1979, the FSLN marched into Managua. After forty-three years in power, the Somoza dictatorship – Somocisimo – was finished.

Political Cycles and Rebellion in El Salvador

As Nicaraguans celebrated the fall of Somoza, junior officers in El Salvador overthrew President (and General) Oscar Romero in mid-October 1979. They quickly formed a governing council with civilian reformers, and the new junta promised to implement social and democratic reforms. The October 1979 coup was not the first time that an officer corps faction had coalesced with opposition politicians to establish a new government. All had failed to end reactionary despotism, and many had been replaced by military governments that repressed opposition activity. Would the latest round in this cycle end in repression (yet again), democratization (as promised), or revolution (as feared)?

The election of Pío Romero Bosque to the presidency in 1927 had unexpectedly led to the first opening of modern politics (Guidos Vejar, 1980). The new president legalized labor unions and held fair and competitive elections for municipal government. Rural laborers began to join unions; fueled by the Great Depression-induced decline in coffee exports and economic activity, they began to protest for an increase in wages. It was in this context that the reformist candidate, Arturo Araujo, won the 1931 elections. Within a month, conservative officers, under the leadership of General Maximiliano Hernández, deposed newly inaugurated President Araujo in December 1931. In response, Indians revolted throughout the western highlands. In a massacre known as La Matanza (the mass killing), the military slaughtered an estimated

20,000 peasants in early 1932 (Gould and Lauria-Santiago, 2008). Both the massacre and General Hernández's twelve-year regime became emblematic of reactionary despotism and signaled the extremes to which its beneficiaries would go to protect their power.

It was a combination of street protests and military factionalism that ended the Hernández regime in 1944 (Parkman, 1988). During the next three decades, no general would come close to repeating his twelve years in office. Factionalism led to six coups and countercoups that would create nine governments (Almeida, 2008: 35–69). Executive instability encouraged the street protests that, in turn, fomented the factionalism of the officer corps. In two of these efforts – those in 1948 and 1960 – officers allied with urban labor unions, students, and political movements to broaden and stabilize their regimes. In both cases, conservative officers reasserted their control to prevent opposition forces from transforming these governments into full-scale regime change.

The cycle of instability came to an end by the early 1960s. After deposing the reformist 1960 junta, the new government convened elections for a Constituent Assembly and formed a new military-backed party known as the Party of National Conciliation (PCN). Although the PCN's candidate, Julio A. Rivera, won 92 percent of the vote in the 1962 elections, it gradually liberalized its rule during the next decade and under the aegis of the 1962 constitution. Between 1964 and 1970, the Christian Democratic Party (PDC), which acted as an umbrella organization of anti-regime forces, won an average of 40 percent of the seats in the country's unicameral legislature (Webre, 1979). The PDC even won the mayoralty of the capital of San Salvador in 1964 and 1968. Unionization rates shot up from 50,000 to 60,000 workers by the early 1970s (Almeida, 2008: 81, 89).

Whether elections could transform the regime became the central issue of Salvadoran politics by the 1972 elections. Initial returns from rural departments put the military's candidate, Arturo Molina of the PCN in the lead. Once returns from the capital, San Salvador, showed the PDC candidate (and Mayor of San Salvador), José Napoleón Duarte, ahead by two to one, the military ordered broadcasters to stop announcing additional returns. Partial results from the capital, where 30 percent of registered voters lived, had unsettled the government. On February 21, one day after the vote, the electoral commission declared that Molina won by approximately 22,000 votes, with 43.4 percent of the vote. In the absence of a majority (e.g., more than 50 percent of the votes), the constitution called on the Legislative Assembly to choose the new president. Five days later, the PCN, which held 65 percent of the Assembly's seats, voted unanimously to make Molina president for a five-year term.

Divisions in the ruling bloc, which had fueled the political opening, turned violent in the aftermath of these elections. One month after the aborted elections, dissident army officers tried to overthrow the government, an action that Duarte endorsed on radio. When the coup failed, the regime captured Duarte before sending him into exile (Webre, 1979: 170–180). Government curtailment of individual rights and opposition activities reduced the share of non-official deputies to 15 and 30 percent in the 1972 and 1974 legislative elections, respectively. The opposition simply boycotted the 1976 legislative and 1977 presidential elections.

Secondary sources all date the rise of rural insurgency to the aborted political opening. In 1970, Cayetano Carpio, leader of the Salvadoran Communist Party (PCS), left with a half a dozen other dissidents to create the Popular Forces of Liberation (FPL). The PFL concentrated on a popular war strategy, one whereby its militants would work with workers and peasants to obtain popular support for the revolution. They left the Moscow-oriented PCS because it renounced armed struggle to topple the government. Two years later, left-wing members of the PDC and other dissidents of the PCS formed the Revolutionary Army of the Poor (ERP). Unlike the PCS or PFL, the ERP did not use a guerrilla strategy, but concentrated on sensationalist tactics to build support for revolution. It lobbed bombs at military and police posts and kidnapped businessmen (Stanley, 1996: 117). In 1975, some members were disgusted with the ERP's murder of Roque Dalton, a poet condemned by the ERP leadership (including Joaquín Villalobos, perhaps its most famous leader) for being critical of its fixation on military tactics. They formed the Armed Forces of National Resistance (FARN) to redirect their efforts on building support among the masses. In 1976, the FARN dissidents created the Central American Revolutionary Workers Party (PRTC) to foment revolution, not just in El Salvador, but throughout Central America. By early 1979, the U.S. Embassy in San Salvador estimated that approximately 2,000 "hardcore insurgents," existed, with 800 in the FPL, 600 in the FARN, and several hundred in the ERP (cited in Brockett, 2005: 84).

Labor unions and civic groups coalesced into several mass organizations, confederations of labor union militants, students, and other political activists by the mid-1970s. Each traced its origins to repression or an economic grievance. In 1974, students, teachers, priests, workers, and peasants formed the Unified Popular Action Front (FAPU) to contest electoral fraud and the rising cost of living. In 1975, university students joined forces with teachers, shantytown dwellers, and others to create the Revolutionary Popular Bloc (BPR) in the aftermath of the university student massacre on July 30. In 1977, university students, market vendors, and peasants formed the Popular Leagues of the 28th of February (LP-28) to honor almost 100 citizens killed by the military for protesting the fraudulent February presidential elections. The BPR would become the largest of these groups, with an estimated 60,000 activists by the late 1970s.

Political mobilization in the face of an unyielding dictatorship occurred as the economy rebounded in 1971 (and kept growing until 1979). Inflation remained low – less than 4 percent – for much of this period; it began to increase as the regime hardened and as a part of the opposition went underground and another sector took to the streets. In 1979, it jumped to 10 percent (Almeida, 2008: 114), the first year that the terms of trade in Central America became sharply negative. To the extent that the mass organizations were calling for the end of dictatorship and preaching about the exhaustion of capitalism, macroeconomic

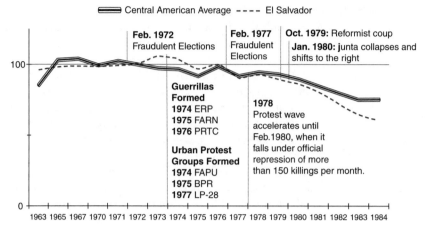

FIGURE 2.5. Repression, protest, and real working-class wages in El Salvador, 1963–84.

Note: 100 = 1963.

Source: Booth (1991: 42).

indicators during the second half of the 1970s, along with the increase in peasant landlessness (partly as a result of the expulsion of Salvadoran peasants from Honduras in the aftermath of the 1969 "soccer war") added plausibility to these claims. In 1976, working-class wages began to fall, and continued to accelerate with the intensification of political protest (see Figure 2.5).

It was political exclusion and broader notions of injustice that apparently encouraged some Salvadorans to support the armed left, especially during the first phase of the civil war (Viterna, 2006; Wood, 2003). In her interviews with 200 peasants in select rural areas, Elisabeth Jean Wood (2003) finds that consciousness about the violation of rights that created guerrilla supporters, not the experience of poverty or exploitation itself. Rural class position, Wood finds, had little to do with support for the FMLN. Members of similarly poor communities sometimes backed the guerrillas and frequently did not. Two-thirds of the residents in her case-areas chose not to collaborate with the guerrillas. The themes that came up in her conversations, which she argues led to support for radical change, were "the injustice of prewar land distribution and labor relations, their desire for land, the contempt with which they were treated by landlords, the brutality with which government forces responded to nonviolent strikes and demonstrations, the fear with which they lived during the war, and the suffering of their families" (Wood, 2003: 230).

Military dictatorship was under attack – not only from the left, but also from the right. Although industrial and commercial elites organized meetings to explore nonviolent solutions to polarization, the agrarian elite criticized Romero for not being repressive enough. Taking their cue from the 1932 Matanza, they began to fund death squads staffed by the lower ranks of the military, who happened on a gruesome way to supplement their meager salaries. Some military officers, in what William Stanley (1996: 117) aptly calls "the military protection racket state," organized kidnappings for personal profit, which they conveniently blamed on the armed left. In May 1979, extreme rightists began plotting Romero's overthrow. Rival officers, Colonels Eugenio Vides Casanova and Guillermo García, planned the president's ouster.

Sensing the regime's weakness, the opposition intensified its activities in the wake of Somoza's fall in 1979. The revolution in neighboring Nicaragua demonstrated the benefits of unifying insurgent efforts. In 1979, the PCS dropped its long-standing policy in favor of a peaceful route to power. It joined the other four guerrilla groups to form the Farabundo Martí Liberation Front (FMLN) in October 1980 to coordinate their efforts in the countryside and their links with the mass organizations. The mass organizations created the Revolutionary Coordinator of the Masses in early 1980 to plan joint actions on the streets of San Salvador. Between 1978 and 1979, the number of demonstrations went up by more than 700 percent: from fewer than five to more than forty in one year. Official statistics record an increase in strikes of more than 400 percent between 1978 and 1979: from approximately 24 to slightly more than 100 strikes in one year. Violent acts – bombs, kidnappings, attacks on military or governmental installations – shot up by more than 100 percent. Insurgents went from committing less than twenty to less than eighty violent acts within a year (Brockett, 2005: 186–190).

It was a group of young officers that ousted General Romero on October 15, 1979. In a televised speech, a junta of two officers and three civilian politicians promised to halt the descent into violence. They announced a cessation of repression, which had already claimed close to a thousand lives. The junta made public its plans to hold fair elections, establish civilian supremacy over the military, and root out corrupt and brutal officers. Most important, it called for an extensive land reform to redistribute property from the land rich to the land poor. The new government could also claim to be broadly representative: Of the thirty-four new cabinet ministers and deputy ministers, sixteen belonged to the left, eleven were from the right, and seven were centrists (Bonner, 1984:145).

By bridging the widening divide, the new junta became the target of the left and especially of the right. On the one hand, the mass organizations and the FMLN reacted with a mixture of disdain and disbelief. They discounted the coup as nothing more than a last-ditch effort to forestall the revolution, which the junta's unexpected actions seemingly confirmed was just around the corner. The mass organizations, in particular, initially rejected the junta's call for a truce, but subsequently became interested in testing the junta's resolve to stop the repression and murder of its militants on the streets of San Salvador (LeoGrande and Robbins, 1980). On the other hand, oligarchs were using back channels to topple the junta and end the dreaded land redistribution. They leaned on conservative officers to continue killing protesters and intensified funding death squads that targeted regime opponents. Members of the country's tight-knit upper class began to divide their estates and hide their landholdings in reaction to the October junta's decree freezing landholdings of more than 241 hectares and nationalizing exports.

The effort to liberalize the political system by strengthening centrist options and thus prevent revolution did not face the opposition of just the old order. It also faced the ambivalence of the Carter administration (Bonner, 1984). For all the right-wing criticism of Carter's human rights policy (Kirkpatrick, 1979), the administration had not turned against Somoza or the Shah of Iran, America's alleged friends in the developing world. At most, the Carter administration's declarations unsettled autocracies already under threat by their domestic adversaries. The Carter administration hoped that dictators would gradually reform, perhaps share power with the opposition, and stop violations of human rights. After the fall of Somoza, however, U.S. policy became more conservative: Within weeks of the coup, it provided the new government with "nonlethal" military aid and U.S. military advisers.

This was a decision with enormous implications for the junta's strategic position, one whose challenges previous reformist efforts had failed to meet. Sending aid signaled that the United States was not committed to reform and a peaceful solution to the escalating conflict. Not holding the security forces accountable for the daily killing of civilians undercut efforts to convince reformers, strcct protesters, and guerrillas that cooperating with the junta could stem the violence. Repression thwarted the formation of a progressive accord, an alliance that could succeed in ending the reactionary coalition at the heart of the Salvadoran political system. It threatened the construction of a new political system in which individual rights would be respected – and oligarchs would lose some privileges and disproportionate influence on state policy.

Military hardliners and right-wing death squads did not stop slaughtering civilians. The monthly death rate went from close to 200 deaths in October to approximately 125 by December 1979 (Brockett, 2005: 300). By early January 1980, the three civilian reformers on the junta and virtually all ministers abandoned their posts, stating that the military was resisting civilian control and doing nothing to stop the violence. Many joined the Revolutionary Democratic Front (FDR), which was rapidly becoming the nonviolent alternative opposition front to the FMLN.

The continuation of violence demonstrated both the right's reassertion of its power and the United States' unwillingness to protect a centrist compromise. It was understandable that the Salvadoran right would wish to scuttle reform. Change meant a reduction in privileges, which it had tenaciously defended for decades. Understanding why the United States backed a government moving swiftly to the right is harder because failure to stem the flight of reformists from government promised to plunge the country into civil war. The Carter administration apparently preferred preventing an FMLN victory to supporting negotiations with the FDR and other opposition forces. No U.S. administration wished to be accused of "losing another country to communism." There was a presidential campaign underway in the United States pitting Carter against a rabidly anti-communist Ronald Reagan, who made much of the fact that Carter had "lost" Nicaragua and Iran, "given away" the Panama Canal, and that the Sandinistas were spreading Marxist revolution in Central America.

Repression began to accelerate and have its chilling effect on social protest. After falling to fifty deaths in January, the monthly death rate climbed every month until mid-year, despite the dramatic fall in social protest between February and April. The number of contentious acts fell from an average of one every other day to one every three days between February and March. The mass organizations held only two protests in April. Right-wing hit squads assassinated Archbishop Oscar Arnulfo Romero in late March while he was saying mass, thirteen days after U.S. Ambassador Robert E. White, a noted reformer, presented his credentials to the Salvadoran government. Between April and September, there were an average of 150 killings a month. Despite the evaporation of street protest, officially sponsored violence produced around 150 deaths every month until September, when it more than doubled until and including the Christmas month of December (Brockett, 2005: 300). In late June, soldiers burned buildings on the national university (including the library), destroyed equipment, killed more than fifty students and professors, and closed and occupied the university.

The quest to stabilize the country around a centrist compromise had failed. During 1980, there would be four separate juntas, including the original one that had collapsed in January. Although U.S. officials claimed that there were still reformers in the Salvadoran government, the incorporation of PDC politicians – including Duarte, who joined the junta in March 1980 – did not stop the spiral into civil war. Although reformers came and went, none had the authority or support of the United States to thwart the militarization of politics. By the end of the year, the security forces and allied death squads had killed government members, including Attorney General Mario Zamora and Agrarian Reform Institute President, José Rodolfo Viera. By December, the last of the military reformers and the only remaining member of the October junta, Colonel Adolfo Majano, was forced to resign (Baloyra, 1982).

With Carter administration support, the military government opted for a strategy of (limited) reform with repression: It used U.S. military aid to battle its opponents while promulgating several reforms to undercut the appeal of the left. In March, it nationalized banks and converted the largest farms (more than 500 hectares) into agrarian cooperatives under the first phase of the land reform program originally announced by the October junta. By late April, it implemented the final stage of a three-phased land reform that would convert tenant farmers into owners of their plots. Yet, vociferous elite protests got the government to postpone the second land reform phase, which promised to expropriate all holdings between 150 and 500 hectares – the size of the most productive coffee farms (Lehoucq and Sims, 1982). By late May, a military judge ordered the release of Major Roberto d'Aubuisson, a notorious anti-communist linked to plotting coups, organizing death squads, and assassinating prominent figures, including Archbishop Romero.

Civil war began in earnest, especially after Ronald Reagan's defeat of President Carter in the U.S. elections in early November 1980 (Montgomery, 1995). As conservatives in El Salvador and throughout Central America celebrated Reagan's victory, protest shifted from the streets of San Salvador to the mountains and valleys of the country. A rural insurgency led by the FMLN faced off against a refashioned conservative government that, over the next decade, received more than a billion dollars in U.S. military aid (Williams and Walter, 1997: 133). Decrying a movement for having received weapons from their ideological counterparts in neighboring Nicaragua, the Reagan administration intensified the battle against communist subversion in El Salvador and Nicaragua. In a widely circulated white paper issued in late February 1981, the Reagan administration claimed that the conflict in El Salvador was a "textbook case of indirect armed aggression by Communist powers through Cuba."

Despite massive U.S. aid, the military government in El Salvador never managed to defeat the FMLN. Nor could the FMLN, despite several final offenses, bring down the government. The revolution was not to be. There was no repeat of the Nicaraguan experience. The war grinded on and became a stalemate.

The Old Order Prevails in Guatemala

Urban protest and rural insurgency reignited in Guatemala by the mid-1970s. They were the latest attempts to confront reactionary despotism, efforts that had begun in decades past. The narrowness of most regimes fueled executive instability that created numerous opportunities for the opposition sectors to contest the regimes, neither of which had much to do with trends in the macro-economy or underlying social grievances. Factionalism did lead to a political opening between 1944 and 1954 (the Guatemalan Spring), in which ambitious officers worked with labor unions and opposition parties to outmaneuver their rivals in uniform. A right-wing military coup in 1954, backed by the U.S. Central Intelligence Agency (CIA) in the name of fighting communism, reinstalled dictatorship in Guatemala. Unable to prevail at the ballot box, the opposition began to battle the regime in a thirty-six-year civil war that ebbed in the mid-1970s before reviving by the end of this decade.

Anti-regime protesters helped rout two personalist dictatorships in the first half of the twentieth century. In 1920, protesters joined with dissident officers to overthrow the twenty-two-year dictatorship of Manuel Estrada Cabrera. Four more coups and countercoups would create a ten-year period of instability that ended with Jorge Ubico's illegal assumption of executive power and founded a regime that lasted for nearly fourteen years (Greib, 1979). In 1944, another coalition of street protesters, unions, and junior officers sent Ubico into exile. A junta led by Federico Ponce Valdés was overthrown three months later by Colonels Francisco Arana and Jacobo Arbenz, who managed to end the latest cycle of instability by promising presidential elections and a new constitution for the country.

Arana and Arbenz's efforts gradually gave way to a more democratic regime (Yashar, 1997). Elections were held for a Constituent Assembly. The 1945 constitution expanded suffrage rights. All men at least eighteen years old obtained the right to vote, although illiterate males were required to vote in public. Literate women got the right to vote in secret. Guatemalans then cast ballots for a new president and congress in 1945, which were won by the social reformer, Juan José Arévalo. Although liberalization stabilized the new system, it did not end the struggle for power that kept governments on the defensive. In 1949, the Arévalo's administration had put down a military uprising following Francisco Arana's assassination (Gleijeses, 1991).

The young democracy witnessed a transition from one democratically elected government to another in 1951, a first in Guatemalan history. Arbenz, a military officer, governed alongside a democratically elected congress. As Arbenz came to rely on the support of labor unions and left-wing parties, he gained legislative approval of reforms that attacked the power of landed elites and foreign corporations. In 1952, his government enacted an agrarian reform expropriating farms in excess of 272 hectares (or 672 acres) that were idle and unused lands in estates between 90 (or 224 acres) and 272 hectares if less than two-thirds were cultivated (Gleijeses, 1991: 150). Nearly a third of the land redistributed to 88,000 families was already in state hands, so many private landowners were unaffected by the measure. The reform also targeted 15 percent of the extensive and mostly uncultivated lands owned by the U.S. United Fruit Company (UFCO). UFCO lobbied Washington to pressure Arbenz's government to reverse the reform, countering that the government's compensation of US$625,000 (based on a US$2.99 per hectare), which it based on UFCO's 1950 tax declaration, should be closer to US$16 million (or US$75 per hectare). Its campaign included a key investor, none other than Central Intelligence Agency Director, Allen Dulles, and pleaded its case before his brother, John Foster Dulles, who was President Dwight D. Eisenhower's Secretary of State (Schlesinger and Kinzer, 2005).

The most comprehensive study of the period argues that it was U.S. anti-communism against a backdrop of Arbenz shifting to the left that ended Guatemala's democratic opening (Gleijeses, 1991). A communist-obsessed Ambassador, John Peurifoy, grew alarmed at the growing influence of left-wing parties, including the Guatemalan Communist Party, in Arbenz's government. The CIA sponsored a coup coalition that included disaffected officers and leading members of Guatemala's oligarchy, a coup that succeeded because the officer corps preferred Arbenz's overthrow to an allegedly imminent U.S. invasion (Gleijeses, 1991). One year after the CIA had helped overthrow the nationalist Prime Minister of Iran, Mohammed Massadegh, Colonel Castillo Armas invaded Guatemala. On June 27, 1954, Arbenz went into exile.

In the years following the 1954 coup, Castillo Armas reversed his predecessor's social reforms. Labor leaders and peasant organizers were jailed or sent into exile. Individual rights and guarantees were suspended. Labor rights were revoked (Levenson-Estrada, 1994). The extensive land reform was undone: Most beneficiaries were required to return their plots to the former landowners (Handy, 1994). With the CIA's backing, Castillo Armas formed the National Committee of Defense Against Communism, which is Latin America's first modern death squad. In 1954, Castillo issued the Preventive Penal Law Against Communism, which increased the penalties for many subversive activities, including labor unionizing. Castillo Armas was assassinated by a bodyguard in 1957, a year after he had postponed presidential elections, enacted a new constitution that permitted him to run for election, and organized legislative elections in which only his party fielded candidates.

Successive military governments maintained a tight grip on politics, even as coups and countercoups destabilized the regime. Ambitious military factions reached out to civilian politicians who could mobilize protesters, who themselves wished to exploit such overtures to expand democratic rights and win presidential elections. Several interim presidents led to General José Ydígoras's five-year administration (1958–63). This administration was cut short by a coup launched by his Defense Minister, Colonel Enrique Peralta Azurdia, to prevent the return of former left-of-center civilian president Juan José Arévalo, whom Ydígoras had permitted to register as a presidential candidate for the 1963 elections. The threat of continued instability led the generals to hold new elections in 1966 to resolve their disputes about political succession. The military nonetheless tightly constrained the left-of-center government of President Julio César Méndez Montenegro (1966–70), which failed to act on campaign promises to broaden democratic freedoms, labor rights, and increase social expenditures. President Méndez Montenegro did not get legislative approval for income and property tax reforms, which kept the state in penury.

Executive instability opened the regime to challenges to its authority. On the one hand, urban-based political activists organized increasing numbers of demonstrations. Between 1958 and 1962, the number of street protests went from less than five to more than twenty a year before falling and then slightly increasing in 1966 (Brockett, 2005: 176). On the other hand, dissident officers began organizing a guerrilla front after failing to overthrow Ydígoras's government in 1960. In 1962, they joined forces with the 13th of November Revolutionary Movement creating the Rebellious Armed Forces (FAR) to stir rebellion in the eastern Departments of Zacapa and Izabal. By 1966, there were approximately 300 insurgents fighting to bring down the government. Between 1966 and 1972, there was an average of seventy-seven terrorist attacks and thirty-six armed encounters reported in the country's daily press, according to a pioneering study of violence by a group of Guatemalan social scientists (Aguilera Peralta et al., 1981: 155), several of whom were assassinated as they were finishing their study.

Guerrilla warfare provoked state repression, which eventually quelled rural insurgency and urban protest. Assassinations and kidnappings averaged 154 and 130 per year between 1966 and 1972, respectively, with a high of 249 assassinations and 237 kidnappings in 1967, which underreports the scale of the violence afflicting the country. While the military and right-wing hit squads targeted regime opponents, the guerrillas went after members of the elite and foreign dignitaries. After a key rebel leader, Camilo Sánchez, was captured by the army, the FAR tried to kidnap U.S. Ambassador J. Gordon Mein, who died in the bungled attempt. Three years later, the FAR executed German Ambassador Count Von Spreti. By 1967, the military had routed guerrilla fronts in the east. Three years later, the Mexican military killed rebel leader Yon Sosa as Colonel Carlos Manuel Arana Osorio, a leading member of the counterinsurgency campaign, won the 1970 elections. By 1972, most FAR leaders had been captured or executed. The estimates are that between 8,000 and 10,000 Guatemalans were killed in the civil war between 1966 and 1972.

The military built a narrowly based regime not only excluding reformers, but also distancing itself from the extreme right and the business class as a whole. Despite the annihilation of the FAR by the early 1970s, generals still targeted opponents and civilians. Although the annual average of terrorist attacks and armed encounters fell to less than twelve by 1976, the average number of assassinations and kidnappings remained high. Between 1973 and 1976, there were a mean of 111 assassinations and 78 kidnappings per year (Aguilera Peralta et al., 1981: 162, 165–173). Paramilitary squads targeted centrist Christian Democratic Party (DCG) leaders for assassination (Trudeau, 1993). Although successive military governments had cultivated ultra right-wing support, anti-communist parties – allowing Mario Sandoval Alarcón of the far-right National Liberal Movement (MLN) to become president of Congress during General Arana Osorio's presidency (1970–4) and vice-president during his successor's rule – dispensed with these alliances by the late 1970s. The regime overturned the 1974 election results when preliminary figures delivered the presidency to General Efraín Rios Montt instead of to President Arana's handpicked favorite, General Kjell Eugenio. General Laugerud García himself facilitated General Fernando Romeo Lucas García's victory four years later. The regime parceled out state agencies to key officers. By the late 1970s, George Black (1984: 52) estimates that forty-six semi-autonomous agencies were headed by military men, including the Institute for Military Social Security and the Army Bank. Generals created a development zone in the north of the country, the Transversal Strip of the North, to reward loyal officers with extensive properties.

The destruction of the FAR and allied groups by 1972 did not stop Guatemalans from founding more guerrilla groups. In 1972, a handful of FAR survivors, members of the Guatemalan Labor Party's (PGT) youth wing, and Roman Catholic students who had been working with peasants in the Department of Huehuetenango entered northern Guatemala from Mexico and formed the Guerrilla Army of the Poor (EGP). It began to work with the rural poor in the heavily indigenous north and west. It later established links with urban protesters as mobilization accelerated in the capital. In 1972, other survivors of the insurgency crushed in 1962 formed the Organization of the Armed People (ORPA). The ORPA emphasized working with the country's poor majority. Unlike the EGP, the ORPA struggled to activate the political opposition of Mayan peasants, who did not see themselves as natural class allies of the ladino (*mestizo* or non-indigenous) rural and urban poor. Like other strictly Marxist-Leninist organizations, the EGP subsumed the ethnic differences between indigenous and peasants in a broader struggle of the poor against the rich. In 1979, indigenous members left ORPA to form the Popular Revolutionary Ixim-Movement.

Political repression led the opposition to mobilize, both in the city and in the countryside. The total number of demonstrations doubled each year between 1975 and 1977, by which point there were more than thirty in the country at large. Opposition activity accelerated after the 1976 earthquake, which left 27,000 dead in the western highlands and the slums of Guatemala City, 1 million homeless, and 20 percent of the country's houses destroyed. By 1978, there were more than seventy demonstrations, an increase that more than doubled the rate of the prior year (Brockett, 2005: 124). In early 1978, peasants formed the Committee for Peasant Unity (CUC) "to fight for the resolution of problems that most afflict peasants: work, land, high prices, kidnappings and robbery of water and forest" (cited in Davis and Hodson, 1983: 47). The CUC, which began to communicate with the EGP, became a prominent peasant organization, one of several political and nonpolitical rural organizations in existence. After the earthquake, the U.S. Agency for International Development (USAID) noted that there were 510 rural cooperatives in the country organized into eight federations with a combined membership of more than 132,000 (cited in Davis and Hodson, 1983: 21).

What caused the renewal of political protest? It was not economic decline. As in El Salvador and Nicaragua, the fall in living standards followed more than it preceded violent conflict. While GDP per capita continued to grow during the 1970s, inflation did lead to a worsening of real working-class wages by 7 percent between 1972 and 1973 (see Figure 2.6). The index of wages hovered around 90 percent of their 1970 level until 1977, when social protest took off. By the late 1970s, it fell by more than a quarter from the base year.

Jeffrey Paige (1983) argues that the livelihood of increasing numbers of landless and near landless peasants – 32 percent of all farming families – slipped below subsistence level by the mid-1970s, when even seasonal migration to large commercial estates in Guatemala's coastal departments could not prevent many of the rural Maya from experiencing a subsistence crisis. That more than 300,000 laborers a year were beginning to travel to coastal plantations, Paige contends, indicates peasants had little more than their labor to sell – and explains why guerrilla activity began to escalate in the rural areas with destitute peasants.

Indiscriminate violence spread the flames of rural rebellion. Jennifer Schirmer (1998: 61), Carol Smith (1988), and David Stoll (1993) argue that, more than socioeconomic grievance, fear of military repression turned peasants into guerrilla supporters. How many Guatemalans backed the armed left? Most estimates claim that there were 6,000 to 7,000 insurgents, although Guatemalan General Héctor Alejandro Gramajo told Schirmer (1998: 41) that there were

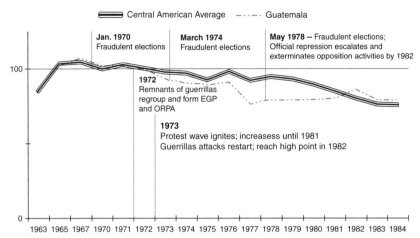

FIGURE 2.6. Repression, protest, and real working-class wages in Guatemala, 1963–84.

Note: 100 = 1963.

Source: Booth (1991: 42).

10,000 to 12,000 insurgents "better armed than the army" with 100,000 serving as part of the guerrilla "infrastructure" and another 260,000 in areas under guerrilla control. Victor Perera (1993: 10), Yvon Le Bot (1995: 195), and the Guatemalan Truth Commission (cited in Brockett, 2005: 124) estimate a similar number of guerrillas and approximately a quarter of a million supporters, although Perera claims that the URNG had double that many followers. Richard N. Adams (1988: 286), the distinguished anthropologist, suggests that the quarter million figure is too low. He cites an unnamed and "long-term resident in the highlands" that there were 500,000 participants by early 1982, the year when four guerrilla groups formed the Guatemalan National Revolutionary Unity (URNG) to coordinate their war against the state.

Ironically, awareness of the poverty in which many Maya lived led the army to conclude, as Schirmer's interviews with Guatemalan officers reveal, that the guerrillas had many more supporters than they in fact did. Belief in materialist theories of rebellion made the military infer that Marxist insurgents were more popular than they were. Ingrained racism led to seeing the Maya as the quintessential "other," a remote and incomprehensible people capable of the misdeed of betraying the Guatemalan nation, as years of anthropological research indicates (e.g., Carmack, 1988; Falla, 1994; Smith, 1990). These beliefs became self-fulfilling prophecies.

Governmental repression intensified social protest and guerrilla activity at first, as systematic research on urban-based protest by Brockett (2005) and Figueroa Ibarra (1991) demonstrates. State-sponsored harassment, illegal detentions, and massacres became commonplace. The number of assassinations increased annually between 1976 and 1982. Deaths zoomed from a decade low of approximately 75 in 1975 to slightly more than 200 in 1976. By 1979, the number of those killed again doubled to more than 400. By 1982, there were more than 18,000 documented deaths in Guatemala (Brockett, 2005: 208, 217). Compilations of the number of disappeared and killed mentioned in the domestic press are even higher. In 1978, there were 879 documented cases of murder and persons disappeared. Two years later, the press reported more than 2,260 Guatemalans killed or disappeared (Figueroa Ibarra, 1991: 139).

Two massacres, in particular, made international headlines and are emblematic of the state's hardline response. In late May 1978, the Guatemalan army killed at least 34 Kekchi peasants in the town of Panzós in the Department of Alta Verapaz, although survivors claim more than a 100 died in the days following the massacre (Grandin, 2004). The massacre was the army's response to a peasant march in which protesters asked the town mayor of the whereabouts of three missing peasant leaders and demanded distribution of land titles promised in an earlier commitment to provide the landless with farmland. In early 1980, state security forces invaded the Spanish Embassy in Guatemala City in response to its occupation by unarmed peasants from Quiché. Soldiers set the compound ablaze. More than three dozen were killed or burned, including twenty-three peasants and a former vice-president and foreign minister of Guatemala (Davis and Hodson, 1983: 47–52, provides a detailed chronology of events between 1976 and 1982).

Street protests and guerrilla attacks accelerated as state-sponsored terrorism increased during the late 1970s. Brockett, in particular, argues that this pattern – which he also observed during the late 1970s in El Salvador – suggests that repression fans marches and strikes if a wave of protest is underway. Moral outrage of state-sponsored murder, he claims, motivated protesters to return to the streets. Both urban and rural-based opposition escalated as guerrilla attacks on the regime emboldened the opposition to increase pressure on the state, especially with the toppling of the Somoza dynasty in Nicaragua in 1978 and the descent into civil war in El Salvador by mid-1979.

Unlike their counterparts in El Salvador, the Guatemalan generals remained united around a strategy of repression. There was no reformist coup, no attempt by regime and opposition moderates to bridge the polarization of society. The closest thing to reform was that a well-known moderate, Francisco Villagrán Kramer (2004; 2009), decided to join General Lucas García's 1978 presidential campaign as the vice-presidential candidate. By September 1980, the centrist politician had resigned his post, only to be succeeded by Colonel Oscar Mendoza Azurdia, who called Villagrán Kramer "an agent of both the United States and the Soviet Union" (cited in Black, 1984: 45). The generals defiantly ignored suggestions to liberalize their rule, even as they took advantage of decades of counterinsurgency training and other support from the CIA and the U.S. army. In 1977, they rejected military support from the United States in response to the Carter administration's critical appraisal of human rights in Guatemala, issued the year before, and the U.S. Congress's later suspension of military aid to the country.

Like the Nicaraguan National Guard, the Guatemalan army dramatically escalated its attacks on the opposition. With Israeli help, the military developed a master plan for identifying urban guerrillas, which helped it turn the tide against both the armed left and urban-based political protest. From a high of close to seventy demonstrations in 1978, protesters organized less than half as many marches in 1979. Within two years, strikes and marches disappeared from urban Guatemala (Brockett, 2005: 176). On the other hand, armed groups stepped up their attacks on the state as urban collective action withered under the unrelenting military assault. The number of armed attacks by the left went from 119 in 1979 to more than 500 in 1980. One year later, they almost doubled to 932 and kept increasing in 1982 (Figueroa Ibarra, 1991: 143).

The Guatemalan state became even more brutal after the 1982 general elections. Weeks after the March election, General Ríos Montt overthrew President Lucas García, preventing General Ángel Aníbal Guevara Rodríguez's accession to power in what the uprising's leaders called a fraudulent ballot. On assuming high office, Ríos Montt led a rejuvenated counterinsurgency campaign against the armed left, their rural supporters, and innocent civilians. During the next two years, it routed the guerrillas in a campaign notable for its ferocity, as anthropologists or eyewitnesses have carefully documented (Carmack, 1988; Falla, 1994; Garrand-Burnett, 2010; Manz, 1988; 2005; Montejo, 1995; Remijnse, 2002; Wilkinson, 2002) and Daniel Jonah Goldhagen (2009) includes in his magisterial study of genocide. Before it was over, the Guatemalan army had killed an estimated 150,000, razed and relocated 626 predominately Mayan villages, raped thousands of women, and sent more than 1 million Guatemalans into hiding in neighboring Mexico or other parts of the country (Ball, Kobrak, and Spirer, 1999; Leiby, 2009).

Why no Civil War in the Rest of Central America?

Guerrillas did not fight governments in the rest of Central America. Costa Rica remained peaceful, even as it underwent economic collapse in the early 1980s. Honduras went from having an autocracy to having a semi-democracy by the early 1980s. Panama witnessed an economic recovery in the late 1970s and its political system began to liberalize (before hardliners reversed reforms later in the 1980s). What does the absence of civil war and revolution in the rest of Central America tell us about the outbreak of violent conflict?

Poverty and inequality had little to do with why Costa Rica, Honduras, and Panama remained quiescent. The two wealthiest countries – Costa Rica and Panama – remained stable, but so did its poorest member – Honduras (see Figure 2.1). All had similar rates of inequality; in each country, the top quintile of the population received between 58 percent and 60 percent of the national income (see Figure 2.2). Two of them – Honduras and Panama – had more than half of their population living in poverty. Costa Rica, alone in the region, had a quarter of its population living in poverty (see Figure 1.4). It was something other than tolerance of social and economic deprivation that kept the peace in these countries.

Regime differences best account for the divergent outcomes in Central America. The assessments of regime types in Figure 1.3 suggest that the political systems of Honduras and especially Panama had a mixed history. Panama spent most of its time since independence in 1904 as a semi-democracy. Honduras's political trajectory, according to this index (Bowman, Lehoucq, and Mahoney, 2005) was more uniformly authoritarian, but resembles Guatemala's, which suggests that it too is not fine-grained enough to measure more fundamental differences between these sorts of regimes.

Two factors distinguish the regimes that fought civil wars from those that did not. First, Honduras and Panama were liberalizing (and Costa Rica's was already democratic) by the late 1970s. These regimes negotiated differences with their opponents, and thus discouraged them from taking up arms against incumbents, even if generals in both places placed limits on protest – and, in Panama, later reversed reforms and resorted to the use of violence to ensconce itself in power. Second, they were less intolerant of individual rights. These regimes did not police and slaughter their citizens; they did not emulate the behavior of their counterparts in El Salvador, Guatemala, and Nicaragua, a point long part of the conventional wisdom among Central Americanists (Munro, 1918; Williams, 1994). Levels of violence, as this chapter discusses, simply do not compare between these two sets of countries.

State policy toward unions also illustrates the less repressive nature of regimes in Honduras and Panama (Bulmer-Thomas, 1987: 219–224). Figure 2.3 reveals that workers did not experience the same fall in incomes in Costa Rica, Honduras, and Panama that they witnessed in El Salvador, Guatemala, and Nicaragua. In Costa Rica, real wages increased impressively between the mid-1970s and 1981, when they were more than 120 percent of their 1970 level. In Honduras, there was some modest growth in real wages until 1979. In Panama, there was a slight decline in real wages in 1979 before equally modest increases in the early 1980s (Zimbalist and Weeks, 1991: 122). These outcomes are a product of fundamental differences between regimes, of what governments allow – or must accept – organizations of peasants and workers to do, and that existing classifications of political regimes fail to capture.

How the Costa Rican political system reacted to its foreign debt crisis reveals how periodic (and fair) elections allow democracies to replace incumbents without endangering their continuation – and illustrates how their underlying resiliency simultaneously promotes accountability, stability, and their ability to correct policy mistakes. The 1973 oil shock and subsequent coffee boom had been accompanied by a major expansion of governmental activities in Costa Rica on the assumption that windfall foreign exchange earnings would continue. In 1979 and 1980, the current accounts deficit shot up to -10.51 percent of GDP from an average of -6.67 percent in the previous eighteen years (see Mesa-Lago, 2000: 513–514). Inflows of private capital fell to U.S. $57 million in 1979 from an average of U.S. $134 million in the previous five years (González Vega, 1984: 382). Just when policy making needed to be flexible enough to deal with an ominous economic picture, minority United Coalition (CU) President Rodrigo Carazo (1978–82) refused to readjust macroeconomic policy. Both Claudio González Vega (1984) and Eduardo Lizano (1999) are critical of the central government's slow and haphazard response to the crisis. Despite repeated warnings to the contrary from domestic and foreign economists since the late 1970s (for several of the dire forecasts, see Lizano, 1999: 15–18), embattled President Rodrigo Carazo refused to unfix the exchange rate. Government declarations to defend the national currency fueled the conversion of colones into U.S. dollars and led to a rapid decline in foreign exchange reserves. Adherence to an outdated fixed exchange policy led to haphazard and ultimately ineffectual foreign exchange experiments that, in the context of trade and fiscal deficits, forced the public debt to go from 56.2 percent to 125.2 percent of GDP between 1980 and 1981 (Mesa-Lago, 2000: 520). In 1982, the government defaulted on its international debt.

Regularly scheduled elections in 1982 provided an orderly change in government. Fed up with President Carazo's behavior, Costa Ricans voted overwhelmingly for the opposition candidate, Alberto Monge, of the Party of National Liberation (PLN), who won the election 59 to the 34 percent obtained by Rafael Angel Calderón of the incumbent CU, a decline of more than 15 percent with respect to the 51 percent that Carazo had won in 1978 (Seligson and Gómez, 1989). An open political system also allowed peasants to organize social movements to protest the ensuing austerity measures, ones that included ending state support for basic grain production (Edelman, 1999). So, the ability of citizens to throw out incumbents and march in the streets is what permitted the Costa Rican political system to weather the effects of a severe economic downturn.

While not democratic, the less repressive regime of General Torrijos of Panama had begun to liberalize authoritarian rule by the late 1970s. In 1978, the National Assembly of Municipal Representatives selected a civilian president, Aristedes Royo. Later that year, parties were legalized. In 1980, voters elected nineteen of the fifty-seven members of the National Council of Legislation, a quasi-legislative party. Torrijos was promising open and competitive elections for the presidency and a full-fledged legislature in 1984. Whether Torrijos would have let liberalization turn into democratization, of course, is unknown; he died in a mysterious helicopter crash in mid-1981. Military hardliners soon reasserted themselves as General Manuel Antonio Noriega became Commander in chief in 1983 and ensconced himself in power (Ropp, 1992; Zimbalist and Weeks, 1991).

Honduras had what I call an inconsistently authoritarian regime or what Jeff Goodwin (2001) calls a "semi-open" regime, one that helped it avert civil war. Honduran political life was simply not as repressive, which Donald E. Schulz and Deborah Sundloff Schulz (1994) claim is the single most important factor distinguishing Honduras from neighboring countries. It is important to emphasize that Honduras barely avoided violent conflict because some regime opponents did start guerrilla fronts in 1983, ones that the military crushed. How did inconsistent autocracy help the cause of peace?

On the one hand, military governments in Honduras, unlike their counterparts in El Salvador, Guatemala, and Nicaragua, proved incapable of decapitating rural social movements (Morris and Soler, 1977). Executive instability, on the other hand, led to the largest number of potential regime openings on the isthmus. There were almost twice as many coups in Honduras than in the average Central American country; the country, in fact, has the third-highest rate in Latin America after Bolivia and Ecuador (Lehoucq and Pérez-Liñán, 2010). Coalitions of military officers and civilians overthrew thirteen incumbents between 1900 and 1980, more than twice the regional average of eight coups during the twentieth century (see Table 1.2). An intense struggle for power, one fraught with high levels of uncertainty, led to possibilities for reform.

Interest in regime survival led officers to ally with social and opposition movements to broaden the base of regimes and thus to stabilize what were tenuous governments, especially by the 1960s (between 1963 and 1980, five presidents were toppled). As a result, labor organizations – of banana workers in the north and peasants throughout the country (Posas, 1981) – obtained wages and benefits that saw small, but gradual increases by the 1960s (see Figure 2.2). Between 1962 and 1979, agrarian reform benefited 46,780 families; more than two-thirds of the beneficiaries obtained land between 1973 and 1976, when General Oswaldo López Arellano (1972–5) was again president (Salomón, 1982). He had become president in 1963 by overthrowing liberal civilian President Ramón Villeda Morales (1957–63), who had enacted the land reform that López Arellano would later champion (Bowman, 2001b). Himself ousted in 1971, López Arellano returned to power in another coup one year later. He accelerated land reform before being ousted from office, yet again, in 1975. J. Mark Ruhl (1984: 52–53) estimates that 8 percent of the country's total farmland and roughly 12 percent (34,364) of its rural families farming in 1980 were still beneficiaries of land reform, which he, like other specialists on Honduras, argue prevented social conditions in the countryside from getting worse.

Inconsistency, but of a semi-democratic regime, also helps explain why there was a brief civil war decades earlier in Costa Rica. Before the mid-twentieth century, the political system was in part democratic because there was a free and vibrant press. Suffrage rights were essentially universal for adult men, and, most important, regularly held elections selected the president and members of congress. It contained authoritarian tendencies because executives could manipulate electoral laws for partisan advantage. Although the 1871 constitution (the predecessor of the current constitution, dating from 1949) empowered congress to certify election results, it was the president who was responsible for assembling the electoral registry, for organizing and naming most officials at polling stations, and for tallying the vote. Far from balancing the executive and legislative branches of government, what I call the classical theory of electoral governance encouraged the president to pack the legislature with his supporters to minimize opposition checks on the abuse of his powers (Lehoucq, 2002). Marginalizing the opposition within congress, however, led to rebellion against standing presidents. So, even if three incumbents imposed their successors on the presidency between 1882 and 1949, their efforts provoked twenty-six insurrections, three of which installed a new incumbent on the presidency. Presidents who governed with plural legislatures finished their terms and stepped down after their four-year term was over avoided being toppled, and after waiting another four years (because consecutive reelection was not possible), managed to be reelected to high office (Lehoucq, 1996; 1998a).

The 1948 elections, the triggering event of the civil war of that year, culminated nearly a decade of struggle between an ambitious president and his often strident opponents (Lehoucq, 1991). Political competition began to polarize once President Rafael Angel Calderón Guardia (1940–4) of the National Republican Party (PRN) deployed the presidential powers to exclude his opponents from the political system. The election of Teodoro Picado to the presidency in 1944 was widely perceived as a product of his predecessor's machinations, even if analysis reveals that officially sponsored fraud was not the reason the opposition lost these elections (Lehoucq and Molina, 2002: 190). Equally destabilizing was the marginalization of the opposition in congress: Between 1940 and 1944, the PRN and the PVP held approximately three-fourths of all legislative seats. By upsetting the delicate balance of power responsible for maintaining political stability, President Calderón Guardia provoked the formation of groups dedicated to using force to capture state power.

It was the mixed nature of the Costa Rican political system that helps explain why the civil war was brief. The *calderonistas*' arbitrary use of state powers helped polarize political competition, but did not prevent President Picado from satisfying most opposition demands for a level playing field in the 1946 mid-term or 1948 general elections (Lehoucq, 1995a). The war was not an effort to overthrow a dictatorship, but the escalation of an intense struggle over political succession, one whose initial results indicated that the opposition had won the 1948 presidential election. Once the semi-autonomous National Electoral Tribunal declared Otilio Ulate of the Party of National Union (PUN) the winner, the PRN-dominated congress used its constitutional right to annul the election on March 1, arguing that the opposition-controlled Electoral Registry had deprived thousands of its followers of electoral identification cards necessary to vote for Calderón Guardia. In the weeks that followed, efforts to negotiate a pact between government and opposition became irrelevant as a ragtag army led by José Figueres, who had been exiled by Calderon Guardia and denied a congressional seat in the 1944 elections, won the two-month civil war (Lehoucq, 1992).

Conclusions and Implications

The cross-national, statistical literature on civil war identifies one key reason for the onset of civil war in Central America. Three of the four poorest
countries of the region – the ones with GDP per capita incomes below the
world average – did see conflict turn violent by the late 1970s. Insurgents in
Guatemala began to battle dictatorship over what became a thirty-six-year
conflict, one that flared in the 1960s before dying down and reaching a new
crescendo by the late 1970s. Honduras, the poorest country on the isthmus, did
not experience civil war.

   Inequality and poverty, however, did not make civil war inevitable in Central
America. Although some studies unearth statistical associations between
inequality and civil war, others do not, largely because the data on income and
land distribution does not exist or is far from ideal. My examination of the
evidence about inequality in Central America suggests that it became notably
worse in El Salvador by the late 1970s. The average incomes of workers fell
in El Salvador, Guatemala, and Nicaragua, but the descent into violence preceded both the fall in real wages and in economic growth. Macro-indicators
also show that life was becoming less miserable in much of Central America.
Illiteracy rates had fallen from 40 to 30 percent of the population between
1960 and 1980. Life expectancy had increased from fifty-seven to sixty-seven
during these years. Infant mortality rates had decreased from 83 to 41 deaths
per 100 live births in this twenty-year period (see Table 1.3). Although Central
Americans had economic or social grievances, dictatorships went to war when
overall conditions had been improving for the average Central American.
Something else caused civil war.

   It was what I call inconsistent authoritarian regimes that helps explain why
political conflict became violent in three Central American countries. Civil war,
however, had little to do with the existence of semi-democratic regimes, as several cross-national studies avow. With the exception of Costa Rica, regimes on
the isthmus were unalloyed autocracies. Most were reactionary despotisms, in
which agro-export interests manipulated the factional struggles of the officer
corps to protect their investments. Most also belonged to a class of what I call
inconsistently authoritarian regimes – systems afflicted by factionalism and
unable to quash opposition activity.

   Executive instability did create (rare) opportunities for reform, ones where
dissident military officers could form coalitions with opposition civilians
to topple incumbent generals. Not infrequently, both would ally with labor
unions to stabilize a new government. It was during these reformist interludes
that these regimes were at their weakest, which only encouraged street protesters and insurgents to redouble their efforts to push for full democracy or revolution. Under such pressure, regimes that split or wavered invited even more
protest, which only a concerted hardline response managed to break, as the
cases of El Salvador and Guatemala in the late 1970s demonstrate. Although
the Salvadoran military eliminated street protest by 1980, it was forced to fight

a protracted counterinsurgency against the FMLN. The Guatemalan military, in contrast, did crush its opponents. Factionalism ended as officers unified around a strategy of unbridled violence that cleaned the streets of protesters, decimated an urban guerrilla movements, and defeated a rural insurgency at the cost of more than 150,000 lives.

The Somoza dictatorship in Nicaragua, after having built a loyal National Guard and having co-opted the country's two historic parties (Conservatives and Liberals), labor unions, and business groups, faltered once this coalition began to disintegrate. By the mid-1970s, upper income groups had begun to distance themselves from Somoza. President Carter's human rights policy, along with the dictator's August 1977 heart attack, made the mortality of the regime a central issue in national politics, one that insurgents, opposition politicians, and businessmen used to organize a united front against the regime. Despite the massive use of force, Somoza failed to stem the revolutionary tide. Internationally and domestically isolated, the Somoza regime fell as the National Guard lost the bloody war against the Nicaraguan people.

It was therefore both political grievance and revolutionary collective action that led to civil war in much of Central America. Enough peasants, workers, and students struggled to change governments that systematically violated their rights and ignored their complaints. They found reactionary despotism objectionable not only for its social inequities, but principally for its political repression. In dozens of clandestine meetings, opponents created the organizations and assembled the coalitions that challenged regimes, three of which allowed insurgents to transform factional disputes within the ruling bloc into full-blown regime crises, ones that a fall in commodity prices only made uglier and more threatening.

3

Stalemates, Peace Negotiations, and Democratization

Introduction

Civil war engulfed Central America in the 1980s. A peace agreement was not signed in El Salvador until late 1992, although the fighting between the government and the FMLN had dissipated to an inconclusive war by the late 1980s. The civil war in Guatemala did not end until 1996, although its military had defeated the insurgents, at a great loss of life, by the mid-1980s. No sooner had Nicaraguans overthrown the Somoza dictatorship than the Sandinistas became embroiled in another civil war, one that pitted them against an irregular army organized by former members of the Somoza's National Guard (the Contras) and supported by the Reagan administration.

The 1980s were the decade of civil war not only on the isthmus, but also throughout the world. At the start of this decade, less than 15 percent of the world's countries witnessed insurgents contesting governments in bloody conflicts. By the end of this decade, civil war had started or continued in more than 20 percent of all countries (Fearon and Laitin, 2003). The equivalent figure for Central America was high: Three of the seven countries, or more than 40 percent of them, were engulfed in bloody civil wars.

The 1980s were also the start of what Samuel Huntington (1991) called the "Third Wave" of democratization. At the start of this decade, autocracies existed in most countries. By the end of the 1980s, however, there were more democracies than dictatorships. By the mid-1990s, the majority of political systems allowed all adults at least eighteen years old to cast ballots in regularly scheduled and competitive elections and, to one extent or another, respected the civil rights of the citizenry (Lehoucq, 2011).

Political developments in Central America echoed international trends. If only Costa Rica was democratic at the start of the Third Wave, every country on the isthmus saw the replacement of military-appointed juntas and executives with elected presidents (and legislators) by the mid-1990s. In Honduras, generals ceded power to civilians in 1981. In Guatemala, a civilian president took office in 1985. In El Salvador, a civilian became president in 1985 in the midst of a civil war. In Panama, civilians took charge after the 1989 U.S. invasion.

These transitions were unanticipated for at least two reasons. First, most of Central America was not sufficiently developed, even if one analyst, Mitchell A. Seligson (1987), suggested that Central America was rapidly approaching the economic threshold making democracy possible by the late 1970s. Second, democratization was unexpected because so many of us took civil war to mean that peaceful solutions to conflicts had failed. No one in or outside the region predicted democracy would emerge once political violence became widespread. In a conversation in the late 1980s with a prominent Salvadoran political scientist, I wondered whether the stalemate between the ARENA government and the FMLN was creating the basis for a democratic peace, an insight that we regrettably did not develop at that time. We did not know then that there was some truth to this speculation, as subsequent events would demonstrate.

This chapter explores why dictatorship gave way to more democratic political systems in Central America, that is, develop the logic of our all too casually dismissed speculations. It first reviews modernization-inspired accounts to suggest that development levels do not explain regime change. It, second, examines whether democratization was a function of changing elite interests (Boix, 2003), a claim that Jeffrey Paige has insightfully made for Central America (1997). Finally, this chapter analyzes the argument about how war transformed the region's political landscape (Rouquié, 1994; Wood, 2000; Zamora, 1997), about why the actions of peasants, workers, and street protesters ended reactionary despotism on the isthmus.

A combination of the second and third arguments best explains regime change in Central America. Civil war produced the realignment of interests that undermined the coalition between military officers and agro-exporters – one that counted on the acquiescence, if not outright support of Washington. It was revolutionary collective action – from organized acts of resistance to the deployment of violence – that liquidated the old order on the isthmus. Where the threat to reactionary despotism was the greatest, as in El Salvador and Nicaragua, the institutional breakthroughs were most dramatic. This is a pattern that holds for Costa Rica, which also forged its democratic institutions, as I show, amid violence and conflict during the first half of the twentieth century.

The absence or defeat of guerrillas made for different transitions in the rest of Central America. In Honduras – as in Guatemala, where the insurgents were largely defeated by the early 1980s – the military negotiated a gradual transition that preserved many of its prerogatives. In both countries, landed elites retained many of their privileges, even if officers agreed to let civilians run the executive and legislative branches of government. In Panama, a surprise invasion finished off a dictatorship, in the wake of which there was a transition to formal democratic rule.

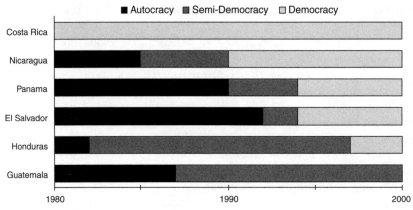

FIGURE 3.1. Regime types, 1980–2000.

Source: Bowman, Lehoucq, and Mahoney (2005); Brinks, Mainwaring, and Pérez-Liñán (2011) for Panama.

Political Regime Change: The Facts

Figure 3.1, which I undertook with two colleagues (Bowman, Lehoucq, and Mahoney, 2005), displays regime types, by year, for Central America. The regime classification for Panama stems from research by Scott Mainwaring, Daniel Brinks, and Aníbal Pérez-Liñán (2008). We code political systems on five dimensions: how competitive their elections are, how extensive voting rights are, whether civil rights are respected, whether national sovereignty exists, and whether civilian authorities exercise control over the military. To be considered a democracy, a regime has to score high on all dimensions; scoring poorly on one dimension would make a regime an autocracy. A mediocre rating on one or more dimension classifies a regime as semi-democratic. This is an admittedly limited conception of democracy, one that emphasizes procedural norms at the core of liberal democratic thought.

Honduras became the first country to leave autocracy. In 1980, Hondurans cast ballots for the Constituent Assembly that produced a new constitution, one that has been in effect since 1982. In late 1981, Hondurans elected Roberto Suazo Córdova of the Liberal Party president. Its political system became semi-democratic in 1982 and remained so until 1996 for three reasons. First, the government did not always respect the civil rights of its opponents. Although human rights abuses did not lead to large-scale assassination, disappearances of 179 regime critics did occur (CNDH, 1994). Second, its military remained independent of civilian control until the 1990s (Ruhl, 1996; Salomón, 1992). Third, the existence of an anti-Sandinista insurgency known as the Contras funded by the U.S. Central Intelligence Agency, one that possessed the blessing of the Honduran armed forces, limited the sovereignty of elected officials (Dillon, 1991).

Of all the political transitions on the isthmus, the Nicaraguan one generated the most controversy. For its supporters, the Sandinista political system was a creative blending of liberal and Marxist theories, one that would overcome the limitations of each (Luciak, 1995; Vanden and Prevost, 1993). In place of geographical-based systems of representation, the post-revolutionary regime relied on local organizing committees and mass organizations to transmit popular preferences to the government. To prevent the centralization of power common among vanguard parties, it created a quasi-legislative body, the Council of State (in 1980), consisting of party and interest-group representatives, to balance the authority of the Junta of National Reconstruction, and implicitly, the Frente's nine-person Directorate. To its critics, the institutions of the immediate postwar political system were little more than window dressing for a Leninist-style dictatorship (Christian, 1985). Even after Daniel Ortega won the 1984 presidential election and the Sandinistas produced the 1987 constitution, the Sandinista's critics denounced these institutions as meaningless given the de facto power the Frente's Directorate held and its control of the armed forces.

We code Nicaragua as an autocracy until 1985 because the revolutionary junta, which saw its conservative members leave in April 1980, and the Sandinista Directorate retained power, despite their willingness to bargain on some issues with the Council of State. With the development of the Contra movement, the junta declared a state of emergency that limited civil rights. It did not convene presidential and legislative elections until 1984, which leading opposition members, egged on by the Reagan administration, boycotted. The elections, judged as fair by international observers (Close, 1988: 132–138; Walker, 2003: 156–159), and the promulgation of the constitution were a political opening that makes Nicaragua's political system semi-democratic in 1985. After the 1990 elections, its political system became democratic. Won by Violeta Barrios de Chamorro, the widow of Pedro Joaquín Chamorro who was the editor of *La Prensa* assassinated in 1978, both the Sandinistas and the Contras recognized the results of the 1990 election. In the following years, each side demobilized its war machine (Hartzell, 2002; Spalding, 1999) and the 100,000-person Sandinista army gradually lost influence on government (Ruhl, 2003).

The Guatemalan political system underwent a transition from brutal authoritarian rule in 1985. As the military was routing the URNG, it held elections for a Constituent Assembly, which produced a new constitution in 1985. Later that year, Guatemalans turned out to vote and delivered a victory for Vinicio Cerezo, the PDC's presidential candidate, giving his party a majority of seats in the congress. This country's political system remained semi-democratic throughout the rest of the 1980s and 1990s. Failure to end civil rights violations continued until the 1990s. The military's independence from civilian authority limited democratization (Ruhl, 2005).

The political system of El Salvador went through a more gradual and controlled transition from repressive military rule, which started when Salvadorans cast ballots for a Constituent Assembly in 1982 (Byrne, 1996). Although the

Christian Democratic Party (PDC) won the largest number of Assembly seats, the right-wing National Republican Alliance (ARENA) and Party of National Conciliation (PCN) together held a majority and planned to make Major Roberto D'Aubuisson, ARENA's leader, and chief suspect in the 1980 murder of Archbishop Oscar Arnulfo Romero, President of the Assembly and of the country. To avoid a Democratic-controlled U.S. Congress's vote against military aide for the country, the Reagan administration mobilized its supporters in the Salvadoran military to pressure the PCN and the PDC to make Alvaro Magaña, a compromise candidate, president of the country (LeoGrande, 1998: 163–165). Despite presidential elections in 1984 and 1989, continuing human rights violations and the lack of civilian supremacy over the military limited political reform (Williams and Walter, 1997). It was not until the signing of the peace accords in 1992 that the Salvadoran political system became semi-democratic. This country's political system democratized in 1994, when presidential elections included candidates from the left and the right, and which ARENA won.

The regime opening of the early 1980s in Panama came to an abrupt halt in 1981, when General Omar Torrijos, the Commander of the National Guard, died in a mysterious plane crash. Apparently his plan was to hold competitive elections for the presidency in 1984. His death triggered a power struggle within the Guard, which was gradually won by General Noriega. In 1984, Noriega's candidate for the presidency, Nicolás Ardito Barletta, won in a fraudulent vote. Noriega deposed him a year later and allowed Barletta's vice-president, Eric Arturo Delvalle, to become president. Following another fraudulent election in 1989, the United States overthrew Noriega. The candidate who allegedly won the 1989 election, Guillermo Endara, was sworn in as president, a post he held until 1994. The National Guard was disbanded and the security forces rebuilt in the wake of the invasion (Arias Calderón, 2000; Caumartin, 2007). During the U.S. occupation of Panama, Brinks, Mainwaring, and Pérez-Liñán (2011) code Panama as a semi-democracy. They code Panama as a democracy with the election of Ernesto Pérez Balladares to the presidency in 1994.

Explaining Regime Change

Levels of economic development or growth do not explain political changes on the isthmus, as modernization theory would have it. Using a database of 135 countries between 1950 and 1990, Przeworski and colleagues (2000) suggest that none of the region's countries, including Costa Rica, had met thresholds of economic development for democracy between 1950 and 1990. Yet, most regimes began to liberalize in the 1980s, and politicians in Costa Rica consolidated their democratic system in the 1950s. The decades when autocrats relinquished control of their political systems were also when GDP per capita fell everywhere, and in some places, dropped significantly.

Even exclusively regional comparisons underscore the limited utility of the modernization thesis. Although Panama has had an economic development level similar to Costa Rica's, its political system was one of the last to democratize

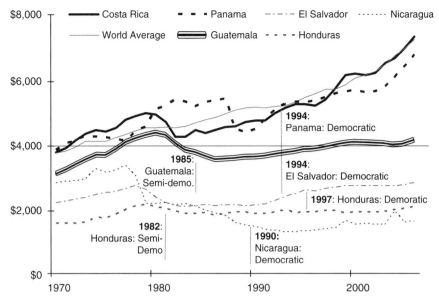

FIGURE 3.2. GDP per capita, 1970–2006 (in 1990 U.S. international dollars).
Source: Maddison (2010) and Figures 1.4 and 3.1.

in the region. Moreover, data on GDP per capita in Figure 3.2 indicates that development dipped as a result of the civil wars of the early 1980s. In two countries – El Salvador and Guatemala – levels of economic development only recovered their mid-1970s rate by the late 1990s. Honduras's GDP per capita levels have stagnated and Nicaragua's took a dramatic turn for the worse during the 1980s. Yet, most of these countries made a transition from authoritarian rule during this period.

Some argue that structural change in upper-class interests undermined reactionary despotism (Paige, 1997; also, see Colindres, 1978, for the analysis of prewar elite interests). Elites went from making profits by planting and exporting coffee – or investments in fixed assets – to generating income in commerce and finance – or investing in movable assets. This is a core insight that Carles Boix (2003) later developed into the finding that democracy is more likely to exist when wealth is less fixed or specific. Some evidence exists for a broad relationship between economic development, the shift from specific to movable assets, and democratization in the region and the world as a whole.

It was civil war, however, that led to political (and economic) change in Central America (Rouquié, 1994; Wood, 2000; Zamora, 1997). Armed conflict preceded the elite's diversification of interests in El Salvador, that is, its shift from fixed investments in agriculture to mobile investments in commerce and finance. It drove the oligarchy from the countryside, an outcome that was the product of what Elisabeth Wood (2000) calls an "insurgent route to democracy," or one in which revolutionaries and popular movements forced a dictatorship to change. Agrarian reform, the occupation of rural estates, and the disruption caused by war led the elite to diversify its investments, which may have lessened its preference for authoritarianism. In Guatemala, the elite survived the war with its fortunes intact (Casaús Arzú, 1992). In Panama, the elite had invested heavily in commerce and finance decades earlier, the revenues from which were shared with autocrats until one of them, Manuel Antonio Noriega, began to encroach on this lucrative economic activity (Ropp, 1992). Decades earlier, as the last section of this chapter explains, the political system of Costa Rica had become democratic by the 1950s as a result of a long-term, simmering stalemate between governments and opposition movements in an economy dominated by coffee exports.

The implication of these findings is that the strategic calculations of regimes and their opponents determine whether there is a transition from authoritarian rule. Chapter 2 concludes that inconsistent dictatorships suffering from factional struggle and instability encouraged the opposition to contest the regime. Instability typically led to a return to autocracy because regime hardliners scuttled the reforms that could progress to democracy (Przeworski, 1991). On the handful of occasions in which regime moderates marginalized hardliners to join forces with the opposition before the 1980s, the United States intervened to tip the balance of power in favor of restoring the old order.

In the following paragraphs, I show how civil war, along with the end of the cold war, broke this cycle and led to transitions away from authoritarianism. Where incumbents and guerrillas fought themselves into a stalemate, democratization became a solution to typically severe class conflict. This insight serves as the core idea that Leonard Wantchekon (2004) uses to explain why democracy sometimes becomes the equilibrium choice of the key actors in post-civil war settings. Acemoglu and Robinson (2006) subsume this argument in their theory about how democracy emerges as a guarantee to protect the core interests of the elite and the majority. Such a framework – one emphasizing bargaining among self-interested rivals – also accommodates the fact that the end of the cold war helped democratization in Central America. Once U.S. policy shifted from siding with anti-communist forces to pressuring them to reform, the negotiations to end civil war and establish democracy became possible.

Renewed Civil War and Democratic Breakthroughs in Nicaragua

Somoza's overthrow ended the commonality of interests between the FSLN and Nicaragua's non-Marxist politicians. The FSLN began to assert its control over the state and economy, even as the Sandinistas did not exclude their former partners from policy making. Businessmen had the capital and technical expertise to run an agro-export economy devastated by the war against Somoza. As in Costa Rica three decades earlier, the tense and often acrimonious relations between revolutionaries and businessmen could have become the basis of a compromise, one with elected officials presiding over a mixed economy. U.S. foreign policy, however, derailed such an accommodation, one that the Frente's pragmatists did little to protect at key moments during the 1980s. The cost of the Reagan administration's hardline policies proved to be enormous: They led not only to death and massive destruction in Nicaragua, but also to repeated violation of U.S. law (and the constitution) in quixotic pursuit of communists, real and alleged, in Central America.

There were disagreements among the nine men on the FSLN's Directorate, although they shared the goal of socialist revolution. Moderates recommended against nationalizing private property and monopolizing the state. The Frente needed cross-class collaboration and international support to rebuild an economy destroyed after the civil war against Somoza. They also pointed out that the Nicaraguan people's commitment to socialism was unclear. Hardliners including Tomás Borge and Humberto Ortega, urged the Frente to move swiftly to protect a revolution so it would not suffer the fate of other reformist governments such as those of Jacobo Arbenz in Guatemala (1954), Victor Paz in Bolivia (1964), and most recently, Salvador Allende in Chile (1973). Each of these was overthrown in military coups supported by the CIA. The Frente did not waste any time organizing a new army under the leadership of Humberto Ortega and the Interior Ministry under Borge.

Although debate continued among Sandinistas, economic realities helped the moderates win several early battles, including respect for private property, consultation with non-Sandinista organizations on the quasi-legislative Council of State, and accommodation with the United States. The Sandinistas left much of the economy in private hands, even as they nationalized the Somoza's family agricultural and commercial holdings, the banking system, foreign trade, mining, fishing, and forestry and established state marketing boards for export and domestic crops. A year after the revolution, public sector spending rose to 37 percent from 15 percent in 1978 (Gibson, 1987; Ruccio, 1987).

Centrist and conservative politicians objected when the Sandinistas demurred on calling for early elections and instead focused on reconstruction and consolidation. The two leading moderates on the five-person revolutionary junta – Violeta Barrios de Chamorro and Alfonso Robelo – resigned their positions in April 1980. They protested the lack of an electoral timetable and the Frente's request that the junta approve expanding the size of the Council of State from thirty-three to forty-seven members to make room for representatives from the Sandinista's new mass organizations. This move created a majority for the FSLN on what was rapidly becoming a policy making arena in which regime opponents could air their grievances and negotiate changes with the Frente (Gorman, 1981).

The Carter administration worked to moderate the Sandinistas, even though it had spent the preceding years unsuccessfully convincing Somoza to step down to prevent a Sandinista triumph. It used the promise of U.S. aid to extract concessions from the Sandinistas, a policy that Somoza's former allies on Capitol Hill and conservative Republicans opposed. The United States recommended that the private sector's peak association, the Superior Council for Private Enterprise (COSEP), which had become a key opposition vehicle, sit on the refashioned Council of State. It also encouraged COSEP to support appointing two new moderates on the junta, Arturo Cruz, the president of the Central Bank, and Rafael Córdova Rivas. The FSLN responded by promising to hold elections in 1985.

The Sandinistas and their opponents reached different conclusions regarding the nature of postwar political arrangements, even as circumstances forced them to accept compromises on key political economic issues. The FSLN claimed that it was establishing a genuine democracy, one that respected private property, the freedom of the press, and allowed the opposition to play a role in policymaking. Businessmen and non-Marxist politicians, in contrast, argued that the FSLN was creating a one-party regime, one based upon nationalizing large swaths of the economy. The sandinistas, in fact, had begun to redirect state policy from stimulating traditional exporters to helping newly created cooperatives on the extensive holdings confiscated from the Somoza family. In protest, large-scale agriculturalists had begun to reduce investment in coffee, cotton, and sugar production and cattle ranching (Colburn, 1986; Spalding, 1994).

By working with pro- and anti-government moderates, the Carter administration protected the fragile agreements painstakingly reached by the left and the right – ones indispensable for establishing the consensus necessary to build democracy in Nicaragua. From the accounts left by Lawrence Pezzullo (Pezzullo and Pezzullo, 1993), the Carter-appointed Ambassador to Nicaragua, and Robert Pastor, the Latin American specialist on the National Security Council, it is clear that the Carter administration did not celebrate the Sandinista's triumph for the same reasons that hardline U.S. foreign policy makers opposed the Frente: It doubted the FSLN's commitment to democracy and free-market economy. Unlike the cold warriors, the Carter administration thought economic aid and diplomacy could deprive Sandinista hardliners of the excuse of U.S. intransigence to ally with Cuba and the Soviet Union. The tremendous need for international assistance in the devastating civil war, they reasoned, would strengthen Sandinista moderates and encourage the Frente to compromise.

Ronald Reagan's election in 1980 upset the delicate balance of power in Managua. Reagan's foreign policy team consisted of cold warriors who read the fall of American allies in Iran and Nicaragua as losses in the United State's struggle with the Soviet Union. On assuming office in January 1981, they turned to stopping revolution in Central America. The rise of U.S. foreign policy hardliners had the predictable effect of allowing FSLN hardliners to scuttle efforts to strengthen incipient democratic arrangements, especially as the Reagan administration began covert support for the former members of Somoza's National Guard assembling in neighboring Honduras and plotting a return to power, as investigative journalists began to confirm (Dillon, 1991; Dickey, 1985).

There were several opportunities to thwart the polarization in the ensuing years. The first crystallized around a trip to Managua made by Thomas Enders, an Assistant Secretary of State, in August 1981 (Gutman, 1988). In meetings held over two days, Enders accused the Sandinistas of funneling arms to the FMLN in neighboring El Salvador as part of a broader plan to spread instability and communist influence in Central America. The Sandinistas charged the United States with sponsoring an armed attack on the revolution and with responsibility for Somoza's numerous crimes. Frank exchanges led to an understanding whereby Enders promised U.S. respect for the revolution in exchange for the Frente not funding left-wing insurgents in Central America and for sharp reductions in the Nicaraguan armed forces.

The tentative agreement reached between Enders and the Sandinistas, which was very much the understanding that the Carter administration had reached with Managua, did not bridge the divide between Reagan and the Sandinistas. For Reagan hardliners, Enders's mission was less an effort to prevent a break with Managua than to convince Congress, controlled by the Democrats, that the Sandinistas were untrustworthy and thus build support of the administration's policy on Capitol Hill (LeoGrande, 1998: 188–224). The Frente's behavior after the August meeting with Enders did little to help its case in Washington. Ender's communiqués with the Frente went unanswered. Daniel Ortega lambasted the United States in his September 1981 address before the United Nations. The United States increased covert support for the counter-revolutionary movement in Honduras as the Sandinistas declared a state of siege in response to the Contras' initial incursions on Nicaraguan territory, an insurgency that grew to encompass peasant soldiers with grievances against the Sandinistas (Brown, 2000; 2001; Horton, 1998) as well as ex-guardsmen (Dickey, 1985; Dillon, 1991). What each side believed was evidence of malevolence spiraled into a series of decisions that seemingly confirmed each side's worst fears of its rival.

Was it U.S. or Nicaraguan intransigence that led to the break in relations? In his comprehensive review of U.S.-Nicaragua relations, Robert Kagan (1996), a former aide to Elliot Abrams, U.S. Assistant Secretary for Human Rights, argues that Ender's mission came to naught because the Sandinistas already had decided to ally with the USSR. Most other accounts of these years suggest that Enders was outmaneuvered by Reagan hardliners, who, like Kagan, already had decided that the Sandinistas could not be trusted. They note that U.S. intelligence agencies reported there was no movement of arms from Nicaragua to El Salvador in its March 1981 assessment, one that Reagan hardliners dismissed (Arnson, 1993: 74–81). Despite the lack of evidence that the Frente was acting in bad faith, the Reagan administration terminated U.S. aid to Nicaragua on April 1. So assessing the Sandinista's intentions in light of their behavior was irrelevant because Reagan administration officials, including CIA chief William J. Casey, were "looking for a place to start rolling back the Communist Empire" (cited in LeoGrande, 1998: 283). Instead of working to establish a mutual understanding with the Sandinistas – and to strengthen moderates in Managua – the administration reinforced the views of the Frente's hardliners.

Pastor (2002: 188) faults the Frente for not trying harder to reach an agreement with the United States, no doubt because the Sandinistas had more to lose than the Reagan administration if relations broke down. The United States could defeat the FSLN and destroy Nicaragua, but the Sandinistas could not get rid of Reagan nor invade the United States. The converse also is true: The Sandinistas posed no threat to the United States. This asymmetry in power between the United States and Nicaragua fueled the FSLN's suspicions that the Reagan administration was plotting to overthrow the revolution, which, as support for the Contras reminds us, it was. That some in Nicaragua saw Pastor's point was later revealed by Sergio Ramírez, a Nicaraguan junta member and later vice-president. In a 2001 interview with Stephen Kinzer, a former *New York Times* journalist, Ramírez reflected, "If you ask me now, sitting in this room, what I think of [Ender's] offer, I'd say it sounds like a pretty good deal. But at the time we refused even to discuss it. You have to put yourself back in that moment to understand the emotions on both sides." Ramírez points out, "We saw it as a trap: the gringos would cut us off from our friends, isolate us, and then attack and destroy us" (cited in Kinzer, 2001b: 32).

The 1984 elections did not bridge the divide between Nicaraguans or between the FSLN and the Reagan administration, despite the fact that the Sandinistas had signaled their willingness to compromise. They had lifted the siege months before the election. They opened competition to all parties renouncing violence to capture the state. In response, many parties did register their candidates for the presidential and legislative races. Leading opposition candidates were barred from competing because they had joined either the northern or southern fronts of the counter-revolutionary struggle. Weeks before the election, the opposition's leading presidential candidate, Arturo Cruz, left the race, a decision that the Reagan administration applauded. So, even if the election was judged honest by international observers, it was inconclusive. Washington ignored an election won by Daniel Ortega, the FSLN's candidate. Even with 67 percent of the vote, the Sandinistas and their foreign supporters could do little to counteract the US.

Failure to reach an agreement led to a U.S.-financed war that imposed a terrible cost on Nicaragua, a country already reeling from the destruction of the war against Somoza, and had led to a 30-percent fall in GDP per capita in the late 1970s. Valpy FitzGerald and Arturo Grigsby (2001: 152) estimate that the direct costs of the war were US$2 billion between 1980 and 1988, which was then the equivalent of one year's GDP. The indirect costs of the war, as a result of the U.S. trade embargo between 1983 and 1990, add to another US$1 billion. What the authors call the "multiplier effect" of lost foreign exchange on national production could total an additional US$5 billion. There also are the incalculable costs of 62,000 victims, half of whom were civilian and military, or almost 1 percent of the national population. The effects of the Contra war included the consequences of economic mismanagement: The centralization of national production, the attempt to create large state enterprises (Colburn, 1990), led to waste and declining exports. By 1989, exports were half of what they had been in 1980 and roughly a third of what they had been in 1977, the year before the final push to overthrow Somoza. Although, by the late 1980s, the regime increased taxes and cut social expenditures to reduce burgeoning fiscal deficits, the war against the Contras, which accounted for 40 percent of government spending by 1987, further reduced the dwindling pot of money the Frente had to reactivate economic production. Even with copious amounts of foreign aid, the state had insufficient funds to stimulate the private sector, establish state corporations, fight a U.S.-financed war, and meet ambitious social objectives. By 1988, inflation had climbed to an annual rate of 43,000 percent and the Sandinistas had contracted a foreign debt of US$9.7 billion, four times the GDP (O'Campo, 1991: 331).

Political scandal, along with a change in presidential administration, changed Washington's policy toward Nicaragua. The sale of weapons to Iran (in exchange for the release of American hostages), whose profits were turned over to the Contras – the Iran-Contra Scandal – deprived the Reagan administration of support for the Contras on Capitol Hill (LeoGrande, 1998). By February 1988, the Democratic majority in the U.S. Congress defeated Reagan's latest effort to fund the Contras. The election of President George H. W. Bush in November 1988 changed Washington's interest in the Contra war. Gone were officials like Elliot Abrams, who, along with thirteen other Regan administration appointees, were prosecuted for lying under oath to congress about the covert war in Nicaragua (Arnson, 1993: 297–301). The new administration wanted to deemphasize the role Nicaragua and Central America occupied in American foreign policy, a trend that accelerated with the rapprochement between the United States and the USSR. Soviet President Gorbachev's decision to permit the collapse of eastern European governments by mid-1989 signaled the end of the cold war.

Loss of U.S. support weakened the Contras, which was one reason the FSLN negotiated with an adversary key Sandinistas swore they would never meet. The possibility of eliminating the Contras – and with the reluctant connivance of Washington – had great appeal to the Sandinistas. A second reason was the economic collapse of the Nicaraguan economy, one making peace a high priority, especially for the Ortega brothers, one of whom was president, and the other – Humberto – defense minister. Ending the war would not only eliminate the Contras, but also generate a peace dividend that would allow the Sandinistas to resume building a new society in Nicaragua. A third was that the Frente had to negotiate with the Contras to discourage conservative Democrats in the U.S. House of Representatives from endorsing Reagan's hardline policy; it was the support of these Democrats that had allowed the congressional Republicans – then a minority in the House of Representatives – to fashion enough votes to pursue their Cold War policies toward Central America (Leogrande and Brenner, 1993).

For these reasons, the FSLN latched onto Costa Rican President Oscar Arias's peace proposal, launched in the Guatemalan city of Esquipulas in December 1987 (Child, 1992). Arias's peace plan appealed to the Sandinistas because it involved ending support for hostile guerrilla movements on a neighbor's territory as part of a broader effort to reduce the region's armed forces and incorporate insurgents into formal political life. Over the next eighteen months, the Sandinistas agreed to many reforms in exchange for a cease-fire and eventual disarmament of the Contras. The FSLN agreed to lift the state of siege and thus relax press censorship, revamp the electoral registry, and guarantee the openness of the 1990 general elections. As part of the ongoing negotiations, the Frente agreed to let none other than former President Carter mediate the 1990 elections. Carter was rapidly becoming an election monitor much in demand, having himself been the target of a stolen election in his first bid for public office in rural Georgia in 1960 (Carter, 1992). On this occasion, the Sandinistas and their opponents took the opportunity to negotiate an end to the U.S.-financed war, one that committed them to accept the results of a hotly contested and internationally supervised election (Pastor, 2002).

The 1990 elections were an enormous gamble for the government and the opposition. Although each side accepted – at least in theory – the possibility of defeat, each concentrated on the ideal outcome: victory and its rival's acceptance of its triumph. It was the enormity of this payoff that led the Sandinistas, the Contras, and the domestic political opposition to negotiate, over many months, numerous electoral reforms and agreements. For the Frente, few of these decisions were uncontroversial; accounts of these years explain how each concession led to bickering among regime factions. The hardliners feared these concessions gave up too much – the possibility of losing control of the state – for the sake of a peace they might win on the battlefield, anyway. Each concession, the more moderate Sandinistas like the Ortega brothers reasoned, made it harder for Washington to ignore a Sandinista victory that would have President Carter's seal of approval. Reforms were worth what they reasoned were minimal risks for the sake of ratifying their government control and ending the war (Kinzer, 2007: 349–353). For the Frente's opponents, each compromise made it more difficult for the Sandinistas to reject their defeat at the polls, which rapidly became the only way the Contras or the domestic opposition retained to dislodge the Sandinistas from the heights of power. The elections acquired an enormous significance because they promised to end the civil war and effect a transition to democratic rule in Nicaragua.

The Sandinistas had an additional reason for submitting their state control to internationally supervised elections. Simply put, they expected to win on February 25, election day. Many polls showed that Daniel Ortega, the FSLN's presidential candidate, was ahead of Violeta Barrios de Chamorro, the presidential candidate of a coalition of opposition parties known as the Nicaraguan Opposition Union (UNO). Preelection surveys revealed that most gave Ortega a comfortable lead over his opponent for much of the campaign (Barnes, 1992; Bischoping and Schuman, 1992; Miller, 1991). The Sandinistas therefore had good reason to believe that the 1990 elections would replay the 1984 elections, in which a grateful people would reward the Sandinistas for the revolution, its social policies, and standing up to the United States. If the Sandinistas had not believed they could win, a simple thought experiment indicates they would not have agreed to hold an election, an argument that leading members of the Nicaraguan opposition also understood. "It was fortunate for us," to cite UNO candidate doña Violeta Barrios de Chamorro (1996: 271), that the opinion polls "created an illusion that the Sandinistas would win with 75 percent of the vote because they would never have risked their power if they had thought they would lose."

Why the opposition continued to participate in elections that many polls showed it would lose indicates that its dilemma was different. Abstaining would continue their political marginalization; continuing the war would, at best, extract concessions from the Sandinistas, but not lead to their defeat, especially as the United States was wavering in its commitment to the Contras. Campaigning for executive and legislative offices would allow the opposition unfettered access to Nicaraguans. They would have months to hold rallies, circulate fliers, and criticize the Frente. "Even if we lost," said doña Violeta, "we would be achieving a lot of good for the democratization of the country." Participating in the election held out the possibility of winning, an outcome that dispassionate analyses suggested was more than a remote possibility. "The people of Nicaragua," doña Violeta (Barrios de Chamorro, 1996: 258) wrote in her autobiography,

> would not forget who had plunged us into a civil war that lasted a decade, killed so many of our sons and daughters, and lowered the country to a level of such severe economic decay that we might never be able to emerge from it. Under the rule Nicaragua had become, after Haiti, the poorest nation in our hemisphere. Who could thank the Sandinistas for that?

This hardheaded assessment, one consistent with the long-standing finding that voters punish incumbents in times of economic distress (Duch and Stevenson, 2008), was infrequently heard in the months before election day because preelection surveys offered comfort to the Sandinistas. Careful observers, like doña Violeta or her campaign director (and son-in-law), Antonio Lecayo (2005), found evidence that the FSLN could lose, which is why they channeled extracted numerous electoral guarantees from the Sandinistas and insisted on international observation of the elections. Surveys revealed that up to a third of Nicaraguans were undecided or would not identify a choice to a pollster, suggesting that many citizens were deliberating and/or unwilling to tell pollsters for whom they would vote. Surveys, such as Victor Borge's, a pollster from Costa Rica, that assured the secrecy of the vote – by, for example, having respondents fill out key questions on paper and away from the gaze of the surveyor – uncovered impressive majorities in favor of doña Violeta, the matriarchal candidate who typically appeared in white and promised to reunite the Nicaraguan family if she was elected president of Nicaragua. It was a credible promise; she had adult children who supported the Sandinistas and others who joined the Contras. As election day advanced, more polls showed that Ortega's lead was dwindling or even that he was behind the candidate the Sandinistas had dubbed "an instrument of imperialism."

Preelection surveys thus generated results to assuage the worst fears of both sides, even as their uncertainty redoubled campaign efforts and investment to level the playing field. For the opposition, polling trends persuaded them that they had a fighting chance of winning. For the FSLN, these trends fueled anxiety. In his memoirs of these years, Sergio Ramírez (1999: 276–278) relates how the Frente was flummoxed by these results, and especially by the finding that virtually all Nicaraguans – 96 percent – thought the Frente would "never be capable of detaining the war," an opinion shared by 56 percent of its own voters. How did the Sandinistas react to these concerns? Ramírez wrote that they "tried to correct the surveys," implying that the Sandinistas scrutinized the results even as they ignored key parts of the story. They hired Stanley Greenberg, a noted Democratic pollster, to help with the campaign. As the number of undecided voters increased, the Sandinistas comforted themselves that, among such voters, Ortega outpolled doña Violeta when asked which candidate was more qualified, more experienced, and more familiar with the economy and international affairs. When these voters were added to the number of respondents intending to vote for Ortega, Ramírez states, the resulting numbers reassured the Sandinistas they would win.

In an election watched by the entire world, the Sandinistas lost 40.8 to 54.7 percent of the vote (with 4.4 percent cast for other candidates), one that saw 87 percent of the electorate turn out to vote. It was a shock for the Sandinistas, one that left the Frente and its supporters dazed, depressed, and befuddled. The opposition coalition also won control of the legislature, with the constituent parties of the UNO coalition splitting control of 55.4 percent of the seats. The Frente went from holding 63.5 percent of assembly seats in the 1984 elections to controlling 42.5 percent of the legislature in the 1990 elections. By early morning on the 16th of February, Ortega conceded victory while the Carter delegation and other international observers worked behind the scenes to ensure a smooth, if wrenching, transition of power.

The Frente's hubris obscures some truths about the 1990 vote, ones that explain the electorate's behavior. Perhaps the most insightful analysis stems from Carlos Vilas (1990a), the Argentine sociologist who spent the 1980s living in Nicaragua and writing about the Sandinista revolution. He attributes Ortega's defeat to economic collapse, a situation that the U.S.-financed war and economic mismanagement caused, and to the war itself. Drastic cuts in government subsidies and expenditures in early 1988 led to a decline of more than 10 percent in GDP in the year before the elections. The unemployment rate shot up to 28 percent (Vilas, 1990b: 336), and real salaries were less than a fourth of what they had been in 1980 (O'Campo, 1991: 335). Surveys confirm Vilas's hunches: They reveal that large majorities held the Frente responsible for the devastation and decline in incomes. By February 1990, more than 60 percent of those surveyed concluded that life was better before the revolution. Most voters also believed that doña Violeta could end the war and the crisis, improve the economy and obtain more foreign aid, bring peace and reconciliation, and build a better Nicaragua (Anderson and Dodd, 2005: 153, 164).

What postmortems suggest is that the Sandinistas misread public opinion. Although the 40 percent of voters who backed Ortega apparently accepted the Frente's claim that their revolution had benefited Nicaragua, a majority saw a vote for the opposition as a way to end a decade of economic privations and material destruction. The attempt to establish socialism and defy the United States had ended in defeat.

War and Gradual Democratization in El Salvador

The effort to fashion a centrist compromise – and thus a democratic transition – in the aftermath of the 1979 coup failed as the reformist junta could not stop the army from slaughtering civilian opponents. By early 1980, the junta (and cabinet) shifted to the right with the departure of its reformers, often to join the Democratic Revolutionary Front (FDR), the social democratic civilian exile group that later allied with the FMLN. With U.S. complicity, the alliance between the military and oligarchs reasserted itself. It assassinated Archbishop Romero in March 1980. It killed six FDR leaders, three American churchwomen, and one religious worker in December 1980. It gunned down the president of the agrarian reform institute and two American labor advisors in January 1981. It killed between 733 and 926 civilians – half of whom were children – in *el Mozote*, a rural hamlet, in December 1981 (Danner, 1994). Before the war was over, the military and right-wing hit squads had exterminated the majority of the estimated 75,000 Salvadorans killed in the civil war. How did this dreadful state of affairs lead to democratization?

The defeat of urban protest led the FDR and FMLN to concentrate on winning the countryside. Government repression led many rural Salvadorans to collaborate with the guerrillas, although only a minority joined one of the FMLN's constituent groups. As several ethnographies explain (Cabarrús, 1983; Pearce, 1986; Wood, 2003), many peasants were enraged by the brutal killing of family members. For many, civil war activated memories of conscious-raising that religious workers, peasant unions, and guerrillas had begun in the 1970s. Cooperation took the form of supplying rebels with food, delivering messages, and passing intelligence on the army's movements, especially once guerrillas began to force large property owners to improve working conditions for laborers and extract taxes from them. Until approximately 1983, a 12,000-strong FMLN was on the offensive, one that would control the northern and northeastern parts of the country and freely circulate in many other parts of the country.

The Reagan administration pushed reform as part of a broader counterinsurgency campaign – and to obtain approval for its initiatives from a Democratic-controlled Congress. As Cold Warriors deepened the hardline stance toward Central America, Democrats obliged the administration to certify progress on respect for human rights before backing its aid requests.

Administration spokespersons repeatedly covered up the Salvadoran government's abuses in contentious committee hearings on Capitol Hill (Arnson,
1993). The administration, much to its ideological dislike, strong-armed the
junta into implementing an agrarian reform that many in the Republican Party
saw as an ill-fated attempt to push socialism on El Salvador and destroy the
mainstay of this country's economy. It also called for elections for a Constituent
Assembly that would draft a new constitution.

The 1982 elections were a victory for El Salvador's right. Distrustful of officers and many U.S. foreign policy makers, the right organized a party known
as the National Republican Alliance (ARENA), which obtained the second
largest number (nineteen) of seats in the 1982 elections for a new Constituent
Assembly. Initially dismissed by reformers as the party of the oligarchy, the
ARENA became a popular right-wing party. It promoted the interests of agro-
exporters, embraced laissez-faire economic policies, and borrowed extensively
from the 1982 U.S. Republican Party's platform. ARENA also struck a responsive chord with thousands of Salvadorans who favored a hardline response
to a growing rural insurgency. It relied on local-level defense committees to
mount a campaign calling on Salvadorans to veto "communist" reforms. The
campaign was lead by the charismatic D'Aubuisson, a now cashiered army
major organizing right-wing death-squads and fomenting barracks revolts
against the government. Only U.S. pressure prevented the PCN, which had
won fourteen seats, the party with long-term links to the military, from backing
D'Aubuisson's bid to become president of the country. Although the Christian
Democratic Party (PDC) – one of whose leaders, José Napoleón Duarte, had
been deprived of victory in the 1972 presidential elections and joined the
junta in March 1980 – had won the largest number of seats in the Constituent
Assembly (twenty-four of sixty), it had failed to secure an outright majority in
the body entrusted with writing a new constitution and legislating on behalf
of the public. Amid protests and threats by ARENA, the U.S. Embassy and
the military high command instead pressured PCN and PDC delegates to support the election of Alvaro Magaña, an apolitical mortgage banker, as provisional president of the country. ARENA gradually relented once it realized that
resistance was futile and D'Aubuisson was made president of the Assembly
(LeoGrande, 1998: 164–165).

The Salvadoran political system had become a hybrid of democratic forms
and authoritarian characteristics (Karl, 1995). Although civilians now participated in the executive and legislative branches of government, it was the military in association with the U.S. Embassy that made many key decisions for
the government. The military was responsible for the largest share of public
spending and directed the war against the FMLN. Even with a new constitution, promulgated in December 1983, the armed forces remained independent
of civilian oversight (Williams and Walter, 1997).

The armed forces, however, were not winning the war, even if they were no
longer losing it (Manwaring and Prisk, 1988). By the mid-1980s, half a billion

dollars in U.S. aid had begun to professionalize a military ill-equipped to fight a long-term war against a well-organized insurgency. U.S. advisors retrained entire battalions. The Salvadoran army obtained sophisticated helicopters and other hardware to wage a counter-insurgency war. The military went from having 7,250 soldiers in 1980 to 51,150 by 1985 (data cited in Benítez Manaut, 1989: 20). In response, the FMLN shifted from deploying large units of guerrillas to battle the army, which the military's superior technology began to detect and destroy. It developed many small units of no more than a half a dozen guerrillas to destroy infrastructure, ambush army units, and maintain a presence throughout as much as the national territory as possible. By 1987, one estimate indicated that the FMLN fielded approximately 6,000 combatants, an almost 50 percent decrease from the 12,000 it had in the early 1980s (data cited in Wood, 2003: 135).

The military stalemate provided opportunities for a compromise, which centrists from the right and left explored. In a speech that caught the Reagan administration by surprise, President José Napoleón Duarte, who had beat D'Aubuisson, 54 to 46 percent in a May 1984 runoff election, used his appearance before the UN General Assembly in early October to call for peace talks with the FDR-FMLN. It was a bold move, especially since the FDR-FMLN had repeatedly called for negotiations to end the war. The rebel alliance had, in fact, called for a "Provisional Government of Broad Participation," in late January, a proposal it had sent Duarte in mid-May (Lungo Uclés, 1996: 199). The FDR-FMLN swiftly accepted Duarte's offer, one that Duarte designed to be rejected, according to Salvador Samayoa (2002: 43), a high-level FMLN official. The FMLN accepted the offer and both sides agreed to meet in the town of La Palma (in the Department of Chalatenango) under benefit of a temporary ceasefire (Karl, 1985). ARENA, the conservative military factions, and many foreign policy officials in the Reagan administration opposed the talks but could not oppose them.

There was a huge constituency for peace in El Salvador, which explains why Duarte broke with precedent to meet with the FDR and the FMLN. Polls conducted by the Jesuit-run University of Central America in San Salvador revealed that a majority of Salvadorans wanted an end to the war (Martín-Baró and Orellana, 1984). Just more than half of those surveyed supported a dialogue with the opposition. FDR politicians, many of whom had left the governing junta because the military would not stop killing civilians, and FMLN members recognized the widespread clamor for peace. For decades, opposition politicians had organized and protested for the right to win in honest elections, which they believed they could win. Both had an additional incentive for ending the conflict: Brokering an end to the war promised an electoral dividend to whomever the voters believed was responsible for peace. It was a message that infuriated and intrigued ARENA, alarmed the military, and surprised the United States.

A political equilibrium in favor of the war's continuation was the paradoxical result of Duarte's initiatives. Neither the meetings held in La Palma nor later that year turned into substantive peace talks. The military, ARENA, and the United States demanded that the FDR-FMLN surrender its weapons and join what the governing coalition called the country's "democratic process." The FDR-FMLN insisted that both sides form a transitional government to guarantee the life and safety of its members and to plan a democratic opening. Regardless of Duarte's real intentions, there was little the PDC could do on its own, although it won a majority in the 1985 legislative elections. The military had no interest in peace. Years of civil war had allowed the military to enrich itself. It was the recipient of more than half a billion dollars of military aid from the United States. The war also provided the military with impunity; as long as it directed the war, it could not be held accountable for its extensive human rights violations. The economic interests behind ARENA – which continued to finance death-squads and plot with dissident officers to limit Duarte's power – also opposed talks because they did not want a settlement that involved relinquishing their substantial economic and political power.

The United States refused to tip the balance of power toward a genuine democratic opening. Duarte's election paradoxically reduced the Reagan administration's interest in promoting peace in El Salvador. That an alleged centrist was president of this war-ravaged Central American country convinced conservative Democrats that the Reagan administration's strategy was working. Duarte's visits to Capitol Hill helped Republicans win approval of Reagan's repeated requests for military and nonmilitary aid for El Salvador. Without congressional pressure, the Reagan administration reverted to a strategy emphasizing defeating communism (LeoGrande, 1998). Like the Salvadoran military, Reagan valued winning the war more than ending it.

The war dragged on, leading to an increase in inflation as the economy stagnated (Segovia, 2002). Although it claimed fewer lives, it remained brutal. Violent repression of regime opponents continued but declined in intensity. By 1983, massive repression had cleared the San Salvador streets of opposition protests (Brockett, 2005). The U.S.-sponsored overhaul of the armed forces changed the security forces' tactics because counter-insurgency doctrines required protecting – not slaughtering – civilians (Peceny and Stanley, 2010).

Guerrilla tactics also changed, largely because of the shift to fighting a prolonged war, one fought by fielding smaller contingents against the state. Ten FMLN urban commandoes kidnapped Duarte's daughter in September 1985. Leftist gunmen assassinated mayors working with the central government and killed several American marines. Another band of guerrillas, disguised as Salvadoran troops, attacked and killed four U.S. marines in the *Zona Rosa*, the chic commercial zone of the capital; when civilians reached for their pistols to fight back, the terrorists killed nine and wounded fifteen café customers (LeoGrande, 1998: 268–273). These acts, which one former guerrilla called "banditry" (Castellanos, 1991: 94), also reflected changes in the FMLN's rank and file. If the first generation of guerrillas were motivated by injustice, subsequent ones joined the struggle because repression made it difficult not to do so or because they had been recruited, and accepted an offer out of a sense of adventure or a desire to avenge crimes of the past, as a systematic study of eighty-two female guerrillas uncovers (Viterna, 2006). In her interviews with 231 FMLN combatants in eastern departments in 1991, Cynthia McClintock (1998: 282) finds that the struggle for political power (50 percent) and whim (20 percent) were the most common reasons they mentioned for continuing to fight.

In an attempt to break the logjam, the FMLN launched a final offensive in late 1989. Although the army held its ground, the FMLN fought its way into the capital, penetrating the wealthy neighborhoods of the north. In retaliation, the army entered the campus of the University of Central America and slaughtered six Jesuit priests, their housekeeper, and her daughter in the weeks before the Christmas break. The priests included Ignacio Martín-Baró (1994), the father of opinion polling in El Salvador, and Ignacio Ellacuría, the university's rector.

That neither side was close to winning gradually softened the preferences of some on the right and left. As in Nicaragua, a regime opening half a world away in the Soviet Union made the less ideological Bush administration more receptive to a peace accord. The newly elected president of El Salvador, Alfredo Cristiani of ARENA (who had won the 1989 presidential election with 53.8 percent of the vote), evinced interest in peace talks, but could not say so publicly because of widespread opposition within his party and the military. Instead, he authorized intermediaries to meet with a high-level FMLN delegation under the auspices of the Arias Peace Plan. Between April 1990 and January 1992, government and FMLN representatives met twenty times to bridge the chasm separating them on issues ranging from wealth and income distribution to the nature of transitional authority (Samayoa, 2002: 157).

Three trends created a balance of power favorable for peace talks. First, the rapprochement between the United States and the Soviet Union led the newly inaugurated Bush administration to talk with the armed left. No longer was it necessary that the guerrillas unilaterally disarm, a precondition that had worked to the military's advantage. Second, the oligarchy's interests had changed. The civil war, along with a partially implemented agrarian reform, had pushed many landowners out of the countryside. Many chose to shift their capital from export farming to commerce and especially finance (Wood, 2000). Although many in the elite were rabidly opposed to negotiating with the FMLN, they understood that business would improve with an end to the war. No doubt some on the right feared that the FMLN would morph into the sort of insurgents battling the Colombian state, ones that relied on drug trafficking, hostage taking, and terrorism to wage war on the state. Third, the right realized that it could organize a successful political party. ARENA's law-and-order approach to the war, its anti-communist rhetoric, and its free-market policies appealed to important segments of the electorate. Although ARENA lost the 1985 election to the centrist PDC, it won the elections four years later, a triumph helped by D'Aubuisson's decision to step aside from candidates less linked to death-squads like Cristiani.

Intensive bargaining under the auspices of the United Nations gradually convinced both sides to negotiate a transition to democracy. Although the military stalemate and the end of the cold war prompted most to become interested in settling their differences, little consensus existed on a host of issues. The FMLN's long-term demands that peace required addressing the socioeconomic inequities of El Salvador terrified the right. ARENA and the military's demand that the guerrillas demobilize before talks could begin had long stalled peace negotiations. At first, both sides agreed on procedures to guide their talks. They then shifted to identifying a timetable for considering the underlying disputes and the steps to implement agreements. In his detailed reconstruction of the peace negotiations, Salvador Samayoa (2002), an FMLN negotiator, credits the UN with playing a vital role. It not only facilitated the dialogue and proposed solutions to protect each side's core interests, but also became the guarantor of the peace process. The UN acted more like an impartial arbiter than a coercive, third-party enforcer of its decisions (Peceny and Stanley, 2001). Deploying hundreds of observers in the country to monitor compliance with the agreement, it resolved the FMLN's long-standing objection to the government's demand that it unilaterally disarm. After months of negotiations, the insurgents dropped their demand to become part of a transitional government because the Cristiani's government agreed to empower the UN Observer Mission for El Salvador (ONUSAL) to verify that the military stayed in its barracks and human rights were respected. It was a temporary encroachment on national sovereignty that met the FMLN's demands the government could accept, and one that set the agenda for subsequent peace settlements across the globe.

The FMLN and the government of El Salvador signed a peace agreement on January 16, 1992. If the Salvadoran people were the beneficiaries of the accord, the military was the biggest loser. Although the FMLN lost its 12,000-person army, they gained the legal right to organize a political party and field candidates in the 1994 elections. Although ARENA and the right were forced to respect the armed left's right to use democratic rights, it gained the FMLN's respect of private property and a market economy. The military was forced to halve its size and dismantle several police agencies and the rural National Guard. The agreement called for establishing a new, professional National Civilian Police outside of the Ministry of Defense and a new State Intelligence Office reporting to the president and the assembly (Call, 2002).

Regime Liberalization in Guatemala, Honduras, and Panama

Regime liberalization in Guatemala, Honduras, and Panama did not require peace negotiations with the left. By the mid-1980s, the military had routed the armed left in Guatemala, although guerrillas remained active in certain parts of the country and in international forums (Torres-Rivas, 1998). There were no guerrillas in Honduras and Panama. Analyzing these experiences demonstrates why civil war is the factor that best explains why transitions were different in Guatemala and Honduras from those in El Salvador and Nicaragua (as well as

Costa Rica and Panama) – and raises the question of why the military decides to extricate itself from the political arena.

Severe economic problems and a wish to avoid factional instability prompted military factions in Guatemala to reform their political system. First, an economy debilitated by capital flight, international isolation, and massive corruption led the military to reach agreements with CACIF (Coordinating Committee of Agricultural, Commercial, Industrial, and Financial Associations), businesses' peak association. Needing funds to pay for the internal war, CACIF repeatedly rejected tax and other economic reforms proposed by the generals, especially when standby agreements negotiated with the International Monetary Fund (IMF) required increasing tax revenues (McClearly, 1999: 26–66). After Ríos Montt was overthrown and replaced by his defense minister, General Óscar Humberto Mejía Victores in early August 1983, the new government conferred with CACIF. Conversations between the generals and CACIF evolved into the special protections for private property and limits on state authority the 1985 constitution contained – including libertarian principles empowering the Constitutional Court to rule that levying many taxes was a violation of property rights. Second, enough armed forces sectors wished to end the factionalism of the officer corps. Defections by junior officers had ignited the insurgency in the early 1960s and, just when the guerrillas were at their strongest, had weakened the state in the late 1970s. Although neither a revenue-poor state nor factionalism required the military's withdrawal from politics, regime liberalization could focus the military's attention on finishing off the guerrillas. These are the reasons that led General Héctor Alejandro Gramajo Morales (1997: 115), the country's defense minister between 1987 and 1990 (during President Vinicio Cerezo's civilian government), to declare that "keeping a military man in the presidency made the war against the communist insurgency more difficult to conduct." In interviews with Schirmer (1998), General Gramajo made much of the fact that the military had evacuated all civilian institutions without ceding its autonomy to conduct the counter-insurgency as they liked.

It was not until the 1990s that civilian politicians began to pursue peace negotiations with the URNG (Pásara, 2003). President Cerezo (1985–90) was the first civilian executive to contact the URNG in the mid-1980s. He did little more than reiterate the official position that the guerrillas must lay down their weapons, an offer the military's defeat of the guerrillas by 1983 made more than generous. That Cerezo was the target of at least two coup attempts – one in 1988 and another in 1989 – limited his ability to propose anything that might unite enough military factions to topple his government. President Jorge Serrano (1990–3) began conversations with the URNG as part of an effort to gain the political initiative in a strategic impasse one in which he had neither a legislative majority, nor independence from the military's extensive prerogatives. His overtures, unlike Cerezo's more limited appeals, dropped the requirement that the guerrillas unilaterally disarm. Serrano's government accepted that a peace settlement must address what the URNG called "the real causes of the war," or the inequities of Guatemalan society. Serrano's successor, Human

Rights Ombudsman Ramiro de León Carpio (1993–6), reinitiated the dialogue with the armed left and expanded it, at the behest of the Roman Catholic Church, to include representatives of all social sectors in what later became known as the "Assembly of Civil Society."

The armed left was ambivalent about peace negotiations. Hardliners wanted to regroup and plan for a long war. Many interpreted their defeat by 1983 as a temporary setback akin to the rout they experienced in the early 1970s, from which they recovered by the end of that decade. Moderates were united more by the goal of not rejecting discussions with the government than anything like a concerted plan of peace. Until the 1990s, the URNG displayed little of the unity of purpose their Salvadoran counterparts exhibited. Defeat – but not annihilation – had thrown the URNG into strategic disarray.

Negotiations gradually convinced the military, CACIF, the URNG, and presidential administrations to reach an agreement by the mid-1990s (Aguilera Peralta, 1998). Meetings sponsored by the UN, largely between presidential emissaries and URNG leaders and held in different cities of the world, starting in January 1994, permitted the key players in Guatemalan politics to become reacquainted with each other. Numerous meetings of the Assembly of Civil Society disseminated ample information about the agreements. With time, the government and the URNG found reasons to conclude their talks. No government could ignore the electoral benefits of bringing peace to the country or the billions of dollars in foreign aid that UN-sponsored agreement could bring for a perennially cash-strapped state (in exchange for reforms to increase taxation above 10 percent of GDP, the western hemisphere's lowest rate). For their part, enough guerrillas concluded that signing the peace agreement was better than fighting a war they had already lost. That the FDNG (New Guatemalan Democratic Front), a party aligned with the guerrillas, managed to draw 7.7 percent of the presidential ballot and win six of eighty congressional seats in the 1996 elections also buoyed the URNG's expectation that organizing electoral campaigns would be more efficacious than armed struggle.

The government and the URNG signed the accords in late December 1996 because they largely refrained from threatening any key player's interests. The ambitious set of agreements recognized the multicultural nature of Guatemalan society, called on the government to respect human rights, and, most important, included a formal cease-fire. Although agreements referred to the (highly) unequal distribution of land in the country, they did not commit the government to enact any legal or constitutional changes. CACIF went along because it got to keep its constitution – including a high constitutional court that declared income and other direct taxation unconstitutional – although it did not succeed in eliminating tax reform from the internationally supervised agreements. The military agreed to disband the Civilian Self-Defense Patrols (PACs) and reduce the armed forces to 31,000 in uniform (Stanley and Holiday, 2002: 448). It did not have to reorganize itself or its autonomy.

Perhaps their most far-reaching component, one that potentially threatened the military's interests, consisted of establishing a "Commission for Historical

Clarification" to investigate the human rights abuses of the past. Despite the decision not to "individualize" responsibility for war crimes, the agreement on human rights was far-reaching enough that Héctor Rosada Granados, the government representative negotiating with guerrilla representatives in Oslo, Norway in 1994, decided to consult with the military, as he terms it, to avoid being put on a death list for such an agreement. After presenting the text of the agreement to a meeting of the 152 military commanders, he waited outside while officers deliberated on the agreement to clarify the atrocities of the past thirty-four years. Only after officers endorsed the agreement did the government agree to sign it with the URNG (Kinzer, 2001a: 52).

The absence of left-wing insurgents also colored the transition from authoritarian rule in Honduras. After approximately two decades in power, key military factions began to liberalize the regime in 1979 as a way to overcome the factionalism wrecking havoc with institutional discipline (Posas, 1989). Executive instability was a chronic problem in Honduras; it was the Central American country that experienced the largest number of coups – thirteen – between 1900 and 1980 (see Table 1.3), which makes it the third most coup-prone country in Latin America, with only Bolivia and Paraguay being more unstable. That three incumbents were overthrown in the 1970s – one in 1972, a second in 1975, and the third in 1978 – led to forming clearer rules governing presidential succession. In 1975, the military created the Superior Council of the Armed Forces (CONSUFFAA), consisting of forty-five top-ranking officers, to reach agreement on key matters before disputes over policy, perks, and promotions split the armed forces. Henceforth, the CONSUFFAA would select the armed forces chief and set policy for the military (Ruhl, 1996: 37).

The military, encouraged by the Carter administration, began meeting with civilians by 1979, especially its allies in the Conservative Party, to safeguard the military's prerogatives and plan a return of civilian government. In April 1980, elections for a Constituent Assembly unexpectedly returned a majority for the Liberal Party, which won thirty-five of the convention's seventy-one seats. Talks between the military and the parties led the Liberal and National Party candidates to accept a military veto over cabinet appointments, the military's primacy in security affairs, and an agreement not to investigate charges of military corruption (Schulz and Schulz, 1994: 71–72). In November of the following year, the Liberals won the presidency with 53.9 percent of the vote and obtained forty-four of eighty-two seats in the assembly. In January 1982, the assembly produced a new constitution, which made the military responsible for maintaining public order. From a list of candidates submitted by the CONSUFFAA, the national Congress would select the Chief of the Armed Forces. General Policarpio Paz García remained chief of staff.

Panama's political system was the last one to liberalize, and, like Honduras, it did not witness a guerrilla movement. Although protesters took to the street's of the country's cities, it was the functional equivalent of an insurgent victory – the 1989 U.S. invasion – that ended the Noriega dictatorship in

1989. Opposition to Noriega and the façade presidency of Delvalle escalated in 1987 with the formation of the Civic Crusade, an umbrella organization of 200 civic and professional groups. It organized almost daily street protests, which the regime repressed, often bloodily. The Civic Crusade contested the 1989 elections, which exit polls showed that its candidate, Guillermo Endara, had won by 55.1 to 39.5 percent for Noriega's candidate, Carlos Alberto Duque (Scranton, 1991: 161). On May 9, the government released figures declaring that Duque had won the election with 71.2 percent of the vote, which its own electoral tribunal annulled a day later. Within a week, the government's bloody crackdown of opposition marches led the Organization of American States to adopt a resolution condemning the regime for its actions. By the end of August, the Noriega-controlled Council of State closed the National Assembly and made Francisco Rodríguez, a former attorney general, provisional president. It announced that it would hold new elections within six months (Ricord, 1991).

The 1989 U.S. invasion surprised the Panamanians and the world. Although the United States no doubt was forewarned about a failed attempt to topple Noriega by 200 Panamanian troops in October, no one expected U.S. forces to become actively involved in replacing Noriega. On December 20, the National Assembly had made Noriega the de jure head of state by adorning him with the title of Maximum Leader. Inexplicably, the assembly declared the republic to be in a state of war with the United States. Five days later, U.S. marines occupied key military installations in Panama, disarmed the Panamanian Defense Forces, and captured Noriega. The general ended up in the Vatican's diplomatic compound, where he remained until turning himself over to the United States. In the meantime, Endara, who had won the 1989 presidential election, was sworn in as president on a U.S. warship.

Why the United States overthrew Noriega is one of the puzzles from this period, one that did little to buoy the FSLN's confidence that the United States would accept their triumph in Nicaragua's elections. The general was an embarrassment to Washington, especially because his role in drug running, corruption, and supply and training of the Contras had become public by the mid-1980s. Noriega was indicted for drug trafficking in Miami in early February 1988. That Noriega had engaged in such activities long before he became persona non grata with the Reagan and later the Bush administration makes it doubtful that this was the decisive factor in U.S. behavior. Portraits of the general, and of United States-Panamanian relations, suggested that Noriega had mastered the art of political manipulation in his country as well as in Washington, DC, whose officials regarded him useful, even if venal. In a review of alternative explanations, Andrew Zimbalist and John Weeks (1991: 136–144) argue that it was Noriega's decision not to expand his involvement with the Contras that turned the U.S. administrations against him. John Dinges's (1990) detailed reconstruction of Panamanian politics does not disagree with this assessment, even if he argues that bureaucratic politics led to the invasion, one that became viable once barracks revolts and opposition protests proved incapable of unseating Noriega. Another journalist's account of these years concurs; it suggests that President Bush sent U.S. troops to Panama when other, less overt, ways of deposing Noriega failed. Bush, as a candidate, had promised to deal with Noriega, and the dictator's survival embarrassed the new Republican president (Buckley, 1991). Perhaps it was that the U.S. Southern Command – the Pentagon's center for Latin American operations – decided its installations were in danger and a U.S. invasion could swiftly put an end to an annoying general. The United States had always considered Panama within its sphere of responsibility, the Panama Canal Treaties notwithstanding.

What About Costa Rica?

Standard comparisons among Central American countries emphasize the violence and transition from authoritarian rule in every country – except Costa Rica. The country did remain peaceful during the 1980s, even as its economy slumped in the early 1980s and became a large recipient of U.S. foreign aid, allowing it to minimize the effects of economic austerity (Clark, 2001). Yet, it would be misleading to contrast the peace-loving ways of most Costa Ricans with the violence of its neighbors. The democratization of its political system also was a result of insurgents forcing incumbents to negotiate an end to war and instability. The inability of any single political force to dominate the political system fueled developing democratic institutions in Costa Rica, where the threat of violence helped construct the region's most stable democracy.

The government's defeat in the 1948 civil war – and Calderón Guardia's flight into exile – covered up the disunity in opposition ranks, a fact with profound consequences for the country's political development. Although the political (and more conservative) and the military (and more progressive) wings worked to defeat the PRN during the 1940s, their divergent aims became manifest during the civil war itself. The PUN wanted to elect Ulate to the presidency. Figueres and his followers wanted an economic transformation of the country. Paradoxically, the PRN's defeat did not end the strategic impasse between rival political parties; it continued as the political and military wings of the opposition split after the civil war.

Stalemate between the left and right forced rival groups to compromise. In control of the only armed force left in the country, Figueres and the insurgents formed a junta that forced the PUN to wait eighteen months (until December 1949) before Ulate became president. At the end of 1948, however, the junta lost the elections for a National Constituent Assembly. The PUN-dominated Constituent Assembly quickly moved to strip the junta of its legislative powers and restrict its ability to issue emergency decrees. Conservatives stymied progressive forces by rejecting the junta's draft constitution calling for a dramatic expansion of the state's role in public affairs. In the end, the pro-junta forces in the assembly got many of their proposals incorporated in the revised version of the 1871 constitution because the assembly approved them as part of a broader compromise that included ratifying the revolutionary junta's decision to ban a standing army (Gardner, 1971). The military absence not only liberated additional funds for human development (Bowman, 2002), but also eliminated its use to crush the opposition or to overthrow the government.

Death, Accountability, and Truth Commissions

Civil war claimed a staggering number of victims in Central America. No one knows for sure how many were killed, disappeared, or tortured. The numbers that exist are estimates, either because assassins concealed their grim handiwork or no one counted the victims. Some estimates are based on newspaper reports, which tend to underestimate the number of deaths in rural areas, especially in Guatemala, where large numbers of Maya live in inaccessible hamlets (Davenport and Ball, 2002). Others were courageous efforts undertaken by Roman Catholic-affiliated human rights organizations (Archdiocese of Guatemala, 1999), which also relied on newspaper reports, testimonies by survivors or the relatives of victims, or visits by human rights workers. At different times during the 1970s and 1980s, international human rights organizations such as Amnesty International or Human Rights Watch publicized these results or conducted their own investigations on the abuse of individual rights. Some of these individuals paid a high cost for recording events and stories; in addition to the six Jesuit priests (and their housekeeper and her daughter) killed in 1989 by the Salvadoran military (Whitfield, 1994), there was the murder of Bishop Juan Gerardi of Guatemala (Goldman, 2008), on the eve of the publication of the Archbishop's human rights report. By far the most influential accounts on the human cost of civil war have been the truth commissions in El Salvador and Guatemala, in part because they built on these earlier efforts to document the scale of the atrocities.

Research suggests that approximately 305,000 Central Americans perished in the civil wars fought near the end of the twentieth century. The most widely cited estimate of victims in El Salvador is 75,000 between 1979 and 1991, which a thorough examination of the evidence suggests is the most plausible figure of the numbers killed (Seligson and McElhinny, 1996). This comprehensive study estimates that 80,000 Nicaraguans died in the war against the Somoza dictatorship (1975–9) and the U.S.-financed Contra War (1980–90). It reports that the range of estimates for El Salvador is between 58,328 and 92,823 victims and between 30,000 and 86,345 deaths in Nicaragua. The most widely used estimate for Guatemala is approximately 200,000 between 1960 and 1996, one that the UN-sponsored Commission for Historical Clarification (CEH, 1999, 1: 93) endorsed as the likely number of victims. Dividing this figure by the share of documented individuals killed or disappeared between 1978 and 1985 (Ball, Kobrak, and Spirer, 1999: 119) leads to the finding that 75 percent of the victims – or 150,000 – died during the high tide of the carnage.

The military, often in association with right-wing hit squads, was responsible for most of these killings. The Truth Commission of El Salvador concluded that the government was responsible for 85 percent of the victims in the smallest of the Central American republics (CVES, 1993). Its counterpart in Guatemala arrived at a higher estimate, one that made the military and its police force responsible for 93 percent of the deaths in this country. The truth commissions reached these figures after documenting 22,000 deaths and disappearances in El Salvador and 37,255 in Guatemala. In Nicaragua, Somoza's National Guard was responsible for most of the 30,000 who died between 1975 and 1979. There is little consensus about who was responsible for most of the 50,000 war-related deaths during the 1980s.

Justice for the victims of human rights abuses has been limited. Only in Nicaragua did the Sandinistas manage to try and jail torturers. In the aftermath of Somoza's fall, the FSLN jailed approximately 1,200 members of the Guard, which they released in early 1989 as part of the Arias peace plan. On the eve of the 1990 elections, the Sandinistas pardoned all former Guardsmen and members of the Contras in jail for human rights abuses (Vilas, 1990b: 342). Neither the FSLN, the Contras (or their U.S. backers), nor post-Sandinista governments established a truth commission to document human rights violations, much less apportion responsibility for killings, disappearances, and torture.

Although the governments and guerrillas in El Salvador and Guatemala agreed to let the UN establish truth commissions as part of comprehensive peace accords (each of which was chaired by a prominent member of the international community), neither empowered the commissions to work with the courts to punish military officers. Honduras saw its Commission for the Protection of Human Rights (CNDH, 1994) issue a report listing 179 cases of disappearances between 1980 and 1992, most of which it attributed to the country's security forces or the U.S.-sponsored Contras based on its territory (Kaye, 1997). No report has led to more than a handful of legal prosecutions, in large part because truth commissions were accompanied by amnesty laws. The National Assembly in El Salvador enacted an amnesty law within five days of its presentation of the truth commission's report on March 15, 1993. Although the original agreement signed between the Guatemalan government and the URNG in Oslo, Norway in 1994 contained no such provision, both sides later agreed to a partial amnesty in December 1996 of war-related crimes, including extrajudicial killings, but excluding genocide, torture, and forced disappearances. Neither commission was empowered to identify individuals responsible for the gruesome acts of violence described in these reports. Both commissions were products of complex negotiations involving armed combatants, those with little interest in a comprehensive reckoning of the past and with the ability to scuttle tentative moves from authoritarian rule (Collins, 2010).

Debate has raged about who, other than the military, shares responsibility for the atrocities in Guatemala. David Stoll (1993) contends that the armed left bears some culpability for these crimes because the guerrillas overreached. They did little to prepare peasants to defend themselves and abandoned them once the army began its razed earth campaign. Suzanne Jonas (1991: 139–142; 2000), based on interviews with former guerrillas and an analysis of their documents, suggests that the guerrillas overestimated their military abilities, failing to coordinate their actions and limit their territorial scope. Piero Gleijeses (2006) points out that the United States has largely failed to accept its responsibility for these killings – and for U.S. policy toward this country since the CIA's help in overthrowing President Arbenz in 1954. The Guatemalan army's rejection of official U.S. military support in 1977 does not relieve the United States of organizing a truth commission on its role in Guatemalan politics, according to Gleijeses, especially since the CIA continued funneling money to the country's notorious security forces through the Reagan, Bush, and the first Clinton administration. He implies that U.S. President Bill Clinton's 1999 public apology in Guatemala for "support for military forces or intelligence units which engage in violent and widespread repression of the kind described in the [UN-sponsored Truth Commission] report" is insufficient in light of the magnitude of the slaughter (cited in Cullather, 2006: 175).

The scale of the killings in Guatemala suggests that the Maya were targets of genocide. The CEH makes the security forces responsible for "acts of genocide" without accusing them of genocide because of the thorny question of whether the army was targeting the Maya or guerrilla supporters, who the army assumed were disproportionately rural Maya, for destruction. The United Nations defines genocide as killings or bodily or mental harm "committed with intent to destroy, in whole or in part, a national, ethnical, racial, or religious group." It is this definition that leads Victoria Sanford (2003) to argue that the military is guilty of genocide because, as the CEH documented, 83 percent of the victims and all of the 626 villages destroyed were Mayan. Two of the most gruesome slaughter of humans for political reasons in modern Latin America, in number and in purpose, occurred in Guatemala and in El Salvador – the murder of civilians in the 1980s and the killing of Indians in 1932 (La Matanza).

Conclusion

The 1980s began violently in Central America. Three of its political systems – El Salvador, Guatemala, and Nicaragua – were in the throes of civil wars that political exclusion, more than poverty or inequality, had caused. The isthmus also became the site of one of the cold war's last conflicts, one that led the Reagan administration to battle the Sandinista government in Nicaragua, support a military-dominated government's struggle against left-wing guerrillas in El Salvador, and applaud the military's defeat of a Marxist insurgency in Guatemala.

At the time, no one predicted that civil war would give way to democracy. The armed conflict, with its large number of massacres, appeared to be the negation of politics. The war appeared to be – and was, in part – the culmination of the incapacity to develop procedures for regulating access to state power and for ameliorating long-standing conflicts of interest. Yet, the wars were long and bloody preludes to internationally supervised peace settlements. Why?

It was not economic development that led to regime change in Central America. Every country in Central America was short of the GDP per capita associated with transitions to democracy. The fall in economic growth experienced throughout the region further weakened the basis for democracy. Although structural change of the economy – the shift from fixed to mobile investments – helped the cause of democracy, it was not responsible for the transition from autocracy.

It was civil war that changed Central America. It was the violent attack on privileges that forced elites to abandon their landed estates, which lessened the preference for dictatorship among the upper classes on the isthmus. It was the behavior of peasant activists, urban protesters, and insurgents that forced the opening of closed political systems. For the reasons I discuss in the first two chapters of this book, reactionary despotism evolved into a resilient, if unstable, autocracy, which restricted possibilities for peaceful change, especially if the United States preferred backing the old order to tipping the balance in favor of the forces of change. In retrospect, we overlooked the fact that civil war was (and is) the continuation of political struggle, to paraphrase Clausewitz, by other, violent means. Only the transformation of such struggles could liquidate the anachronistic dictatorships of the past.

Change in the international system contributed to democratization in Central America. While a central characteristic of the global system – the cold war between the United States and the USSR – had helped prevent regime change, events half a world away, in the Soviet Union, made domestic-level changes possible in Central America and in the developing world. As Mikhail Gorbachev began to reform an economically bankrupt USSR, United States and Soviet leaders reassessed the cost of supporting revolutionary or counterrevolutionary adventures in the Third World. A change in U.S. administrations – from Reagan to Bush – led to a change in priorities, which included opening negotiations with the Sandinistas in Nicaragua and pressing the Salvadoran military to sign an accord with the FMLN. Outcomes are consistent with the claim that international linkages undermined what Steven Levitsky and Lucan Way (2010) refer to as a "competitive authoritarian" system in Nicaragua.

War and global change transformed the balance of power in Central America and political outcomes on the isthmus. Where governments and insurgents were unable to defeat each other, as in El Salvador, bargaining over the nature of the transition and democratic institutions became possible. Military standoffs also caused the democratization of the Costa Rican political system, which decades of confrontation between incumbents and opposition movements gradually turned into a more democratic system. Where revolutionaries won power outright, as in Nicaragua, an electoral or competitive autocracy replaced the dictator, an outcome that U.S. foreign policy may have encouraged, even if it did not cause. The unwillingness to share power, along with the Reagan administration's active encouragement of counter-revolutionary forces, sent Nicaragua into another destructive civil war. A transition to democracy occurred with the hotly contested 1990 elections, ones that the Sandinistas lost to an opposition coalition. Where insurgents lost, as in Guatemala, autocrats largely dictated the terms of transition. Why the Guatemalan generals relinquished the presidency is a puzzle, one that begins to resolve when we recognize that they gave up little more than control of the executive and legislative branches of government. Abandoning formal control of government also was an effort to end the cycle of coups and countercoups that had undermined the unity of the armed forces and thus its ability to wage an effective counterinsurgency.

Violence also was the trigger for regime change in Panama and even in Honduras. In Panama, a U.S.-led invasion overthrew a dictator – Manuel Antonio Noriega – who the opposition had been fighting for years. In the absence of the autocrat, civilians negotiated a transition to democracy. The sporadic appearance of guerrillas, along with executive instability, encouraged generals in Honduras to negotiate a return to formal democratic rule with civilian politicians. As in Guatemala, retreating generals in Honduras retained important prerogatives that limited the extent of civilian supremacy.

This chapter confirms a pattern that analysts both familiar and unfamiliar with Central America have noted. Democratization results from a series of interactions between incumbents and opposition movements in which each side accepts that unilateral control of the state is not possible (Rustow, 1970). The inability to quash an opponent leads to the negotiation of the institutions of democracy, a process that rewards key interests with political representation and allows them to protect their core economic interests (Acemoglu and Robinson, 2006). What the transitions in Central America during the 1980s and 1990s also reveals is that the international community (Doyle and Sambanis, 2006) can facilitate the negotiations that end civil wars and help enforce the terms of the peace necessary for transition to a more open political system.

4

Economic Stability, Lackluster Growth, and Social Change

Introduction

Until the late 1970s, the Central American economies were growing, although only the growth rates of Costa Rica and Panama surpassed the average annual GDP per capita of the world. In hindsight, this record, for all its limitations, was a golden age on the isthmus as it was for much of the world. Since 1990, most Central American countries have fallen farther behind, with Nicaragua failing to recover the ground it lost since the late 1970s. The inability of dictators to reform imposed painful costs on most Central Americans.

Ill-timed external shocks compounded the effects of war. As states battled insurgents, the sudden drop in the terms of trade in 1979, along with the rise in interest rates on foreign loans, led to a contraction of economic activity. Both external shocks were central components of a generalized economic crisis highlighting the weaknesses of a growth model that relied on exporting agricultural commodities, ones whose prices were volatile and whose benefits concentrated among landowners, as I showed in Chapter 1.

Although many of them were waging war, Central American policy makers had little choice but to stabilize their economies. They devalued currencies, renegotiated foreign debts, and balanced state budgets, which reduced incomes and worsened recessions. Like their South America counterparts, Central American states opted to shrink their role in the economy as they stabilized (Kingstone, 2011). By the end of the decade, policy makers in both countries – even Costa Rica, the country with the region's largest state and most successful economy – had returned to the libertarian doctrines of the past, ones associated with decidedly mixed results for economic growth and development.

The principal goal of this chapter is to explain why, with one or two partial exceptions, growth rates have been meager since 1990. Although Costa Rica and Panama have recovered their pre-crisis strength, no other country has been able to build on the growth record of the three decades before the 1980s. In Honduras and Nicaragua, in fact, growth rates have been paltry or nonexistent. After identifying the economic and political sources of unimpressive

TABLE 4.1. *Average Annual GDP Per Capita Growth Rates, in Central America and Select World Regions*

Country	Average Annual Growth Rates			Years for GDP Per Capita to Double Based on Growth Rates during	
	1950–1975	1980–1990	1990–2008	1950–1975	1990–2008
Costa Rica	2.9%	−0.3%	2.9%	23.9	24.2
El Salvador	2.0%	−1.8%	1.8%	35.8	38.4
Guatemala	1.9%	−1.8%	1.7%	37.0	40.6
Honduras	1.1%	−1.2%	1.1%	62.1	65.5
Nicaragua	3.0%	−3.5%	0.9%	23.1	75.3
Panama	2.9%	0.2%	2.3%	24.3	30.5
Averages[a]					
World	2.7%	1.2%	2.1%	26.1	33.2
12 Western European	3.7%	1.8%	1.5%	18.8	46.4
8 Big Latin American	2.5%	−0.3%	1.7%	28.0	41.0
15 Small Latin American	2.2%	−0.3%	1.3%	31.7	51.9
57 African States	1.8%	−0.4%	1.1%	38.2	62.1

[a]Weighted averages
Source: Maddison (2010).

growth rates, this chapter discusses changes and continuities in the region's production profile, ones that show much of the region continues to depend on exporting agricultural products and cheap labor.

Economic Growth Over the Long Run

The region's growth rates since 1990, the decade since the calamitous eighties, have been mixed. The average annual rate of GDP per capita growth in Honduras and Nicaragua has hovered around 1 percent. It has been less than 2 percent in El Salvador and Guatemala, which places them below the global average. Only Costa Rica and Panama have surpassed the rates among the developed world (the twelve core economies of Western Europe) and the world average. Table 4.1 contains these figures. Most economies of the isthmus have fallen behind since 1980, with two (Honduras and Nicaragua) underperforming, two (El Salvador and Guatemala) producing below average growth rates, and two (Costa Rica and Panama) slightly exceeding mean per capita growth rates.

It was the 1980s that accelerated the divergence among Central American countries, as the data in Table 4.1 show. In all countries but Costa Rica and Panama, average annual growth rates fell by more than four to six times the big eight or fifteen smallest economies of Latin America, in which they dwindled by less than 3 percent in the 1980s. In Nicaragua and Guatemala, the decline was substantially larger. In Nicaragua, civil war and economic misman-agement shrank per capita income by almost 40 percent during the 1980s. In El

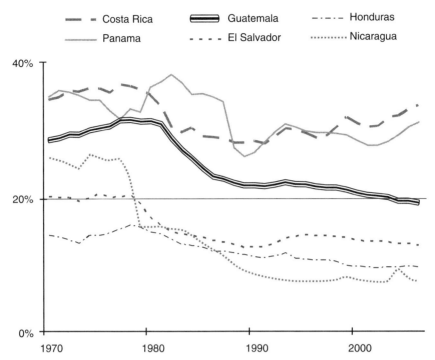

FIGURE 4.1. Trends in GDP per capita, 1970–2008 (as a share of Western European average).
Source: Maddison (2010).

Salvador and Guatemala, GDP per capita decreased by a fifth or a total of 20 percent. Only in Costa Rica and Panama did the average income deteriorate at the broader regional average.

Another way to interpret these results is by comparing Central America's GDP per capita rates with those of the twelve most important economies of Europe. The percentages in Figure 4.1 show that only Costa Rica and Panama have held their own with respect to the developed world. Their GDP per capita rates have remained at a third of the Western European rate. All other economies of the region have fallen, in relative terms, since 1980 or 1990, although the decline rate has shrunk since 1990. Most of the isthmus has a GDP per capita rate that, by the late 2000s, is less than 20 percent of the Western European average.

The cost of low growth rates is not low. At the current (since 1990) growth rates, it will take most of these economies more than forty years to double their GDP per capita. Although it will take El Salvador and Guatemala less than forty years to double their per person income, it will take Honduras and Nicaragua more than sixty-six and seventy-five years, respectively, to achieve the same objective. Both Costa Rica and Panama can double per capita GDP in twenty-four and thirty years at the post-1990 rate. The number of years to double average GDP per capita would have been lower if autocrats would have loosened their grip on power. Amazingly, Nicaragua would only have needed twenty-three – not seventy-five – years to double its per capita income if it had continued to grow at its mean annual growth rate between 1950 and 1975. With the exception of Honduras, it would have taken none of the other economies more than thirty-seven years to double their average incomes.

External Shocks and Macroeconomic Policy

The debate about why economic growth has been mediocre in Central America is inextricably linked with the market-friendly or neoliberal policy reforms of the 1980s. In most of Latin America, governments were forced to reform their economies once, beginning with Mexico in mid-1982, so many of them halted payment on foreign debts burgeoning with the global rise in interest rates. This led to a lost decade of growth throughout the region, not just in Central America. It also led to adopting economic policies that championed developing new exports from the isthmus. Understanding why economic growth has been limited since the 1980s reveals that macroeconomic stability, whose achievement was the aim of neoliberal reforms, has been insufficient to spark high and sustainable growth rates.

Just as escalating conflict was dampening economic activity in the late 1970s, the economies of the isthmus saw their balance of payments turn negative. The initial source of the excess outflows of monies was an exogenous shock: The sharp oil price increase in 1979 raised the cost of imports. The second source was ballooning interest rates of loans denominated in U.S. dollars, and thus payments on the foreign debt, once international capital became scarce. Third, the resulting slowdown in the international economy led to a decrease in demand for the region's exports. The rapid fall in the price of coffee was especially unsettling because it had crested just a few years earlier. To make matters worse, inflows of capital, which had historically covered the region's chronic deficit in the current account (or exports minus imports), reversed themselves. Political crisis led to capital flight as many of the region's wealthy sent their money abroad. Estimates suggest that between 2 to 6.5 billion U.S. dollars were sent abroad between 1980 and 1987 (Cáceres, 1990, cited in Pelupessy and Weeks, 1993: 8). All countries therefore fell victim to the effects of the war, capital flight, and the sudden drop in the terms of trade (Bulmer-Thomas, 1987: 237–244; López, 1986).

Central American policy makers were forced to stabilize their economies, that is, to reverse the slide into national insolvency, a situation in which they would no longer be able to pay for their imports. Economic authorities enacted policies to reduce the incomes of producers and consumers, actions that lowered demand for goods and services (especially imported ones), pushing their economies into recession. Negotiations with the Inter-American Development Bank (IADB), the International Monetary Fund (IMF), and the World Bank led to loans at preferential rates for Central America in exchange for reforms to eliminate balance-of-payments crises and reignite economic growth.

The first reform was to devalue national currencies. The first countries to devalue were Nicaragua in 1979, right before Somoza's fall, and Costa Rica in late 1980. Most policy makers began by establishing multiple exchange rate systems (making dollars cheaper for some imports than for others) for their currencies before fixing their price at a unified, lower rate during the 1980s. The small size of Central American economies meant that monetary authorities never opted to float a currency; only large economies have enough buyers of their currencies to prevent a big investor or interest from profiting by speculating against it. For most countries of the region, readjusting their currency value was the end of a decades-long adherence to fixed exchange rates with the U.S. dollar (García-López, Larrain B., and Tavares, 2001). Honduras, which changed its fixed rate in 1990, had maintained it since 1918 (Esquivel and Larrain B., 2001: 343). By making it more expensive to buy U.S. dollars or other hard currencies, devaluation raises the price of imports as it lowers the price of exports. By making its exports cheaper in global markets, devaluation increases demand for the region's products, helping reignite economic growth.

The second reform involved half of the countries – Costa Rica, Nicaragua, and Panama – renegotiating the terms of their (public and private) external debts because the interest rate on their bonds (set in U.S. dollars) mushroomed. Although every country saw its debt burden become larger, it soared in the three countries that had borrowed the most. By 1983, one year after the Mexican government stopped making interest payment on its debts, Costa Rica and Panama's debt took on the value of 133 and 100 percent of their GDP, respectively. Nicaragua, destroyed by the struggle to oust Somoza, saw its foreign debt increase to 147 percent of GDP by 1983, a figure that continued to grow until the early 1990s, when it reached more that 600 percent of annual GDP (Edwards, 1995: 2). The growth in Nicaragua's external debt was the product of contracting new loans and the implosion of its economy (O'Campo, 1991).

Third, economic stabilization required control of fiscal deficits to remove incentives for governments to contract more debt and/or to print money. By 1980, the average imbalance among central states was in excess of 5 percent of GDP, with Guatemala having the lowest average annual deficit spending rate between 1970 and 1996. Nicaragua easily had the largest deficits throughout the 1980s. By 1984, it was approximately 25 percent of GDP. Since 1995, most fiscal adjustment came through cutting expenditures (Offerdal, 2004). Figure 4.2 contains these figures.

Revamping the economy to block the state from indebting itself was the core objective of structural adjustment, that is, part of a broader effort to minimize the state role in the economy. The architects of neoliberal reform argued that a small state would create an environment in which the private sector could flourish and the economy could grow. Privatization of state enterprises and governmental activities would promote efficiency and thwart corruption, two afflictions affecting many state enterprises in the region (Chong and López de Silanes, 2005). It would also eliminate the ability of state officials to raid the public purse, pad the public payroll with their supporters, and take actions

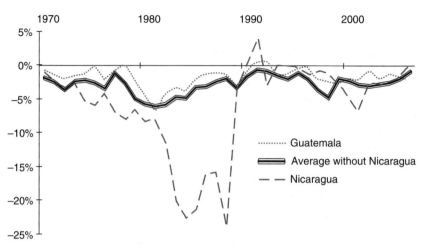

FIGURE 4.2. Fiscal deficits in Central America, 1970–2006.
Note: The lowest and highest average deficits are displayed.
Source: IMF (2010).

that would augment fiscal deficits. Liberalizing finance would spur foreign investment. Reducing tariffs on imports would force domestic firms to become more competitive. These were the key elements of what became known as the "Washington Consensus," named in honor of the advice of the multilateral institutions in Washington, DC and the U.S. government (Williamson, 1990).

Policy advice about empowering the private sector represented an unmistakable return to the (very) recent past for Central Americans. Unlike larger countries in the Latin American region, most Central American states did not develop industrial policies, even if they erected trade barriers during the 1960s and 1970s with the Central American Common Market (CACM). All relied on privately owned agriculture to spearhead development. Economic liberalism was the status quo ideology and policy in a region dominated by small, agro-export economies.

Only in Costa Rica, and briefly in El Salvador and Nicaragua, did states seek to tame capitalism. Since 1949, when a revolutionary junta had nationalized the major banks, governments in Costa Rica had expanded the state role in the economy (González Vega and Céspedes, 1993; Rovira Mas, 1982). Public utilities were in state hands throughout the region, but only the Costa Rican Institute for Electricity (ICE) sought to provide electricity and telecommunications throughout the national territory to spur development. By the 1970s, the administration of President Daniel Oduber (1970–4) created the Costa Rican Corporation of Development (CODESA), whose board consisted of the president and his council of ministers, that invested in food production, fertilizers, and other activities. After the 1979 coup, the military junta in El Salvador nationalized banks and implemented an agrarian reform that struck at the power of the wealthy agro-exporters. These governments established a marketing board for coffee and cotton (two key exports), and, in the context of a full-fledged civil war, regulated the prices of many goods (Pelupessy, 1997). In Nicaragua, the Sandinistas rapidly expanded the role of the state in the economy, a task facilitated by nationalizing Somoza's vast properties and business holdings. They also nationalized the financial system, foreign trade, large-scale gold mining, forestry, and fishing. In the shift from patrimonial to public ownership of property, the Nicaraguan state ended up controlling 20 percent of land and accounting for 40 percent of GDP (O'Campo, 1991: 336).

Activist states, as limited as they were, did not escape neoliberal reform. In Costa Rica, presidents of both the center-left Party of National Liberation (PLN), the party that had spearheaded social democratic reforms in earlier decades, and the United Social Christian Party (PUSC) of the center-right assembled legislative coalitions to enact market-based reforms. During the 1980s, they dismantled CODESA; closed the Anglo-Costa Rican Bank, one of the state's banks; and eliminated the public banking sector's monopoly on private bank accounts (Clark, 2001; Wilson, 1994, 1998). Before CODESA was shut down, it had consumed 18 percent of internal credit (or 50 percent of the credit available to the public sector) and had generated enormous public debt (Meléndez and Ramírez, 1993). In 2008, the ICE lost its monopoly on telecommunications in a first ever referendum that saw a bare majority of Costa Ricans vote in favor of ratifying the Central American Free Trade Agreement (CAFTA; Vargas Cullell, 2008). Opposition to many neoliberal policies thwarted efforts either to privatize pensions or the ICE, although both underwent reform. Formal sector workers started private retirement accounts as they kept contributing to the pay-as-you-go system in the mid-1990s (Martínez Franzoni, 2008b). These reforms did shrink the size of the state during the 1980s and 1990s, which, however, never fell below 30 percent of GDP, as measured by total public sector spending; by the late 1990s, it returned to the trend of approximately 38 percent of GDP (Straface and Vargas Cullell, 2008: 98).

In El Salvador, the private sector government led by ARENA President Alfredo Cristiani (1989–94) reversed many reforms of the previous decade. It liberalized interest rates, freed the prices of many regulated goods, abolished the state marketing board for coffee and sugar exports, re-privatized the banking industry, and established the autonomy of the Central Bank. ARENA President Armando Calderón Sol (1995–9) privatized the state communications and electric monopolies, established a new calendar for reducing tariffs, and increased VAT from 10 to 13 percent (Segovia, 2002: 36–45). It became the only country on the isthmus to privatize its social security (e.g., old-age pension) system (Madrid, 2003). At the beginning of the administration of President Francisco J. Flores (1999–2004) ARENA fixed the national currency to the U.S. dollar, a measure wanted by bankers but not by exporters or consumers (Towers and Borzutsky, 2004). For slightly more than a decade after signing the peace accord with the FMLN, the ARENA won three presidential elections, which permitted it to assemble legislative majorities, allowing a return to many free-market policies agro-exporters had championed.

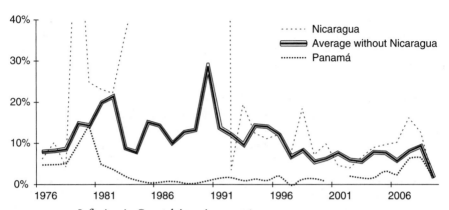

FIGURE 4.3. Inflation in Central America, 1976–2009.
Note: Lowest and highest average inflation rates are displayed.
Source: CEPAL (2009).

In Nicaragua, the Sandinistas began to readjust the economy and reduce the size of the state. Between 1985, soon after winning the elections of the previous year, and 1990, when they were defeated at the polls, the Frente implemented three austerity packages (Close, 1999: 123–125) to rein in an inflation that reached 33,000 percent by 1988. They made credit more available to the private sector to reactivate the moribund agro-export economy, one that, in 1989, exported slightly more than half of what it had a decade earlier (O'Campo, 1991: 339–340). A return to a minimal state occurred during the first post-revolutionary government headed by Violeta Barrios de Chamorro (1990–6), when the state payroll was cut by a quarter (or 30,000 jobs). Economic austerity claimed a larger share of reductions because the Sandinistas had eliminated 20,000 public sector jobs in the two years before they left office (Stahler-Sholk, 1997: 88). By the time Barrios de Chamorro left office, inflation had been tamed, after the second of two stabilization programs brought down the inflation rate to approximately 10 percent. The president and her team liquidated 351 state corporations. By the end of her mandate, the state only owned the National Institute of Electricity (INE), the Telephone Corporation (TELCOR), and National Institute of Water and Aqueducts (INAA).

Macroeconomic stability was achieved by the mid-1990s. First, data in Figure 4.3 shows that inflation fell everywhere in the 1990s. The average inflation rate in Central America went from 15 in the 1980s to 8.4 percent between 1995 and 2009. It became virtually nonexistent in Panama by the mid-1980s. Outside of Nicaragua, only Costa Rica's inflation rose above 30 percent, when it hit 82 percent in 1982, right before the economy entered a severe recession. Nicaragua's bout with hyperinflation (not shown) galloped between 1985, when it was 334 percent, and 1990, when it went to 13,490 percent. It fell dramatically in 1991, when the final attempt at stabilization succeeded in bringing down inflation. Since 1993, it has been less than 10 percent. Second, the average fiscal deficit in Central America during the 1990s was almost half of what it had been during the previous decade (see Figure 4.2).

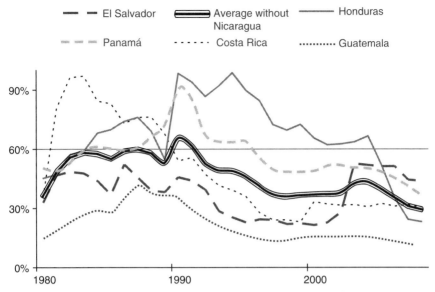

FIGURE 4.4. External public debt, 1980–2008 (as a percentage of annual GDP). *Source*: CEPAL (2009).

Finally, the external public debt also fell. The average for the region (not including Nicaragua) went from 57 to 47 percent of GDP between the 1980s and 1990s, respectively. It fell even further in the first decade of the new millennium, when it reached 37 percent. Figure 4.4 displays these trends. Nicaragua's debt (not shown) reached a high of 720 percent in 1988 before dropping to 186 percent in 1996. It fell below 100 percent of GDP only in 2006.

Neoliberalism and Growth Rates: A Balance Sheet

Sustained growth remains elusive. Only two countries, Costa Rica and Panama, have grown consistently since 1990 (see Figure 4.1). Why? Neoliberals argue that the reforms did not go far enough. Proposals shifted to recommending that governments make labor markets more flexible (e.g., reduce labor rights), establish independent central banks (focused on inflation targeting), fight corruption, adhere to international standards of financial conduct, and reform corporate governance. Many of these reforms aimed to eliminate the crony capitalism that had accompanied agro-export development whereby key business interests had colonized state agencies for their benefit. Some "second-generation" reforms, to use the term coined by Moisés Naím (1994), a former Venezuelan finance minister, included creating social safety nets and anti-poverty efforts, progressive ideas similar to the social security and health care programs often reformed or privatized during the 1980s and 1990s. The new emphasis on fighting poverty was to redirect resources from the urban constituencies that typically received the lion's share of social welfare benefits to the poorest sectors of the population (Lindert, Skoufias, and Shapiro, 2006).

Central American states concentrated on enacting the first-generation reforms associated with economic stabilization. By 1999, Guatemala and Nicaragua each scored above the Latin American average on the Structural Reform Index developed by Eduardo Lora (2001) of the Inter-American Development Bank. Costa Rica and El Salvador achieved rankings placing them slightly below this mean. Honduras, along with Mexico, Uruguay, and Venezuela, was one of the least reformed economies by the end of the 1990s. First, policy makers in Central America had liberalized their trade regimes. By 1999, the average tariff in Central America was 7.1 percent, less than the Latin American average of 12.6 percent. Second, they curtailed regulations controlling interest rates, even if they did not always strengthen the rights of borrowers. Third, these states reduced marginal tax rates on individuals and corporations while increasing value added taxes (VAT), the standard tax on consumption. Every country but Nicaragua scores above the Latin American mean on these measures of financial liberalization. Fourth, several states, especially in El Salvador, Guatemala, and Nicaragua, privatized state corporations. Outside of Costa Rica, which only privatized the small corporations of CODESA, selling state assets in Central America meant privatizing industries nationalized or established in the early 1980s. Finally, most states on the isthmus made labor laws more flexible, that is, made it easier for firms to offer short-term work contracts or dismiss laborers, both on the assumption that firms would hire more workers if the costs of reducing the work force declined.

The available evidence suggests that structural reform has had a limited impact on growth rates. An econometric study by Eduardo Lora and Felipe Barrera (1997) of the IADB concludes that the more profound reformers in the region did grow faster, but the effects of these reforms were small. An earlier study by Eduardo Fernández-Arias and Peter Montiel (1997) estimates that macro reforms, ones aiming to achieve economic stability, added 1.3 to average annual growth rates. The structural reforms contributed half a percent to growth. Another study that uses Lora's index produces similar conclusions (Escaith and Morley, 2001), which find that fast reformers grew faster, but the overall effects of reforms often cancelled each other out. The studies uncover evidence that tax and capital account liberalization, which Lora's index does not measure, have positive and long-term effects on growth. A more comprehensive study finds that stabilization policies help growth (Loayza, Fajnzylber, and Calderón, 2005). This study, like many others about the impact of reforms, assesses variables – such as price stability, a positive balance-of-payments ratio, or the absence of systematic banking crises – that are the alleged outcome of structural reforms, not the trickier question of whether the Washington consensus-inspired reforms caused these outcomes.

It was economic stabilization – solving balance-of-payments deficits and cutting inflation – more than caging the state that restored growth. Moreover, economies resumed growing once the terms of trade for their exports became more favorable and, most important, their civil wars ended. Growth had less to do with the decisions taken or not taken by policy makers, although blunders worsened the slump in Costa Rica in the early 1980s (Lizano, 1999) and contributed to the macroeconomic disasters in Nicaragua during the Sandinistas' audacious efforts to remake their economy. It was the harsh facts of being small, open economies that got the region into macroeconomic trouble as the 1970s ended. It was the consequences of dictatorship that snowballed into civil wars of enormous devastation that wrecked the possibility of returning to previous growth rates, much less to improving rates of growth.

Labor, Capital, and Productivity

Economic growth has been paltry in Central America because investment and productivity have been small. Growth accounting, as economists call the statistical exercises that quantitatively measure the role of labor, capital, and productivity in the growth of GDP, reveals that the single-biggest contributor to GDP per capita rates in the region is increased labor supply (Agosín and Machado, 2006; Esquivel, 2001; Loayza, Fajnzylber, and Calderón, 2005; Ros, 2006). That more individuals have entered the labor force accounts for approximately one-half of growth since the end of the civil wars of the 1980s. Physical capital, as measured by the share of private and public investment as a share of GDP, contributed approximately a third to GDP growth between 1991 and 1999 in a series of models with data from Costa Rica, El Salvador, Guatemala, Honduras, Nicaragua, Panama, and the Dominican Republic. The share of growth not explained by increases in labor or capital stems from what economists call total factor productivity, that is, more efficient ways of combining workers with machinery (Agosín and Machado, 2006: 109–114).

That not more than a quarter of GDP growth stems from productivity improvements explains why economic growth, outside of Costa Rica (Rodríguez-Clare, Sáenz, and Trejos, 2004) and Panama, has been trivial. Its role has been the largest in these countries and in El Salvador, which experienced a short postwar boom in the 1990s (Segovia, 2002). Agosín and Machado (2006: 114) estimate that greater investments in physical and human capital would have boosted GDP by almost a quarter. If gross investment in capital would have been at least 25 percent, the average growth rate of Central America would have been nearly 5 percent instead of the actual rate of 4.1 percent. If the number of years of schooling would have been twice as large, the average annual GDP growth rate would have been half a percent higher. At this rate, it would have taken 13.2 years for the Central American GDP to become twice as large instead of 17.7 years. (All figures are based on calculating averages by excluding the Dominican Republic, which augments them because its average annual growth rate was 5.8 percent during the 1990s.)

The implications of growth accounting research are far reaching. First, these statistical exercises remind us that cheap labor and the absence of long-term capital investments – key components of the agro-export development model – remain central characteristics of the region's economic development. This was a finding of an important study on the region's economy, authored by Reynolds

(1978), who used data from the 1960s and 1970s to demonstrate that growth was largely a function in the increase in low-wage labor, noting, too, that owners of capital obtained most gains from this development model. Second, these findings help explain why key parts of Central America – El Salvador, Guatemala, Honduras, and Nicaragua – are caught in a growth trap in which the causes of low-growth solidify and produce a low-growth equilibrium. Jaime Ros (2005) suggests that some of these countries have even suffered growth collapses. Like a proverbial black hole, economies such as Nicaragua's have imploded under the weight of civil war and mismanagement. Civil war so set back the economies of El Salvador and Guatemala that growth rates duplicating global averages cannot generate the investments necessary to accelerate development.

Low Return Rates and Unimpressive Growth Rates

Central America has several puzzling cases of development, ones that shift the focus to the social and political constraints on growth existing on the isthmus. The first is Costa Rica, a country with the largest state, but with the region's highest GDP per capita and the best standard of living. The second and third are El Salvador and Guatemala, whose governments implemented some of the most ambitious structural reforms in Latin America. Yet Costa Rica and Panama (which is not measured on Lora's Index of Structural Reform) have grown faster than El Salvador and Guatemala. El Salvador's mediocre growth record has generated a fair amount of reflection, in part because it grew impressively during the first half of the 1990s before falling into a slump.

The short-hand solution to these puzzles is that most of Central America remains unattractive for investors because return rates on capital are not high. In El Salvador, for example, a major study of the country's competitiveness, one seeking to identify the most binding constraint to growth, concludes that large-scale immigration – initially triggered by civil war violence and then by evaporating employment opportunities – deprives the country of its most talented citizens and reduces the growth of labor and thus of productivity (Zegarra, Rodríguez, and Acevedo, 2007). The existence of many Salvadorans in the United States leads to a large and predictable flow of remittances, which have been in excess of 10 percent of GDP since 1990. They do not serve as a pool of investment funds nor add to demand for domestically made products. On the contrary, they augment the consumption of imported goods and, most important, have led to a decline in the real exchange rate. Until 2001, when El Salvador adopted the U.S. currency as its own, the flow of U.S. dollars into the economy created a bit of "Dutch Disease," that is, the cheapening of foreign currency that raises the prices of other exports in international markets.

This study echoes the common wisdom about El Salvador, that little can compete with finance for returns on investment. Segovia (2002: 42, note 55) reports that return rates on banks in the 1990s were 18 percent a year, which meant that, within roughly four and a half years, shareholders recovered their initial investment. Financial intermediation became attractive with the rise of remittances. The owners of newly privatized banks (including President Cristiani and the director of the Central Bank) made easy profits charging fees on transfers by lower-income Salvadoran working in the United States to their relatives in El Salvador. Maquila production, undertaken in tax-free zones, is another area offering returns on investment, involving little more than reliance on cheap and unskilled labor. Neither activity has managed to absorb the 40 percent of the labor force working in the informal economy, or to create backward or forward linkages to other parts of the economy. Nor have local investors capitalized on the proximity of the U.S. market to create new exports, which Ricardo Hausmann and Dani Rodrik (2005) argue suggests that the country's entrepreneurs lack the creativity and drive to discover and market new products.

Remittances seem to have generated less pressure on the exchange rate in neighboring countries, in part because they have become key sources of foreign exchange only in the early 2000s. Since 2004, they represent close to 10 percent of the value of GDP in Guatemala, which an econometric study suggests is not related to the sluggish growth of exports (cited in Artana, Auguste, and Cuevas, 2009: 254). They have been more than 10 percent of GDP in Nicaragua since 2003. They have been more than 10 percent since 2002 in Honduras, where they skyrocketed to the equivalent of 30 percent of GDP (Orozco, 2007: 8). Studies of the binding constraints to growth in Guatemala and Nicaragua, unlike the one for El Salvador, list a multiplicity of factors – high crime rates, insecure property rights, poor education – that discourage long-range investment because rates of returns are low or uncertain.

Low rates of return lead to low rates of investment, a factor that feeds on itself. The fastest growing parts of the world, East Asia and the Pacific, have had investment rates substantially higher than those of Latin America. During the first decade of the current millennium, the proportion of private investment to GDP has been more than double the ratio in Latin America. It has averaged 14 percent in Latin America and 32 percent in Asia. It has always been higher in Asia, with the spread increasing since the 1970s, which helps explain why GDP per capita rates have been lagging throughout Latin America, especially in Central America (Agosín, Fernández-Arias, and Jaramillo, 2009: 2–7).

Defective States and Meager Growth Rates

Most countries on the isthmus suffer the consequences of possessing small and primitive states. If states are defined in economic terms by their functions, especially by how well they provide the basic services of law and order, physical infrastructure, and education, then most Central American states are failing. Underfunding states has been a long-term objective of laissez-faire doctrines, which rationalize an economic order in the short-term interests of exporters and wealthy financial groups. As the example of Costa Rica demonstrates, however, larger and more sophisticated states underwrite policies that foment economic growth, an outcome that is in the interest of investors and society as a whole. The costs of political inaction – of not raising revenues and modernizing state structures – remain high.

Several indicators of state weakness demonstrate the shortsightedness of minimalist state theories. Criminal organizations have overwhelmed several states on the isthmus. Homicide rates have skyrocketed. In El Salvador, they went from a whopping 51.2 to 61.3 per 100,000 between the 1990s and the 2000s in what remains the least peaceful country on the isthmus and, by the first decade of the twenty-first century, the most violent country in Latin America. (Homicide rates fell from 79.3 per 1,000 persons to 52.5 per 1,000 persons in Colombia, the previous most violent country in Latin America.) In the middle-ranked countries of Guatemala and Honduras, the rates have gone from 21.6 per 1,000 and 33.8 per 1,000 to 18.6 per 1,000 and 46 per 1,000, respectively, during the same period. In Nicaragua and Panama, murders have gone from 11.3 and 17.5 per 1,000 persons to 11.1 and 12.4 per 100,000 persons from the 1990s to the 2000s, respectively. Only in Costa Rica have rates remained low, at 5.4 to 8 per 100,000 individuals during these years (Mainwaring, Scully, and Vargas Cullell, 2010). This makes Costa Rica slightly more murder prone than the United States, which has a homicide rate at least double the advanced states in Europe.

The lack of adequate crime statistics is another indicator of the incapacity of states to maintain law and order. The 2008 *Estado de la Región* points out that none of the states possesses a comprehensive listing of crimes by the categories reflected in penal codes or data on suspects and convicts (PENR, 2008: 470–471). Data collected by the police is not used by the courts to facilitate information about, for example, what percentage of suspects is convicted and what punishments they receive.

Short of funds, states are unable to build the physical infrastructure required of a modern economy. Using surveys of businessmen, the 2009–10 *Global Competitiveness Report* indicates that impressions of the quality of physical infrastructure are not high. The average for Central America is 3.95, on a 7-point scale, 7 being a country perceived as having a high-quality road network, efficient ports, and sophisticated telecommunications. Costa Rica and Panama rank highest at 4.25 and 4.21, which places them 55th and 59th of 133 countries. Panama scores highly on ports (eighteenth), and Honduras, Guatemala, and El Salvador obtain slots above the global mean. Costa Rica performs well on perceptions of its electrical supply (40th) and the density of its telephone network (37th). However, these countries do poorly on the other components of the World Economic Forum's competitive reports. Costa Rica obtains an abysmal ranking of 128th on the quality of its port infrastructure and a 107th slot on the quality of its roads. Panama scores around the global mean on most of these components. El Salvador scores 4.02 on the quality of its infrastructure, with a ranking of 77th. In prior years, El Salvador scored slightly higher than Costa Rica. Guatemala and Honduras score just below the regional mean, which places them in the eightieth and eighty-ninth slots. Nicaragua comes in last with a score of 3.44, placing it 115 out of 133 countries surveyed on the quality of its infrastructure.

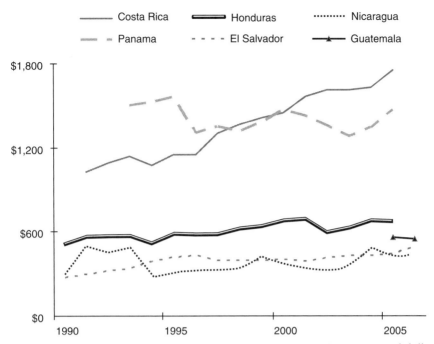

FIGURE 4.5. State revenues per capita, 1990–2006 (in 1990 U.S. international dollars). *Sources*: ICEFI (2007: 195–200) and Maddison (2010).

Hamstrung states cannot make the investments to improve public education. Although all primary age children, by 2005, are attending school, many adolescents are not enrolled. In Guatemala and Honduras, fewer than half of children eligible to be in secondary school were enrolled in post-elementary schools. In El Salvador and Nicaragua, the ratio increased to less than two-thirds. In Belize, Costa Rica, and Panama, the percentage of adolescents in secondary school increased to 69.5 percent, 70.2 percent, and 75.6 percent, respectively (PENR, 2008: 588). These figures conceal the fact that older generations did not often go to school. If the (projected) 2010 average rate of illiteracy in Latin America and the Caribbean is 9.5 percent, only two countries – Costa Rica (with 3.2 percent) and Panama (with 6 percent) – have literacy rates below the mean. Around a fifth of the population fifteen years or older does not know how to read and write in El Salvador (16.6 percent) and Honduras (19.4 percent). A quarter of this population is illiterate in Guatemala (25.6 percent) and somewhat less than a third cannot read and write in Nicaragua (30.3 percent).

The absence of a policy consensus in favor of modern states leads to revenue-poor states. Data in Figure 4.5 show that the revenues of the nonfinancial public sector (essentially the three branches of government and autonomous institutions) in Costa Rica and Panama are equivalent to more than twice what they are in the rest of the isthmus. In 1990 international dollars, the states of Costa Rica and Panama had an average income of US$1,381 per capita versus US$488 per capita in El Salvador, Guatemala, Honduras, and Nicaragua between 1990 and 2006. The most modern states of Central America possess incomes almost three times as high as those of the other isthmus states. The shortcomings of the Guatemalan state are illustrated by the fact that no reliable figures exist for total public sector revenues, a conclusion reached by a comprehensive study of Central American public finances (ICEFI, 2007). All of these states have resources that, in proportional terms, are substantially less than the OECD average, which was in excess of US$12,000 during this period.

The costs of defective states are not low. Several econometric studies indicate that the inability of most states to halt violent crime costs between 8 percent and 12 percent of GDP. The costs in Costa Rica and Nicaragua, which have some of the lowest homicide rates on the isthmus, are less than 1 percent (PENR, 2008: 473). In their econometric study of productivity on the isthmus, Agosín and Machado (2006: 124) find that the lack of institutional development (using the rule of law index developed by the International Country Risk Guide) impairs not only stock of human capital, but also investment in machinery and equipment. In a world with numerous investment opportunities, most countries on the isthmus cannot outshine other places, even for local investors. Low return rates reflect many structural factors, which, combined, inhibit long-range investment and condemn the region to economic stagnation and high levels of social exclusion (Pérez Sáinz and Mora Salas, 2007).

Continuity and Change in the Production Profile

Twenty years after the end of civil war, the isthmus's economic structure has not fundamentally changed. The region remains an exporter of primary products. Data in Figure 4.6 reveal that manufactures remain a minority export of most countries. Only the economies of Costa Rica and El Salvador mostly send manufactures abroad. The construction of an Intel assembly plant in Costa Rica by the second half of the 1990s led to a swift displacement of primary products from its export profile. El Salvador has become an exporter of light consumer goods or maquila. In both countries, manufactures have replaced primary products as these countries' principal exports. In Costa Rica and El Salvador, and, to a lesser extent, in other countries of the region, new exports shape its integration with the rest of the world (Robinson, 2003).

The composition of primary product exports has changed. Although the region continues to export coffee and bananas, these products no longer are the major sources of foreign exchange. Even in Guatemala, El Salvador, Honduras, and Nicaragua, where coffee remains the largest export by value, coffee accounts for less than a quarter of exports since 1990 (Segovia, 2004). Its weight in what these countries sell to other countries continues to decline. Only in Panama are bananas key exports (PENR, 2008: 542–552).

Panama has the most globalized economy, as data in Figure 4.7 shows. Imports and exports are the equivalent of more than 100 percent of GDP. Costa Rica and Honduras, the richest and poorest economies, are also quite globalized. By the mid-2000s, imports and exports are approximately 100 percent of GDP. Guatemala remains the least globalized economy, a place it has held since the mid-twentieth century (see Figure 1.2). This reflects the existence

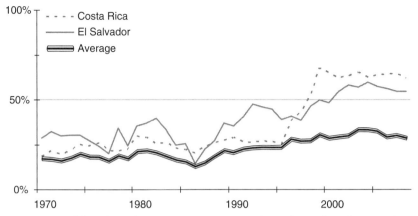

FIGURE 4.6. Manufacturing exports, 1970–2008 (as a share of total exports).
Source: CEPAL (2009).

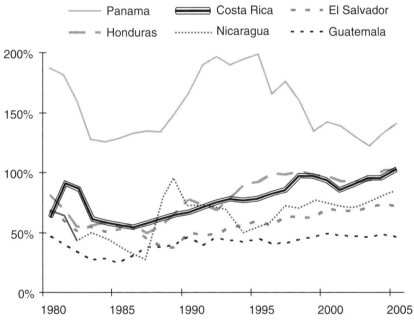

FIGURE 4.7. Trends in globalization (imports and exports, as a share of GDP).
Source: Huber et al. (2008) database, using world development indicators (2007).

of a large subsistence sector in Guatemala, one made up disproportionately by the country's indigenous population.

Some countries have pioneered a new export: labor. The shortage of jobs has led hundreds of thousands of Central Americans to immigrate, largely to the United States. The wave of immigration started in El Salvador, where rural and urban workers fled the violence of the 1980s for the security and jobs of

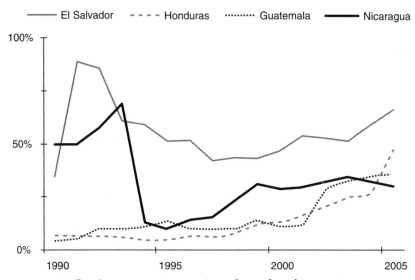

FIGURE 4.8. Remittances, 1990–2005 (as a share of total exports).
Note: Costa Rica and Panama not shown because their annual averages are less than 3 percent.
Sources: Orozco (2007), using Central Bank data and CEPAL (2009).

the United States. By 2006, 15 percent of individuals of Salvadoran descent lived abroad, mostly in the United States. The outflow of poor Salvadorans was subsequently joined by large numbers of Guatemalans, Hondurans, and Nicaraguans. The equivalent of 7, 9, and 5 percent of nationals from these countries reside mostly in the United States. More than half the Nicaraguan diaspora lives elsewhere, largely in Costa Rica (PENR, 2008: 252). Data in Figure 4.8 show that these immigrants have had an enormous impact on their countries. Remittances from El Salvadorans in the United States now consist of the equivalent of more than half of exports. By the early 2000s, remittances from Guatemalans, Hondurans, and Nicaraguans equaled a quarter of the value of exports. By 2005, they were the equivalent of about half of exports in Nicaragua and approaching that proportion in Honduras.

Tourism has also begun to generate foreign exchange by the late 2000s. It accelerated in Costa Rica in the 1990s. By 2006, it was generating nearly US$2 billion in earnings, which is the equivalent of 17 percent of its exports of that year. Tourism brings in 25 percent (or US$1.1 billion) and 13 percent (or US$1.4 billion) of exports in El Salvador and Panama, respectively. The ratio for Guatemala is the highest on the isthmus, at 26 percent of exports (or US$1 billion), largely because the country's exports are less than 40 percent of Costa Rica's, which is the region's largest exporter of goods and services. Dollars spent in Honduras and Nicaragua by tourists are equal to 14 percent (US$490 million) and 16 percent (US$237 million) of exports, respectively (PENR, 2008: 542–552).

Central America also has become less rural. By 2010, slightly more than 40 percent of the region's population was classified as rural by national

TABLE 4.2. *Populations in Central America, 1990–2010*

Country	Population (in Millions)			Rural Population (as a Share of Total)			Population Density (Per Km²)		
	1990	2000	2010	1990	2000	2010	1990	2000	2010
Costa Rica	3.1	3.9	4.6	50%	41%	34%	61	77	92
El Salvador	5.1	6.3	6.2	50%	45%	40%	247	303	299
Guatemala	8.7	11.4	14.4	66%	57%	43%	81	105	133
Honduras	4.9	6.5	7.6	60%	55%	50%	44	58	68
Nicaragua	3.8	5.1	5.8	47%	45%	42%	32	42	48
Panama	2.4	2.9	3.5	46%	38%	31%	32	39	46
Total	28.2	36.3	42.5						
Averages									
Central America	2.6	3.4	4.5	52%	48%	41%	55	71	83
Latin America	10.2	13.4	17.4	30%	24%	21%	22	25	29
Developing	20.5	25.3	31.3	64%	59%	55%	45	53	60

Sources: Population data for the isthmus is from PER (2003: 406). All other data is from CEPAL (2009), with the exception of Latin American and developing world averages population and population density figures, which are from World Bank (2011).

census authorities. As a share of the region's population, this is twice the Latin American rate, but little more than half the average for the developing world, as data in Table 4.2 shows. Costa Rica and Panama have become the most urban of Central American societies. Only about a third of their populations live in the countryside. Honduras has the most rural society, with half its population not living in cities. The rest of the isthmus has populations that are predominately urban, although each has about 40 percent of their inhabitants living in rural areas.

The largest number of Central Americans labor in the tertiary or service sector of the economy. By 2010, more than half the employed population in Costa Rica (66.1 percent), in Panama (63 percent), and in El Salvador (59.4 percent) performed services in exchange for a salary or payment. The proportion everywhere else on the isthmus was at least 40 percent of the economically active population. Approximately a fifth of the isthmus's population worked in manufacturing. Differences among republics were greatest in regard to the population working as farmers. Although only 12 percent of economically active Costa Ricans worked in agriculture, more than a third of the economically active population labored in the agricultural sector in Guatemala and Honduras. In El Salvador and Panama, the proportion working as farmers was about 17 percent by 2010 (CEPAL, 2009: 1.2.5).

The largest number of Central Americans works in the private sector. For the region as a whole, nearly one-half – 46.7 percent – have private sector employers, according to national-level household surveys (circa 2006). Approximately a third of these individuals work for small firms; the remainder are employed by medium- and large-scale companies. Less than one out of ten work for the public sector. Less than 1 percent labor in homes as domestic, mostly female, servants. Slightly more than 40 percent work for themselves. Most are members of the urban, informal sector, that is, they sell services or hawk goods on the streets of the region's cities and towns (Pérez Sáinz, 1994). This proportion is highest in Honduras (49.7 percent), Guatemala (46.5 percent), and Nicaragua (45 percent). A third of the economically active population is self-employed in El Salvador (35.4 percent) and Panama (33.6 percent). It is the smallest in Costa Rica (21.6 percent), where 14.5 percent of the labor force works for the state. A comparable share of the working population is employed by the public sector in Panama. Everywhere else in the region, less than 9 percent of the labor force is a member of the public sector, with the Guatemalan state employing one out of twenty members of the economically active population (PENR, 2008: 151).

Conclusions

Economic growth has diverged in Central America. The best performers in the region – Costa Rica and Panama – have grown barely enough to maintain their distance from the twelve core economies of Europe. This is partly a result of the "lost decade," the recession of the 1980s that put all of Latin America ten years behind the rest of the world. The other Central American economies have done much worse since the 1980s, largely because of the destruction of civil war, of the failure of dictatorships to reform themselves. Misguided economic policies contributed to undermining Nicaragua's productive sector. If the three decades after the end of World War II were, in relative terms, the region's golden age, the post-1980 decades have been a period of sustained decline for four of the six economies of the isthmus.

It is not having the "wrong" economic policies that has hurt the region. Most countries have followed the sound money, small government advice of the Washington Consensus; for most of Central America, this has been a decades-long orthodoxy. With the partial exception of Costa Rica, none of the countries of the isthmus closed their economies and adopted active industrial policies. Short of raising tariffs on imports, which were adopted to stimulate the CACM and raise tax revenue for chronically underfunded states, Central American states remained vehicles of market-friendly policies. The socialist experiment in Nicaragua and some interventionist policies in El Salvador during the 1980s were the glaring exceptions to this rule. All had no choice but to devalue their currencies and pare fiscal deficits when the value of their exports fell by the late 1970s. Several countries saw interest payments on their foreign loans soar in the 1980s, which forced them to restructure international obligations, raise taxes, and cut spending. By the mid-1990s, once the terms of trade improved and the civil wars were largely over, all had conquered inflation, slashed budget deficits, and adopted much of the Washington Consensus.

Growth has been disappointing in most of the isthmus because, with one or two exceptions, productivity has been stagnant. Economic growth has been meager because it has done little more than take advantage of abundant cheap labor. With the partial exceptions of Costa Rica and Panama, firms do not invest in technology to make labor more productive. They cannot take advantage of physical or human capital improvements because the private sector has done little to fund and establish states capable of shifting the domestic terms of trade toward higher-wage and more sophisticated manufacturing and services. Only proximity to the United States beacons as an incentive for investors. Costa Rica and, to a lesser extent, Panama are the only states with enough investments to shift the terms of this equation. Only two or three of these economies therefore are productive enough to keep up in a global race for markets and capital.

Continuities outshine changes in productive structure since the mid-twentieth century. Most countries of the region remain dependent on exporting agricultural products, although coffee and bananas – the region's chief exports before the 1980s – are no longer the only items on the export menu. Two countries – Costa Rica and El Salvador – have become exporters of light manufactured goods that can employ a share of the burgeoning urban sector. Most depend on the export of cheap labor. Remittances from nationals working abroad have been, since the early 1990s, equivalent to half the value of exports in El Salvador. In Guatemala, Honduras, and Nicaragua, remittances are bringing home, by the late 2000s, something like a third of the income generated by exports. Whether working in the isthmus or abroad, it is the poorest Central Americans who remain the mainstay of these economies.

5

Democratization, State Capacity, and Redistribution

Introduction

Military governments no longer rule the isthmus. Citizens elect presidents, leg-islators, and municipal councilmen in each country of the region. This perhaps is the single most important conquest of the civil wars of the 1970s and 1980s. It was a hopeful outcome, and not only because overthrowing dictatorship was a central goal of so many who died in the region's violent conflicts.

Have elections made a difference? There are good reasons to believe that they should. Parties offer different platforms in exchange for votes, and the party or parties that win elections then convert these preferences into laws. This is the virtuous circle of accountability that democratization should unleash. In the context of underdeveloped societies with legions of poor voters, competitive elections should increase redistribution and social spending. Democracy, in other words, should placate the majority and promote the common good.

The goal of this chapter is to explain why this question cannot be easily answered in the affirmative. Although elections have met minimal standards of openness and fairness, clashes between presidents and other branches of government have tainted the quality of the region's democratic institutions. They have led to conflicts in which executives sometimes have prevailed and other times have been exiled. So, even while democracy remains consolidated in Costa Rica and has become stronger in Panama and El Salvador, it has fused with some blatantly autocratic elements in the other republics of the isthmus. A blemished political record bodes poorly for the functioning of democratic institutions, effects that I document and explain in this chapter.

Effective states narrow the gap between the rich and the poor, which I sug-gest is a litmus test for assessing the extent of democratization – and why this chapter analyzes the impact of spending on education, health care, and old-age pensions on income distribution. It is a test that most states of the region do not pass, despite the fact that Central Americans, like most Latin Americans, overwhelmingly favor policies to combat persistently high levels of inequality.

Costa Rica is still the least unequal society on the isthmus, although it has become less egalitarian since the turn of the century. Honduras and Guatemala remain the most unequal places in the region. I evaluate several hypotheses to explain why there has been little reduction in inequality in Central America, even if there have been modest improvements in key social indicators, including a decline in the share of the population living in poverty. It is the most accountable party systems – ones that allow citizens to reward parties that enact promised policies – that have been able to construct states capable of ameliorating the accidents of birth. It takes time, as I show, for parties to learn how to convert citizen preferences into effective public policies.

Having explained why transitions from authoritarianism have produced meager results, I assess the impact of paltry economic growth rates on the deterioration of democratic institutions in Central America. This chapter ends, in other words, by addressing another central issue of political economy, one that requires linking the findings of the last with those of the current chapter. I suggest that economic stagnation does not advance the cause of democracy, but largely for political reasons – and that it has little to do with popular dissatisfaction with democracy. Incumbents engineer ways to stay in power because control of the state confers privileges that take on added significance at low levels of development, that is, in economies that generate few lucrative (and legal) job opportunities.

Democratization: Central Achievements and Shortcomings

Holding competitive and fair elections, long a demand of opposition groups and social movements, has become the norm on the isthmus. Former guerrillas, who took up arms to battle right-wing dictatorships, compete in elections for the presidency, congress, and municipal offices. Christian democratic, social democratic, or other reformist parties, whose members were often targets of military or paramilitary repression, also participate in elections. What have been the achievements – as well as shortcomings – of postwar political systems?

Electoral Governance

Establishing electoral tribunals became a vital (and often ignored) component of postwar settlements in Central America. One country – Costa Rica – helped pioneer the nonpartisan organization and administration of elections, in both the region and the world (Lehoucq, 2002). In the mid-1920s, politicians established an independent body to tally the vote and resolve election-related complaints. Under threat of civil war, incumbents agreed to empower an autonomous electoral agency to run elections and tally the vote, an institution that became enshrined in the 1949 constitution and as an independent branch of government in 1975 (Lehoucq, 1995a; 2000). Although an electoral tribunal existed in Panama since the 1940s, it had become co-opted by military regimes. It was rebuilt after the 1989 U.S. invasion (Scranton, 2000). Much like their Costa Rican predecessors, it was the reality or threat of civil war that prompted the incumbents to create these electoral management bodies.

Most Central American systems have implemented first-generation electoral governance reforms, those ensuring minimal conditions for a fair vote: that every citizen is registered to vote, that ballots are printed in time, that polling stations open on schedule, and that votes are tallied accurately. El Salvador, along with Guatemala and Nicaragua, however, has had problems maintaining an updated electoral registry and distributing electoral identification cards (Artiga-González, 2008). In 2005, the switch to open-list proportional representation (PR) in Honduras overwhelmed its electoral tribunal (Taylor-Robinson, 2007); it took days to issue a preliminary verdict for the presidential race and months to calculate votes for individual candidates and each party's share of the vote, which is what closed-list PR requires (and what every other country on the isthmus uses). Only in Guatemala are citizens not automatically registered to vote. Until 2007, citizens could cast ballots only in municipal capitals (Azpuru, 2008), a factor discouraging turnout (Lehoucq and Wall, 2004).

Electoral governance is the most consolidated in Costa Rica and El Salvador because each has passed the acid test of preventing close or polarizing elections from triggering armed conflicts. Although Nicaragua seemingly passed this test in 1990, when the presidency went from the Sandinistas to UNO, international scrutiny and support was crucial for insuring this outcome (Pastor, 2002), either for good (Lecayo, 2005) or for bad (Robinson, 1992). Subsequent developments in electoral governance have undermined the legacy of this achievement, as I will explain in this chapter, although anti-Sandinista candidates and parties accepted Daniel Ortega's return to power in the 2006 and 2012 elections (Lean, 2007; Ortega Hegg, 2007).

A modern system of electoral governance helped thwart armed confrontation a decade later in Costa Rica when the incumbent party lost another hotly contested election (Bowman, 2001a), even though it did not stop the descent into civil war after the highly charged 1948 elections (Lehoucq and Molina, 2002). That an independent agency ran these 1958 elections made it impossible for the National Liberation Party (PLN) to claim that fraud had deprived it of another four years in office. More recently, the Supreme Tribunal of Elections (TSE) arbitrated post-electoral conflicts when a third-party candidate, Ottón Solís of the Citizen Action Party (PAC), narrowly lost to Oscar Arias in the latter's second (and barely successful) 2006 bid for the presidency. Despite accusations that the tally was manipulated in Arias's favor, an independent analysis concludes there was no bias in the vote count (Alfaro Redondo, 2007). Debate about electoral governance in Costa Rica has shifted to reforming electoral laws as part of a broader agenda (second-generation reforms) seeking to revitalize its democracy (PEN, 2001; Vargas Cullell, 2004), one that includes reversing declining voter turnout rates (Raventós Vorst et al., 2005), citizen apathy (Seligson, 2002), and limiting the role of money in politics (Casas-Zamora, 2005).

First-generation electoral reforms were partially in effect for the 1994 elections in El Salvador, ones featuring participation by the FMLN. Although no one contested the results of this election, an estimated 22 percent of Salvadorans were unable to cast ballots, either because they had not received their identification cards in time or never retrieved them (Lehoucq, 1995b; Spence, Lanchin, and Thale, 2001). The effectiveness of electoral governance was untested because ARENA won by a wide margin: The FMLN lost the 1994 elections by more than 24 percent of the vote, a margin that was largely repeated over the next three general elections, when ARENA defeated its adversaries by an average of 23 percent of the vote. Unable to dislodge the right from the presidency, elections became regular and passionate jousts between the civilian successors of the armed left and paramilitary right, ones whose legislative elections turned over an average of 35 percent of the congressional seats to the FMLN between 1994 and 2009. It was not until the 2009 campaign that the FMLN managed to defeat ARENA, a victory achieved by nominating an outsider, Mauricio Funes, a famous television anchorman, to be its presidential candidate. Signaling moderation persuaded increasing numbers of voters to identify with the left and enough centrist voters to cast ballots for Funes instead of the ARENA candidate (Azpuru, 2008). It was an election that the FMLN won by 2.6 percent of the vote (Artiga-González, 2009), and one whose results ARENA did not impugn.

With these important exceptions, the strength of electoral governance in Central America remains unclear. In the first place, several electoral tribunals of the region are more partisan and less professional than they could be (Rosas, 2010). On the isthmus, the Costa Rican electoral tribunal is the agency with the most professional or formal independence. Parties cannot appoint its staff, its officials have long tenures, and judiciaries help select its members. The TSE minimizes the role that parties play in selecting its magistrates or top-tier officials. Its electoral management body is the second most autonomous in Latin America, with Panama's coming in second in Central America (and sixth in Latin America). El Salvador's tribunal ranks third on the isthmus (and seventh in the broader region). It experienced decay in its formal autonomy between 1998 and 2006, which helps account for the persistence of legal and administrative shortcomings in this country's elections (Wolf, 2009). The electoral tribunal of Nicaragua ranks fourth in the region (and is at the median in Latin America). The electoral management bodies of Guatemala and Honduras rank fifth and sixth in Central America (and eleventh and fourteenth in the broader region).

In the second place, most electoral governance systems have not been tested. They have not had to arbitrate a close election, nor one in which a party of the left has made a serious bid for power. Since 1990, the winners of presidential elections have won by margins in excess of 7 percent in all countries, except Costa Rica, where party system fragmentation has led to multiple presidential candidates and an increase in the average margin of difference from less than 3 percent in 1998 to 7.5 percent in 2002 and 21.8 percent in 2010. Whether former (mostly left-wing) insurgents can come to power after defeating their rivals helps gauge not only the resilience of an electoral tribunal and of the electoral system writ large, but also the strength of democracy as a whole. Whether right-wing and conservative parties formerly allied with the military is much less of a test because they had little trouble winning elections, especially when democratic rights were restricted. In Guatemala, the party of the URNG has not won more than a handful of legislative seats since 1999, when it first ran candidates for elected office. There are no parties of the left in Honduras or Panama.

Electoral governance has suffered most in Nicaragua. A deal hatched between President Arnoldo Alemán (1996–2001), the corpulent Liberal Constitutional *jefe supremo*, and Ortega included electoral reforms to reinforce their domination of Nicaraguan politics. Approved in 2000, these reforms created barriers to entry for smaller and newer parties. Between 1996 and 2001, the number of parties whose registration was approved dropped from thirty-six to six. Most important, the infamous pact lowered the percentage of votes needed to win the presidency from a majority (e.g., more than 50 percent) to 40 percent or 35 percent, if the first place winner had a 5-percent margin on his nearest rival. In 2006, sixteen years after Chamorro had defeated him, Ortega returned to the presidency. He finished the race with 38 percent of the vote and won because he was the least unpopular of the candidates in the race. His chief rival, Herty Lewites, a former Sandinista, unexpectedly died during the campaign; and, his liberal and conservative opponents refused to coordinate around a single candidate (Martí i Puig, 2008). Two years later, international observers refused to certify the 2008 municipal elections as fair, an action taken after the regime did not accredit observers from Etica y Transparencia, the local branch of Transparency International and the Organization of American States. Despite criticism from abroad, the conservative-dominated assembly desisted from pursuing a bill to annul these elections (Anderson and Dodd, 2009). By mid-2010, the Sandinistas got the supreme court, stacked with sympathetic magistrates, to declare unconstitutional the prohibition on consecutive reelection for presidents, permitting Ortega to run and win as an incumbent in 2011.

Few countries on the isthmus or in the world have implemented second-generation electoral reforms, ones seeking to equal the playing field among candidates and parties. There are only a handful of countries that have restrictions on private contributions to campaigns. Individuals, political or social organizations, corporations (except Honduras), and government contractors (except Honduras and Nicaragua) can make campaign donations freely. Although all Central American states furnish public funding to parties, the best estimate suggests that private donations account for less than one-third of campaign expenses in elections (circa 2000) in Guatemala, Honduras, and Panama and approximately half in Costa Rica and Nicaragua (Casas-Zamora, 2003; data for El Salvador was not available). Evidence, according to the most comprehensive study, suggests that

Private funds are raised through processes characterized by strong participation by presidential candidates, the quest for funds among a very small group of major business people, the variable presence of foreign funds, and the subtlety and contingency of exchanges of favor between donors and politicians (Casas-Zamora and Zovatto, 2005: 260).

There are efforts to improve oversight and transparency of campaign finance in Central America. The Legislative Assembly of Costa Rica passed a new Electoral Code in September 2009, which tightens restrictions on private campaign contributions and creates sanctions for violating them. It reestablishes advances on campaign finance, even as it reduces total public campaign financing (Sobrado González, 2010). Reforming campaign finance, as well as improving voter registration, are topics on the reform agenda in Guatemala, Honduras, and Panama. In El Salvador, the Constitutional Court declared closed-lists unconstitutional in 2010. Before the 2012 legislative elections, deputies will have to reform electoral laws in light of this ruling and address concerns in campaign finance, districting, and absentee voting (Artiga-González, 2010).

Executive-Legislative Relations

The region illustrates why the separation of powers can aggravate conflicts and why presidentialism can put democracy under stress (Pérez-Liñán, 2010; Shugart and Carey, 1992). When presidents cannot amass the congressional votes to pass their bills, they have confronted the other branches of government. One – President Serrano of Guatemala in 1993 – tried to close congress. Another – President Zelaya of Honduras in 2009 – tried to force the other government branches to accept his bid for a consecutive term in office, despite the constitutional prohibition against doing so. A third set of presidents – in Nicaragua by 2001 – came up with the most ingenious solution to repeated confrontations between the president and the legislature: Rival parties reformed the constitution to restrict access to the electoral arena and thus deter challenges to executive authority.

Central American presidents are not that powerful, a surprising, perhaps even welcome outcome, given their autocratic proclivities. A comprehensive ranking of their legislative powers, as listed in current and past constitutions, lists two presidential systems on the isthmus above the Latin American average (Negretto, 2008). The Panamanian constitution of 1994 and the Nicaraguan constitution of 1987 endow their presidents with more than average legislative powers. The Costa Rican constitution of 1949 and the Honduran charter of 1982 grant their executives the fewest legislative powers. The 1983 constitution of El Salvador provides its president with less than the mean number of powers, and the Guatemalan president, as outlined in the 1985 charter, is marginally stronger than his Costa Rican and Honduran counterparts. After the 1995 and 2000 constitutional amendments, the Nicaraguan president became the least powerful on the isthmus. Each of these three is approximately as weak as the U.S. president, which helps make the point that most Central American executives are not that powerful.

The chief executives of the region have not been able to count on the support of stable congressional majorities – the other, perhaps more crucial dimension along which the power of presidents is measured. Only two, on average, are elected with majority support in the legislature: Nicaragua (53.4 percent between 1984 and 2006) and Honduras (52.5 percent between 1981 and 2010). The presidents of Panama and Costa Rica count on the support of 47.8 percent (1994–2009) and 46.3 percent (1982–2010) of legislative deputies. Those of El Salvador and Guatemala rely on even less support: 41.8 percent (1985–2009) and 39.7 percent (1985–2007), respectively. The averages for Costa Rica and Guatemala reveal a trend of declining majorities in congress. In the last two elections of this period, the president's party has won 40 percent and 31 percent of deputies, respectively.

Presidents holding larger majorities in congress seem to meet with more success. The presidents of Honduras and Panama, who have among the largest legislative delegations, get more than three-fourths of their bills passed in congress (Saiegh, 2011). The president of Costa Rica gets better than half of what he wants from congress, although other research shows that this share has been dwindling (Lehoucq, 2008). A different, but complementary assessment of the legislative success of presidents reaches similar conclusions: It is the presidents of Honduras and Panama that are responsible for most – more than two-thirds – of enacted legislation. The presidents of Costa Rica and Guatemala leave their imprint on dwindling shares of legislation (García Montero, 2009). Less systematic research on the legislative politics of El Salvador and Nicaragua suggests that presidents reach compromises with other parties to get key parts of their agenda enacted. In El Salvador, for example, ARENA assembled coalitions with the PCN to enact its neoliberal agenda. Collaboration between ARENA and the PCN prevented the standoff between the leftist FMLN and the rightist ARENA from polarizing further (Artiga-González, 2003).

Conflicts between the elected branches of government have escalated into regime crises when presidents could not assemble majority coalitions in congress. Perhaps the most emblematic crisis occurred in Guatemala in 1993 (McClearly, 1999). Three years into his five-year mandate, President Jorge Serrano tried to mimic the behavior of his Peruvian counterpart, Alberto Fujimori, who had closed congress the year before. His party, the Solidarity Action Movement (MAS), had won only 16 percent of the legislative seats, even less than the 24 percent of the vote he won in the election. (Serrano won the runoff with 68 percent of the vote.) Unable to obtain legislative approval of electrical sector and tax reforms, Serrano announced that congressional obstructionism was forcing him to disband the legislature. Over the next several weeks, a coalition of business owners, generals, and civil society movements opposed Serrano's actions. It was an unlikely coalition because capitalists had been quarreling with generals over raising the country's low taxation rate for more than a decade (Fuentes and Cabrera, 2006). Business owners and the military viewed social movements with alarm, and non-elite groups distrusted the dominant players of Guatemalan society and politics. Each concluded, however, that they had more to gain by opposing Serrano's behavior. Capitalists and social movements did not want a return to the arbitrariness of military rule; enough army factions decided it was not convenient to rebuild a dictatorship with a temperamental president. These decisions prevented a clash between the elected branches of government from turning into a full-blown breakdown of democracy. When Serrano left for exile, elections were held to select a new Congress, whose members chose Human Rights Ombudsman, Ramiro de León Carpio, to complete Serrano's presidential term.

A second crisis was a product of an overly ambitious president, one whose agenda had been stymied not only by congress, but also by the supreme court. The military's overthrow of Liberal Party President Manuel Zelaya in mid-2009 was the product of more than a year of clashes between the president and the institutions of horizontal accountability. Despite unusually explicit language in the constitution banning consecutive reelection for the presidency, Zelaya tried to get a ballot measure adopted whereby the Honduran people could endorse his call for a Constituent Assembly to reform the 1982 constitution and permit his consecutive reelection. After the Court of Administrative Litigation and the electoral tribunal refused to sanction the referendum, Zelaya fired the military chief for not complying with his order to help the statistics bureau hold the poll. When the supreme court reinstated the military commander, the chief prosecutor (amazingly) obtained the high court's approval to have Zelaya arrested. In carrying out the court's order, the military put Zelaya on a plane for Costa Rica instead of turning him over for trial. Soon afterward, Congress selected the National Party congressional president, Roberto Micheletti, interim president. By the end of his term, Zelaya held the loyalty of less than the 48.4 percent of the deputies elected on the Liberal Party ticket in the 2006 elections. After months of a standoff that drew world attention, new elections were held that saw National Party rancher, Porfirio Lobo Sosa, elected president in the regularly scheduled November 2009 elections, with results that were not recognized by many countries (Ruhl, 2010).

Nicaragua has been the site for institutionally induced crises and the cleverest, if anti-democratic, solutions to recurrent confrontations between the branches of government. In 1990, the fragmentation of the UNO legislative delegation, holding 55.4 percent of the seats, empowered the Sandinistas, with 42.3 percent of the seats and a more cohesive party, to corner the Chamorro administration. The Frente not only stopped much of Chamorro's legislative program, but also fashioned a coalition with renegade UNO deputies to scale back the president's powers after Chamorro used executive decree authority to enact economic reforms, which turned the Nicaraguan presidency into the weakest one on the isthmus. The UNO president refused to acknowledge these amendments, ones that stripped the president of the ability to promulgate tax measures and agreements with international financial institutions unilaterally. This unlikely coalition also amended the constitution to prevent close relatives of the president from running for election – a measure aimed at taking Antonio Lecayo (2005), Chamorro's key advisor and son-in-law, out of the 1996 race for the presidency. For several months in 1995, the president and the assembly recognized different constitutions. Although she prevailed insofar as her policies remained the law of the land, she lost because she accepted the reforms she originally refused to promulgate (Dye, 2004; Dye et al., 1995; Spence and Vickers, 2000).

Confrontation morphed into collusion in Nicaragua as the elected branches of government dismantled constitutional checks on their authority. The 1996 elections maintained the standoff between the Frente and its liberal opponents, with the former obtaining 39 percent and the latter winning 45 percent of the assembly's seats. By the end of the 1990s, Ortega and President Alemán (1996–2001) deployed their deputies to promulgate a series of constitutional reforms that undermined the rule of law and Nicaraguan democracy. Alemán exchanged protection from the aggressive pursuit of official acts of corruption by the comptroller for Ortega's interest in reducing the competitiveness of elections and receiving legal protection from incest accusations made by his stepdaughter (ones that her mother, Ortega's wife, ignored). The erstwhile opponents agreed to split the executive boards of the leading institutions of horizontal accountability, including the comptrollership, the supreme court, and the supreme electoral council between their parties. They gave outgoing presidents and vice-presidents lifetime seats in the National Assembly (Hoyt, 2004).

For Alemán at least, there is a cruel irony in this clever institutional engineering. His own vice-president, Enrique Bolaños (who was elected president in 2001), led the successful fight to strip his predecessor of immunity (Close, 2004). Alemán was prosecuted and jailed for acts of corruption. Although the infamous pacts between the Sandinistas and Alemán deactivated the institutions entrusted with checking the power of the elected branches of government, it did not prevent a former president from being found corrupt (Anderson, 2006).

Democratization: A Preliminary Balance Sheet
The data in Figure 5.1 indicates that the political systems on the isthmus have gone down one of two paths. On the one hand, the political systems of Costa Rica, El Salvador, and Panama have stayed democratic, although democratic institutions in El Salvador and Panama are not as vibrant as those in Costa Rica. On the other hand, democratization has stagnated or even been reversed in the rest of the cases. Guatemala's political system has remained semi-democratic since 1990. It has experienced shortcomings in its electoral laws, a regime breakdown in the mid-1990s, and presidents unable to bring the armed forces under civilian control (Ruhl, 2005). Honduras's political system became autocratic when Zelaya was ousted; elections held the following year created a regime, like Nicaragua's, containing autocratic and democratic elements. How does this record compare internationally?

Systematic research demonstrates that new regimes tend to be more open or at least less autocratic than their predecessors (Gurses and Mason, 2008; Toft, 2010: 64–65). Civil wars that end with internationally supervised negotiations

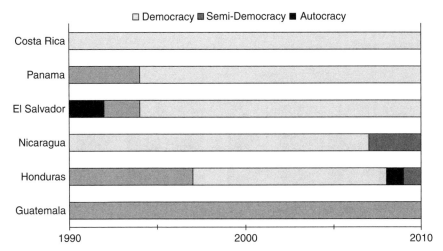

FIGURE 5.1. Regime types, 1990–2010.
Sources: Bowman, Lehoucq, and Mahoney (2005); Brinks, Mainwaring, and Pérez-Liñán (2011) for Panama and all cases between 2001–7; Lehoucq's calculations for 2008–10.

between governments and insurgents, as they did on the isthmus, have the highest rate of regime improvement (Toft, 2010). Of 130 civil wars in the world between 1940 and 2000 (excluding 13 continuing as of 2003), 20 percent (22) involved a cease-fire as part of an extensive agreement on a range of political and socioeconomic issues. Forty-eight cases or 41 percent ended because the government won. Insurgents defeated the government in 28 percent (thirty-three) of all civil wars. Stalemates that end in cease-fires account for 11 percent (13 cases) of civil war. Between five and twenty years of signing a comprehensive accord, the Polity IV regime index rates the average post-civil war system as democratic, even if the quality of its political system decays with time. No other outcome of a civil war – a cease-fire, stalemate, or victory by the government or rebels – does much better than becoming a semi-democracy, even if an insurgent victory outperforms a negotiated settlement twenty years after the war is over.

Postwar trajectories in Central America are consistent with these patterns and help explain why negotiation and military victory led to more open political systems that discourage reinitiating conflict (Walter, 2010). The country with the most stable and highest quality democracy – Costa Rica – had a brief civil war in 1948, won by the opposition. The 1989 U.S. invasion and overthrow of the Noriega dictatorship in Panama, the second most robust democracy on the isthmus, was the functional equivalent of an opposition-led civil war. Negotiated settlements have been the backdrop to uninterrupted democratic rule in El Salvador and the end of civil war in Nicaragua (Spalding, 1999; Spence, 2004). Opposition-led victories are associated with as much democratization as political settlements, perhaps even more. Guatemala, which Toft classifies as a negotiated settlement, is more accurately an instance of a government

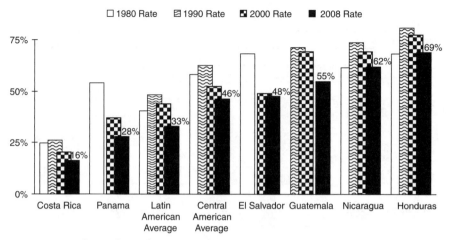

FIGURE 5.2. Share of population in poverty, 1980–2008.
Sources: IICA-FLACSO (1991): 121; CEPAL (2009).

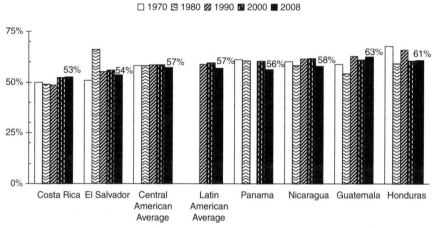

FIGURE 5.3. Top quintile's share of national income, 1970–2008.
Sources: IICA-FLACSO (1991): 122; CEPAL (2009).

victory, in which the peace negotiations, as I point out in Chapter 3, were fundamentally about administering the terms of the URNG's surrender so as to declare a formal cessation of hostilities.

Poverty, Inequality, and Redistribution

Before identifying the reasons democratization has helped some states redistribute more than others, this section analyzes continuities and changes in rates of poverty and inequality on the isthmus. Civil war and the fall in the price

TABLE 5.1. *Leading Social Indicators, 1990–2010*

Country	Illiteracy Rate (as a Share of Adult Population)			Life Expectancy at Birth (in Years)			Infant Mortality (Per 1,000 Live Births)		
	1990	2000	2010	1990	2000	2010	1990	2000	2010
Costa Rica	6%	4%	3%	76	78	79	15	11	9
El Salvador	28%	21%	17%	64	70	72	40	26	18
Guatemala	40%	32%	26%	64	69	71	55	39	23
Honduras	32%	25%	19%	68	71	73	43	31	25
Nicaragua	37%	34%	30%	66	71	75	48	26	18
Panama	11%	8%	6%	73	75	76	27	21	16
Averages									
Central America	25%	20%	17%	69	73	75	37	25	18
Latin America	15%	11%	8%	69	72	75	38	26	19
Developing	30%	22%	20%	63	65	67	153	112	94

Sources: All data is from CEPAL (2009), with the exception illiteracy and life expectancy rates for the developing world, which are from World Bank (2011). These data are for 2008.

of the region's exports sent hundreds of thousands of Central Americans into poverty. Both also exacerbated already high levels of inequality. How has peace changed the social matrix on the isthmus? Before identifying the reasons that democratization has helped some state redistribute more income than others, this section analyzes continuities and changes in rates of poverty and inequality on the isthmus.

The Essential Facts

Data on the population living in poverty in Figure 5.2 reveal that slightly less than half of Central Americans – 46 percent – lived at or below subsistence level by the late 2000s. This is a decline from an average high of almost two-thirds – 63 percent – of the population living in destitution in 1990. The (unweighted) average rate for the isthmus remains higher than for Latin America as a whole: One-third of the region's populations (again, unweighted) live in poverty. Data in Figure 5.3 on the top quintile's share of national income suggest, however, that income distribution has not fundamentally changed. With a few minor exceptions, the top 20 percent of the population receives more than half the national income, and perhaps significantly more than half. Income concentration is no doubt underestimated because wealthier individuals tend to be underrepresented in national-level surveys, which also can fail to include foreign-earned income or returns on stocks and other investments.

Both sets of figures make several other points, including that Costa Rica has the lowest poverty rate and Honduras the worst rate of destitution. Costa Rica has the least amount of income concentration and Honduras, again, the worst

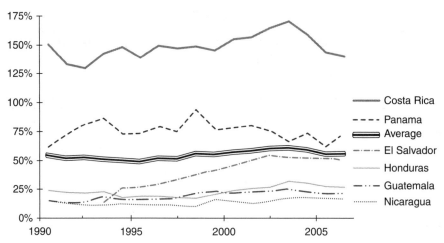

FIGURE 5.4. Social expenditures per capita (as a share of the Latin America average).
Source: CEPAL STAT (2010).

income distribution. Panama and, surprisingly, El Salvador vie for the second best slot on the isthmus. Although Panama has just more than a quarter of its population living in poverty – the second best rate in the region – the share of income its top quintile receives is higher than in El Salvador. This ranking underscores the fact that inequality and poverty rates have dropped the most in this country. Although El Salvador's measures on these indicators ranked with Guatemala, Honduras, and Nicaragua before its civil war, it has distanced itself from what remain the three most unequal societies on the isthmus, which also have the highest poverty rates. The data reveal that inequality has increased slightly in Costa Rica. Although the uppermost quintile received half of all income since 1970, its share has expanded by several percentage points. Rates of indigence in Costa Rica have dwindled to 16 percent of the population, a fall of nearly a third since 1980.

Other important social facts about the region continue to improve, as the data in Table 5.1 reveals. Average life expectancy in Central America equals the Latin American mean. In 2010, it is highest in Costa Rica, almost eighty years, and in Panama, seventy-six years. It is shorter in El Salvador, Guatemala, and Honduras, where it is in the low seventies. Of all the social indicators, life expectancy shows the least divergence among the Central American cases. The mean infant mortality rate in Central America is slightly lower than the Latin American average. The number of deaths before the age of 1 per 1,000 live births has fallen to 9.3 in Costa Rica, substantially lower than in Panama, where it is roughly 15 such deaths. It is highest in Honduras and Guatemala, where it is 24.6 and 22.6, respectively. At eighteen, El Salvador and Nicaragua's infant mortality rates are not far behind those of the worst performers on the isthmus. Illiteracy rates are worse in Central America than in Latin America.

By 2010, the Central American average was almost twice as high as the Latin American mean: 17 percent vs. 8.3 percent.

A review of the data on public expenditures for health, education, and pensions suggest that they track the central pattern identified here, one whereby Costa Rica and Panama routinely outperform their counterparts on the isthmus on key social indicators. If the average Central American country spends half of the Latin American mean, only Costa Rica spends in excess of it, with Panama spending about three quarters of the regional average between 1990 and 2008 (see Figure 5.4). In per capita terms, their expenditures have fallen with time, with Costa Rica channeling about 125 percent of the regional mean, down from a high of 171 percent in 2003. Guatemala, Honduras, and Nicaragua spend the least on social programs, with Guatemalan and Honduras vying for last place on the isthmus. Although social expenditures per capita in Guatemala, Honduras, and Nicaragua have doubled between 1990 and 2007, they have grown more distant from the regional mean with time. El Salvador no longer ranks among the worst performers; indicators suggest that it is inching toward the opposite pole. The government of El Salvador has increased its per capita expenditures at the fastest rate on the isthmus. They doubled between 1993 (the first year for which data is available) and 2002, when they reached 55 percent of the Latin American mean. Since this high point, they have begun to fall.

Social expenditure patterns reflect divergent approaches to social protection. Only in Costa Rica and Panama has the public sector created universal social programs. These two states compensate for some of the market effects and prepare citizens to participate in a modern economy. In the remaining countries, state-supplied social programs only complement family-based efforts to maintain health, educate children, and take care of the elderly (Martínez Franzoni, 2008a). In no Central American country does the state organize insurance programs for the unemployed.

Per capita social expenditures, in other words, are not high on the isthmus. The unweighted mean for Central America between 2000 and 2005, the region's peak, was US\$278 (in constant 2000 U.S. dollars), 58 percent of the Latin American average during that period. For twenty-eight members of the Organization of Economic Cooperation and Development (OECD, 2010), the average spent on social programs per resident was US\$5,269 (in constant U.S. dollars), nearly twenty times as much. Although the Central American (and all Latin American) figures include spending on education, health, pensions, and a small array of housing and anti-poverty programs, the OECD average does not include education, but does contain the other expenditures as well as unemployment benefits and active labor market policies, programs unknown in the region.

The Redistributive Capacity of the State

Comparing social indicators with public expenditures raises the question of the effectiveness of social programs. If these expenditures are the cornerstone of the social welfare state, it becomes relevant to ask whether they reduce social

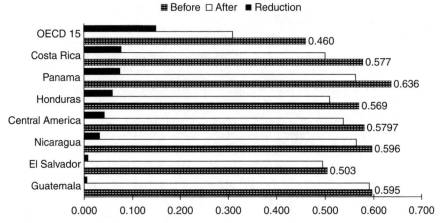

FIGURE 5.5. The impact of taxes and transfers on income inequality (Gini coefficients, mid-2000s).

Source: Barreix, Bes, and Roca (2008): 36, 88.

inequalities. A crucial way of measuring the effectiveness of the state, one vital for comprehending a state's impact on development, is whether it can modify the inequality of society. A standard way to measure the public sector's impact on inequality is to use surveys that ask citizens to identify the sources of their income and whether they benefit from social programs. In the mid-2000s, a group of researchers, sponsored by the European Union and the Inter-American Development Bank, used national-level surveys to estimate "autonomous" income (before taxes and government transfers) and "real" income (after taxes and transfers) (Barreix, Bès, and Roca, 2009). The difference between these figures, as aggregated across members of the sample, uncovers the ability of social policy to reduce inequality.

Taxes and transfers only slightly improve income distribution. Figure 5.5 displays data on the distribution of income before and after taxes, as measured by Gini coefficients. (Lower scores indicate more equality.) It shows that Panama has the most unequal distribution of autonomous income (0.636) and that El Salvador has the least (0.503). The average for Central America is 0.580. Data on the distribution of post-tax and –transfer income indicate that Costa Rica and Panama have the most effective states. Each reduces income inequality by 13.6 percent and 11.4 percent, respectively. Each therefore does better than the Central American mean, which redistributes 7.4 percent of pre-tax and pre-transfer income. There are good reasons to believe that the Costa Rican state did a better job of lessening inequality in the past, although the absence of adequate surveys before and after taxes and transfers hampers these calculations, especially before the 1990s. The other states on the isthmus have little or no effect on income distribution. The Guatemalan and El Salvadoran states reduce inequality by 0.9 percent and 1.7 percent of autonomous income, respectively. The Nicaraguan state decreases the pre-tax and pre-transfer Gini coefficient by 5.4 percent.

Figure 5.5 shows that even the most effective states on the isthmus do not match the success of developed states. The Costa Rican and Panamanian states redistribute at half the rate of OECD countries. After the effects of taxes and transfers are calculated, the Gini coefficient for the OECD falls by a third. The OECD average post-tax and –transfer Gini coefficient dwindles to 0.31, which is a bit more than half the Central American average of 0.537. Impressive reductions in inequality are a product of the fact that developed states have substantial resources, which reflect both their ability to collect taxes and that they grew in tandem with their economies. Central American states, in contrast, spend less on social programs because their states collect little revenue, either in relative or absolute terms. If, by 2008, the average Central American state obtained slightly less than 14 percent of GDP, the average OECD government received more than 40 percent of the GDP. By the late 2000s, the mean per capita size of the Central American economy was slightly more than a fifth of the per capita GDP of the twelve richest European economies.

The Political Economy of Income Distribution

The inability of most Central American states to curtail the privileges of birth and class raises the question of causes. Why do some states redistribute more than others? Existing research shows that electoral competition in Latin America fuels social spending (Huber, Mustillo, and Stephens, 2008) and lessens inequality among Latin American and Caribbean countries (Huber, Nielson, Pribble, and Stephens, 2006). There are good reasons to believe that democratization helps fuel social spending, although the debate about why some democracies redistribute more than others both clarifies and muddles, as I show, the mechanisms linking competitive elections with redistributive spending.

One response to this question argues that competitive elections encourage public officials to cater to the interests of median voters. A frequently cited set of papers in political economy contends that the size of government increases as the distance between the income of the median and average voter widens (Meltzer and Richard, 1981; Romer, 1975). In elections in which candidates must win a plurality of votes, median voters become decisive voters. If lower-income voters cast ballots for the left and upper-income voters vote for the right, the candidate or party that obtains the support of the median voter wins the election. So, as inequality increases (and even if average incomes increase), median voters side with lower-income voters. Progressive social policy is then the result of this electoral coalition.

The evidence for this explanation is surprisingly thin. Simple correlations between Gini coefficients and levels of social spending (as a share of GDP) suggest more equal countries spend more on reducing inequality than more unequal countries. This finding, which has come to be known as the "Robinhood Paradox," also applies among developed countries. The existence of this paradox has shaped research on the political economy of advanced, industrial countries (Iversen, 2005), which suggests that median voters are decisive voters – ones that can swing an election and therefore determine which party wins high office – in more egalitarian societies. In more unequal countries, median voters are not pressuring elected officials to increase the size of the welfare state, either because they do not care about inequality or because politicians face few incentives to increase social spending.

Central Americans care a great deal about lowering inequality. Survey respondents in all Central – and virtually all Latin – American countries approve of state efforts to improve conditions for lower-income families. In every country but Honduras, at least 70 percent of survey respondents agree that "governments should adopt firm policies to reduce inequality" in the 2008 round of the Americas Barometer. One exception is Honduras, in which just a bare majority uphold using the state to fight inequality. (The other exception is Venezuela.) Interestingly, some of the least unequal societies (e.g., Costa Rica and Uruguay) in the region exhibit as much public support for redistribution as the most unequal societies (e.g., Panama and Brazil). Contrary to basic models in political economy, there is no cross-national support for the claim that attitudes toward redistribution vary with inequality levels.

This finding raises two implications for the political economy of redistribution, one theoretical and the other practical. The first-generation models of redistribution assume a world that is frictionless, which does not exist. It is one in which majority rule is the only feature that structures the political environment. Decades of political science research remind us that governments, even in robust democracies, retain a degree of autonomy from citizen preferences (Przeworski, 2010). How governments get elected and the structure of the state, to name two categories of rules, distort the signals sent by citizens – and empower certain aggregations of citizens (interests) at the expense of others. As a result, what citizens want has a complicated relationship with what governments do. Some governments are more responsive than others. Why?

Research on comparative political economy suggests that there are several reasons some democracies reduce inequality more than others. One approach suggests that governments are responsive to the interests of organized labor (Korpi, 1983). The larger the share of the work force that is unionized, the more likely states will respond to the interests of workers as well as to the interests of capital. Another explanation contends that ethnically complex societies undermine the social solidarity necessary to reduce inequality and fight poverty (Alesina and Glaeser, 2004; Roemer, Lee, and van der Straeten, 2007). Minorities will receive scant help from voters belonging to the majority because enough of them refuse to raise taxes to spend money on voters from different ethnic or racial groups. Yet, a final explanation emphasizes the impact of electoral laws on social spending, an argument that has received its most systematic development by Torben Iversen (2005) and also is discussed by Alesina and Glaeser (2004). More proportional electoral systems should redistribute more income because they are more inclusive of low-income voters; legislatures dominated by parties representing these interests will enact more progressive laws.

I develop statistical models to determine which of these factors shapes the redistributive effectiveness of states in Latin America and their social spending habits. I broaden the sample beyond Central America to increase the reliability of the models and place the isthmus in the broader perspective of the Latin American region as a whole. The models use the average unionization rate between 1995 and 2000 to measure the power of labor organizations. They rely on the index of ethno-linguistic fractionalization that Alberto Alesina and his colleagues (2003) developed to measure ethnic complexity. The models use the average effective number of parties (ENP) to test for the proportionality of electoral laws; I choose this indirect measure instead of using dummy variables to distinguish between plurality and proportional electoral laws because all Latin American countries use PR laws. They include a simple count of years of democracy (each of which is worth one point) and semi-democracy (each of which is worth 0.5 points) in each country since 1900. The coding was developed by Bowman, Lehoucq, and Mahoney (2005) and Mainwaring, Brinks, and Pérez-Liñán (2008) to determine whether democracy foments social spending. I use the average share of revenues, as a share of GDP between 1990 and 2004 to test for the impact of state strength on social spending. At the end of the last section of this chapter, I noted that the social spending necessary to lessen inequality expands as a state's revenue increases. The models also have GDP per capita and Gini coefficients to control for development and inequality levels.

The models use ordinary least squares (OLS) regression because Gini coefficients and social spending as a share of GDP are continuous variables. Ideally, I would model the difference between pre- and post-tax and transfers across Latin America, but such data is not available for many countries. Instead, I follow the lead of Evelyne Huber and her colleagues (2006) and use Gini coefficients of the income distribution, on the assumption that they measure the inequality of real income, that is, after taxes and transfers. I rely on cross-sectional models in 2000 and 2005 because it was not until the 1990s that political systems in Central America democratized. Most key independent variables – rates of unionization, ethnic fractionalization, and Gini coefficients (in the models of social spending) – do not change much. Moreover, there are good theoretical reasons to believe that inequality is a product of long-term historical legacies, whether economic, social, or political. As cumulative effects of the past, their impact can be measured cross-sectionally.

The first set of models suggest that unionization rates, ethnic complexity, the ENP, duration of democracy, and state strength have no discernable impact on why some countries have higher or lower rates of inequality in 2000 or 2005. In fact, these models, whose results are not shown here, reveal that none of these factors nor GDP per capita explain different rates of inequality in Latin America. Neither organizational efforts nor democratic history have much impact on reducing inequality. These results are not that different from those reached by Evelyne Huber and colleagues (2006). In a pooled time series

TABLE 5.2 *Regression Model of Social Expenditures in Latin America, 2005*

Variable	Model 1 Gini	Model 2 GDP pc	Model 3 Unions	Model 4 Ethnic	Model 5 Demo	Model 6 Revenue	Model 7 both	Model 8 Demo	Model 9 Revenue
Gini (2005)	-19.718						2.125	3.459	-5.688
	(35.136)						(28.349)	(31.024)	(29.096)
GDP per capita		0.0006					-0.000	-0.0003	0.000
(2005)		(0.000)					(0.000)	(0.0005)	(.000)
Unionization			0.346 ^{a}				0.302	0.383 ^{a}	0.242
(1996–2000)			(0.162)				(0.158)	(0.166)	(0.159)
Ethnic				-4.849			-2.916	-3.831	-2.813
Fractionalization				(6.294)			(5.131)	(5.589)	(5.367)
Years Demo since					0.110 ^{a}		0.090	0.135 ^{a}	
1900					(0.048)		(0.063)	(0.069)	
Average Revenue,						0.939 ^{b}	0.604		0.793 ^{a}
1990–2005						(0.308)	(0.338)		(0.325)
Constant	22.587	5.986 ^{a}	8.026 ^{a}	14.525 ^{b}	8.268 ^{b}	-0.786	-1.488	-4.382	1.683
	(18.096)	(2.470)	(2.457)	(2.933)	(2.139)	(4.445)	(15.689)	(16.793)	(16.245)
R^2	0.0193	0.124	0.232	0.035	0.24	0.367	0.635	0.519	0.560
Adj. R^2	-0.0420	0.070	0.181	0.024	0.198	0.327	0.416	0.300	0.36
F-Test	0.310	2.28	4.55 ^{a}	.59	5.20 ^{a}	9.29 ^{b}	2.90	2.37	2.81
N	18	18	17	18	18	18	17	17	17

^{a} $p < 0.05$
^{b} $p < 0.01$

analysis of inequality rates between 1970 and 2000 of Latin American and Caribbean countries, they find that the effect of democratic legacy is statistically significant: This variable adds 6 percent to the total explanatory power of their statistical modes. (The R^2 increases from 0.62 to 0.66.) Models that include measures of the legislative balance of power and social security expenditures double the size of this effect (the R^2 goes up to 0.73), indicating that what progressive parties do in office improves income equality. These authors also find that ethnic heterogeneity has the largest impact on differences in inequality rates, which they measure in a nonstandard way (as a dummy variable, taking on the value of one when at least 20 percent, but not more than 80 percent of the population is ethnically diverse).

The second set of models – of social spending as a share of GDP in 2000 and 2005 – shows that unionization rates, democratic history, and state strength are each associated with increased social spending. For every percentage increase in the share of the work force that was organized at the end of the twentieth century, social spending would have grown by a third of a percentage point (0.38) in 2005. For every additional year of democracy reached by 2005, social spending would have increased by 0.13 percent. Almost a percentage point of more revenue leads to a percentage point increase in spending on education, health, and old-age pensions. No other factors are statistically significant. Ethnic fractionalization does not explain cross-national variation in social spending in Latin America in 2005. Levels of development, as proxied by GDP per capita rates, are only statistically significant in models where this variable appears without any other independent variables.

Some coefficients in Table 5.2 suggest that a bundle of political factors help explain social spending levels across Latin America. Models with most variables and years of democracy (model eight) or state revenues (model nine) show that each remains statistically significant. A model with all variables neutralizes the impact of every variable (model seven) because there are important correlations between years of democracy and GDP per capita (0.676) and years of democracy and revenues (0.455).

In the aggregate, these models generate several important conclusions. First, it is incredibly hard for states to reduce inequality. The results are meager, although a history of democracy and a strong state are associated with a slightly less inegalitarian income distribution. Second, social spending is not that progressive, which is consistent with the finding that most states in Central America do little to reduce income inequality (see Figure 5.5). My model, along with the paper by Huber and her coauthors (2008), helps explain why states do a meager job of reducing inequality in the region. Although democracy allows voters to reward politicians for increasing social spending, urban-based unions channel large shares of it toward old-age pensions for urban workers and professionals (and their families) working in the formal sector. Clientelistic relations between poor voters and the state may dilute the redistributive impact of state expenditures (Taylor-Robinson, 2010). Social security systems tend to exclude the poorest citizens, which are disproportionately located in rural areas

or in the urban informal sector. The urban bias in social spending suggests that
Central American states have reproduced the duality between insiders – those
benefiting from modern social insurance programs – and outsiders – which, in
Central and South America, consist of workers in the urban informal and rural
sectors (Rueda, 2005).

These findings help explain why social spending is below the regional mean
in every Central American country, except Costa Rica. With its long democratic history (84.5 years) and a just below average share of the labor force
in unions (13.1 percent), it is not hard to understand why the Costa Rican
government spends more than 17 percent of the GDP on social programs. The
country with one of the lowest social spending rates, Guatemala (7.59 percent
of GDP) has the least experience with democratic practices (seventeen years)
and smallest share of unionized workers (4.4 percent). El Salvador, Honduras,
and Nicaragua each spend slightly more than 11 percent of GDP on social
programs and have been democratic for less than twenty years each. Although
the Sandinistas helped build a large union movement (22.6 percent of the labor
force), El Salvador and Honduras have less than 6.5 percent of their work
force in unions. With forty-three years of democratic history, the government
in Panama spends substantially below the mean. It spends 7.53 percent of its
GDP on social programs, a figure that underestimates the extent of such spending because its GDP per capita is more than twice as high as El Salvador's and
three times as high as Honduras or Nicaragua's.

Social expenditures, at these modest rates, barely decrease inequality. Despite
the shift to more open forms of political competition, spending on the poor,
the old, the young, and the sick remains low on the isthmus. Data in Figure
5.4 reminds us that only in El Salvador has democratization brought a democratic dividend. Although its per capita expenditures that have doubled since
the mid-1990s, El Salvador's social spending is half the Latin American average. Most other places, in per capita terms, are stuck at spending a quarter
of the Latin American mean. Outside of Costa Rica, Honduras, and Panama,
social spending does little to reduce the privileges of birth and class, as Figure
5.4 reveals.

Higher and Lower Quality Democracy

Persistently low levels of social spending in most of the isthmus raise troublesome questions about the nature of its democracies. Central Americans want
the state to reduce inequalities, as the Americas Barometer reveals, but states
do not comply. Why not? Is this the result of a deficient party system that
encourages elected leaders to neglect citizen preferences? Is it low voter turnout
rates? Or do weak states hamstring elected officials (and citizens)?

Comparative assessments of democracy indicate that, with the exception
of Costa Rica (and the partial exception of Panama), most of the isthmus's
democracies do not rank highly, although each is rated above the mean for
the 128 developing countries that are regularly studied by the Bertelsmann

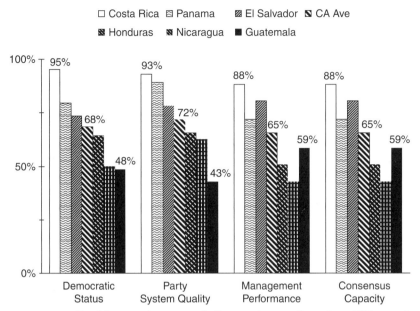

FIGURE 5.6. Rankings on democracy indicators (percentile rank on BTI, 2010).
Source: Bertelsmann Transformation Index (2010).

Transformation Index (BTI; Bertelsmann Stiftung, 2010). Data in Figure 5.6 show that the status of democracy in Costa Rica and Panama is the highest in Central America. On this composite measure of key items on the BTI questionnaire, Costa Rica's democracy ranks at the 95th percentile (or sixth best in the world). Panama's comes in at the 80th percentile (or twenty-sixth highest). El Salvador is ranked in the 73rd percentile (or thirty-fourth best), meaning it surpasses the Central American average (which is equal to the Latin American average) at the 68th percentile (or fortieth slot). The quality of democracy in Honduras, Nicaragua, and Guatemala fall in at 64th, 50th, and 48th percentile (or forty-sixth, sixty-fourth, and sixty-sixth from the top).

Figure 5.6 contains information useful for assessing the quality of democratic institutions on the isthmus, each of which was used to compute the democratic status index. The quality of the party system, which is measured by a question about how stable, socially rooted, and moderate a party system is, echoes the overall ranking of the democratic status index. On the ability of each country's political leadership to chart and maintain a policy course, the ranking remains the same, although there is a slight fall in percentile category under management performance. These results are repeated under consensus capacity, that is, the ability to build overall support for development policies. Guatemala and Nicaragua switch places regarding the democracy measures (the first two sets of columns in Figure 5.6) and governance indicators (last two sets). The most populated country on the isthmus performs the worst on two

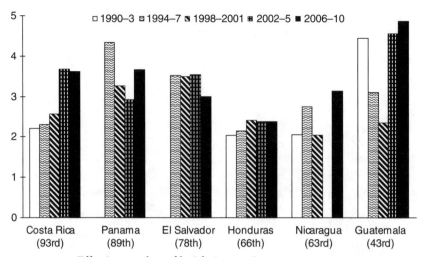

FIGURE 5.7. Effective number of legislative parties, 1990–2010.
Note: Percentile ranks on party system quality on BTI 2010 are in parentheses. Missing bars either mean that an election was undemocratic or was not scheduled during the chart's intervals.
Sources: McGallagher (2010) for most countries; Jones (2008) for Guatemala.

democracy measures, especially regarding the quality of its party system. The Nicaraguan executive comes in at last place in its ability to manage political conflicts and build consensus for national-level policies.

Ranking on this international index of democracy is highly correlated with the age of democracy on the isthmus. Costa Ricans have been practicing democratic politics for 73 years (or 84.5 years if each year of semi-democracy is added at half a year rate), from 1900 until 2005. Panamanians have racked up 20 years of democracy (and 43 years of democracy and semi-democracy). Salvadorans come in third place, with twelve years of democracy (and seventeen years with the combined score). Nicaraguans come in fourth place with ten years of democracy (and a total score of 19.5 years). Hondurans have had a regime that meets minimal conditions for seven years (and twenty-two years for a combined score). Guatemalans have been practicing semi-democratic politics for a total of seventeen years.

Party Systems
The rankings in Figure 5.6 about the quality of the party systems on the isthmus parallel the overall nature of democracy itself. Costa Rica, notwithstanding the turbulence of the first decade of the twenty-first century, has the most stable, socially rooted, and ideologically centrist party system in Central America; Guatemala has the least structured, socially or ideologically anchored party on the isthmus.

These rankings are no surprise for observers of the Central American scene. Regardless of their approach, studies of the parties and party systems would agree that the most responsive and democratic parties systems exist in Costa Rica, Panama, and, to a lesser extent, in El Salvador (Artiga-González, 2008; España-Najera, 2009; Jones, 2008; PENR, 2008). There is widespread agreement that the other party systems of the isthmus should score substantially lower, with Guatemala's falling below the developing world's mean.

Figure 5.7 shows that the effective number of legislative parties does not vary with rankings on the BTI's Party System Quality index. Excluding one-party systems, which typically exist in autocracies, the number of parties does not shape the stability, rootedness (or popular acceptance), or ideological thrust of a party. With the exception of El Salvador and Honduras, most party systems have been volatile. The number of parties has fluctuated since 1990.

In Costa Rica, the bipolar system – one that pits a cohesive party against a coalition of adversaries, according to Fernández González (1991) – that came into existence in 1982, fell apart and swiftly transformed into a three-party system by 2002. The shift from bipolar to multi-party competition results from more than two decades' worth of criticism of a system dominated by the Party of National Liberation (PLN), founded by José Figueres and the other social reformers in 1951, and the United Social Christian Party (PUSC), created by smaller parties in the early 1980s, including parties that fought on opposite sides of the 1948 civil war (Rovira Mas, 2001). More educated urban voters found this bipolar system, dating from 1982, antiquated, unresponsive, and too neoliberal (Sánchez, 2007). Since 2002, the PLN has come under fire from a party disputing its position on the center-left. The Citizen Action Party's (PAC) surprise showing in 2002 and 2006 not only put it in reach of the presidency by 2006 – coming within a percentage point of winning this race – but also forced the PLN and PUSC into a runoff in 2002, the first since 1936 (Lehoucq, 2004). The fragmentation in the party system also was a product of the PUSC's implosion by the 2006 elections. The party's fortunes precipitously fell when two of its leaders – Rafael Angel Calderón Fournier and Miguel Angel Rodríguez – were placed under house arrest for charges of corruption and influence trafficking in 2004. The inability of its last president, Abel Pacheco (2002–6) to enact a tax reform or approve a free-trade agreement, also contributed to its dramatic fall in the polls. Since 2006, the Costa Rican party system has revolved around three main contenders in the assembly.

In Panama, volatility is a result of newness, of parties struggling to find popular support. The effective number of parties competing for the presidency is an average of 4.53 between 1994 and 2004. It climbs to 6.26 for congressional races. This divergence between the number of parties fielding candidates for the presidency and the assembly is a result of the fact that legislative districts are, on average, the most disproportional not only in Central America, but in Latin America as a whole. Disproportionality indices reveal that this ratio is more than twice the Latin American average, with Guatemala slightly more disproportional than the regional average, and every other Central American legislative electoral system at or below the Latin American mean (Payne, 2007: 61). Almost half of legislative seats are apportioned in single-member, often rural districts, whose seats go to the candidate amassing more votes than his or her rivals. Parties respond to these incentives by coalescing in presidential elections, but running separate and highly local campaigns for the assembly, where many compete, but few win congressional representation. The effective number of legislative parties, as a result, drops to an average of 3.5 in Panamanian elections (Brown Araúz, 2009: 93, 141).

In El Salvador, the three-party system has remained stable since 1994 (Artiga-González, 2004; 2009). Next to Honduras's, this country's party system has displayed the most stability. Its key parties are the FMLN on the left and ARENA on the right. In between the left and the right, smaller groupings exist, including the Christian Democratic Party (PDC) and the Party of National Conciliation (PCN). Each party was much more influential in the past. The PDC led a decade-long opposition to military governments in the 1960s, and apparently won the 1972 elections before election results were annulled. It resurfaced in the 1980s before winning the 1985 presidential elections, the last time it had control of the presidency. The PCN was the party military governments organized in the years before the civil war. As both centrist and pragmatic (or, as their critics allege, opportunistic) parties, the PDC and the PCN have become the minor, but indispensable members of coalitions led by ARENA. Not once in six legislative elections, which are held every three years, has the president's party held a legislative majority. Only since 2009, when the FMLN finally won the presidency, have they begun to negotiate with the FMLN to enact the executive's legislative agenda.

Two-party or at least bipolar systems exist in Honduras and Nicaragua, although the latter's has become less predictable with time. For decades, Honduran politics has been dominated by competition between the Liberal and National Parties. Its parties are the oldest in Central America, dating from the first decades of the twentieth century. Nicaraguan politics was for decades swamped by a rivalry between the Conservative and Liberal Parties, one that the four-decade-long Somoza dictatorship pacified. After the Sandinista's 1990 election loss, partisan competition revolved around a plethora of smaller parties, based on Liberal Party and defunct Conservative Party factions, battling the FSLN. Factionalism is reflected in the increase to three parties in the 2006 Nicaraguan elections.

In Guatemala, the volatility in the effective number of parties reflects two characteristics of the underlying political landscape. In the first place, it stems from parties that cannot establish roots in the electorate. In Guatemala, few survive beyond two electoral cycles (Sánchez, 2008). No one but Vinicio Cerezo (1985–90), who became the first elected president when the military returned to the barracks, has been elected as a Christian Democrat (DCG) for president. Neither Jorge Serrano (1990–3) of the Solidarity Action Movement (MAS) nor Alvaro Arzú (1994–9) of the National Advancement Party (PAN) helped build parties capable of winning future elections. President Serrano tried to pull off an *auto-golpe* or, more accurately, an incumbent takeover, one involving closing congress so he could govern unimpeded by legislative oversight. Selected in a congressional vote, his successor, Ramiro de León Carpio (1993–5), the human rights ombudsman, finished Serrano's term without founding a new party. The attempt by former military president, Efrain Ríos-Montt (1982–3), to return and establish a long-lasting presidency came to naught. Unable to run for the presidency because of a 1985 constitutional ban on de facto presidents running for office, his party – the Guatemalan Republican Party (FRG) – nominated Alfonso Portillo, who won the 1999 ballot. Holding the presidency and a comfortable majority in congress, the FRG manipulated several laws that permitted the former dictator to register his candidacy for the 2003 elections. After more than a decade of efforts, it was the voters who refused to hand him the presidency. Ríos-Montt came in third place, polling less than 18 percent, in a race won by Oscar Berger, a former mayor of Guatemala City, of the National Grand Alliance (GANA) (Azpuru, 2005). Neither he nor his successor, Alvaro Colom of the National Unity of Hope Party (UNE), appears to be establishing more than ephemeral parties.

In the second place, an inchoate party system reflects the absence of partisan attachments among legislators and citizens. A major study reveals that 43 percent of deputies have switched parties since 1990 in Guatemala (Fortín, 2010), a figure with no rival on the isthmus. In terms of the percentage of citizens who identify with a party, Guatemalans come in last place in surveys of all Latin American countries (and Belize, Canada, Guyana, and the United States). An average of 15 percent of Guatemalans surveyed in 2006 and 2008 identify with a political party. The average for Panama is 26 percent. The regional mean is 35 percent. Comparative averages for the other countries on the isthmus are 33 percent for Costa Rica, 36 percent for El Salvador, 45 percent for Nicaragua, and 46 percent for Honduras. Above average regional rates in Nicaragua and Honduras are a product of dominant and long-lasting parties. Although the Sandinistas have failed to attract the support of a majority of Nicaraguans, they have the allegiance of a large minority of voters. Liberal and National Party identities among Hondurans reflect support for long-lasting electoral vehicles, ones that date since the beginning of the twentieth century. Average rates in Costa Rica are the result of a long-term process of dealignment, a product of the growth of an educated and urban electorate and of a party establishment's difficulty in reconnecting with a more demanding citizenry (Sánchez, 2007).

Most party systems on the isthmus are non-ideological. Parties appear to be vehicles of electoral strong men, in which adherents openly identify themselves as members of a hierarchically organized party faction. Their policy platforms play a secondary role in parties that make personality-oriented appeals to voters. The Guatemalan, Honduran, and Panamanian party systems score 1.52, 0.75, and 0.57 on a scale of 1 to 10, with 10 being a party system having rival and even polarized ideological appeals (Jones, 2010: 34; also, see Zoco,

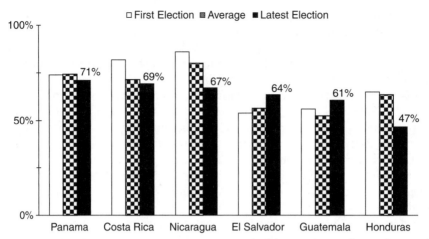

FIGURE 5.8. Voter turnout rates, 1990–2010 (valid votes, as a share of registered voters).
Source: Artiga-González (2008).

2006). These scores reflect the absence of leftist parties, an ideological vacuum that encourages right-wing and centrist parties to emphasize leadership-based appeals and patronage-oriented politics (Taylor, 1996). Without a popular party espousing an anti-establishment discourse, conservative politicians face few incentives to develop parties able to defend established privileges and attract widespread support.

The party systems of Costa Rica are also largely non-ideological, scoring 0.7 on Jones's scale. Unlike Guatemala, Honduras, and Panama, however, the absence of ideological polarization does not signify the absence of progressive social and economic policies. Rather, the slight differences between center-left and center-right parties mean that most parties are reformist in orientation. In Costa Rica, even the defunct Social Christian Unity Party (PUSC), a creature principally of President Rafael Angel Calderón Fournier (1990–4) and secondarily of Miguel Angel Rodríguez (1998–2002), became a successful center-right party because it never called for dismantling the country's welfare state. A Libertarian Movement (ML) remains small, if occasionally a key player in legislative coalitions, because a majority of voters endorses the social welfare policies that have created societies with the best social and political indicators in the developing world (Sandbrook et al., 2007).

The most ideological systems are those in El Salvador and Nicaragua. The Nicaraguan parties, with a score of 5.66, are the second most ideological on the isthmus and in Latin America. The party system of El Salvador obtains a ten, making it the most ideologically polarized party system of Latin America. Policy differences reflect the intense struggle between left and right, between the FMLN and ARENA in El Salvador, and the Sandinistas and their ideological opponents in Nicaragua. It is no accident that the two societies that

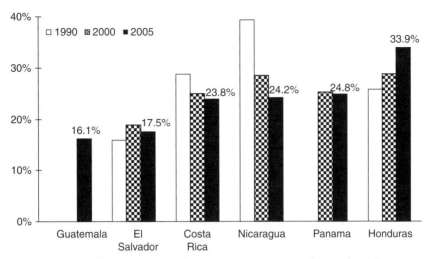

FIGURE 5.9. Public sector expenditures, 1990–2005 (nonfinancial public sector, as a share of GDP).
Note: Data is not available for Guatemala for 1990 and 2000 and for Panama 1990.
Source: ICEFI (2007).

exploded in civil war in the 1970s and 1980s remain polarized, although no longer at war. In both countries, powerful left-wing movements either forced the right to negotiate a peace accord (El Salvador) or revolutionaries overthrew a right-wing dictatorship (Nicaragua). Ideological polarization has undercut the viability of centrist parties because large numbers of voters identify with the left or the right, a characteristic that helps maintain partisan polarization.

Voter turnout rates help explain why accountability improves with the age of democracy. Data in Figure 5.8 shows that the average turnout rate between 1990 and 2010 roughly follows how long a country has been democratic. That Nicaragua has the largest mean rate of participation reflects, in part, its ideological polarization (Barnes, 1998), a factor often associated with turnout because parties have incentives to mobilize support, preventing their rivals from winning elections. (This factor is much less predictive of social expenditures in the statistical model in Table 5.2, which makes the point that it is an intervening variable.) That Costa Rica does not have the highest turnout rate is a product of the fact that its rate of electoral participation fell during the 1990s as a result of citizen disenchantment with established parties (Raventós Vorst et al., 2005). Low average rates in El Salvador and Guatemala help explain why their social expenditures are below expectations. Along with the FMLN's inability to win a presidential election until 2009, low voter turnout explains why spending on education, health care, and pensions are meager in El Salvador. Indeed, the failure of the left to win a presidential election until 2009 contributes to citizen apathy in this country. Low voter turnout rates in Guatemala are another mechanism that explains why lack of a democratic history leads to the chronic underfunding of social programs in Guatemala (Lehoucq and Wall, 2004).

State Capacity

Underfunded and poorly staffed states hamper progressive social reform. Precisely where democratic institutions do little to respond to majority wishes, elected officials are saddled with defective states. One state – Guatemala – has not begun to construct a social contract in which exporters and other investors accept taxation in exchange for growth-enhancing public investments. Effective rates of taxation remain low – the lowest in Latin America – because capitalists and financiers refuse to fund a state they perceive as parasitical (Fuentes and Cabrera, 2006), one whose penury maintains its backwardness and seemingly confirms the fears of Guatemalans who can afford to pay for a better state. In El Salvador, the right's acceptance of the left's 2009 presidential victory signals the deepening of this consensus, one vital for the social investments needed to improve the country's economic competitiveness.

Data in Figure 5.9 reveal the states that redistribute the least (see Figure 5.5) – Guatemala and El Salvador – also spend the least. These are essential components of a set of characteristics found in an impressive review of taxation and expenditure patterns (Fuentes, 2007). They have the smallest states, as a share of GDP. The four other states have public expenditures that are roughly a quarter of GDP. These figures reflect spending by the central state apparatus, which consists of the three branches of government (including the executive ministries), and the nonfinancial public sector. Non-central state expenditures stem from spending by the decentralized agencies, state institutions often containing sources of revenue and constitutionally protected autonomy. Although not an insubstantial amount of money, most states spend far less than the OECD average, which is in excess of 40 percent of GDP.

Most states are organizationally primitive (Ramírez Cover, 2011). More than a quarter of the 946 ministries, bureaus, and agencies of the isthmus's public sector are in the region's second least populated country, Costa Rica. There is a state agency for every 17,000 residents in Costa Rica. With only 313,000 inhabitants, the 102 agencies of Belize make a weightier state in these terms. Panama and El Salvador, respectively, come in third and fourth place with a state body for every 32,000 and 38,000 residents. Nicaragua and Panama have a public agency for every 55,000 and 82,000 individuals, respectively. Guatemala has the smallest state: There is scarcely a state body for every 150,000 individuals.

These ratios reinforce the existence of bureaucracies of inferior quality, with one exception. Virtually all states rank substantially below the Latin American mean in an assessment of the quality of public bureaucracies in the mid-2000s sponsored by the Inter-American Development Bank. On a scale of 1 to 100 (with 100 being the best score), the mean for the Functional Capacity Index – essentially, how existing procedures and practices strengthen civil servants' commitment to public service – is 30. With the exception of Costa Rica, all

Central American states score 17 or worse, with Honduras coming in at last place having a score of 11. On this measure of bureaucratic quality, Costa Rica comes in third of 19 countries, with a score of 48. (The civil service in Brazil and Chile achieve scores of 61 and 57, respectively.) Much the same rankings obtain in a Merit and Civil Service Development Index (Zuvanic, Iacoviello, and Rodríguez Gusta, 2010).

These facts reveal a profound truth about the design and nature of public institutions in the region's most advanced state (Lehoucq, 2010). It was the long-term and simmering political stalemate – one that could turn violent if any party became politically marginalized – that not only prompted politicians to abandon violence, but also encouraged them to develop an innovative constitutional design that would be the backdrop for above-average public policies. The 1949 Constitution entrusts the central and decentralized government sectors with different government functions, a principle of constitutional design that embodies what Bruce Ackerman (2000) calls the new separation of powers. Health care, old-age pensions, and monetary policy are among the areas whose budgets the executive does not propose and the legislature does not approve. Unlike the checks and balances (or Madisonian) version of the separation of powers, the new separation of powers does not compel the parts of government to share responsibility over all or even many governmental functions. The 1949 constitution instead isolates key bureaucratic responsibilities from the vicissitudes of partisan politics. By fragmenting state power, the constitution promotes consensual styles of policy making that, in tandem with regularly held elections, keep elected officials focused on the median – lower income – voter.

That the elected government branches are isolated from electoral administration and adjudication is the best example of the functional specialization at the core of the Costa Rican constitutional tradition. Constituent Assembly delegates built on the 1946 Electoral Code to create the TSE. They scrapped a central tenet of classical constitutional theory, which had entrusted the executive with organizing elections and had delegated certifying their results to the legislative branch of government (Lehoucq, 2002). Made a branch of government equal to the other three in 1975, the TSE is solely responsible for calling elections, appointing members of all polling stations, and interpreting legal and constitutional provisions relating to electoral matters.

Creating the decentralized sector or the autonomous institutions was part of the constitutional convention's effort to remove functions of the modern state from the purview of the elected branches. As of 2004, there were more than fifty-five autonomous institutions in Costa Rica, twelve of which were created in the years before 1950 (Alfaro Redondo, 2004). Rodrigo Facio, a social democratic delegate at the 1949 Constituent Assembly (and a distinguished author), argued before the assembly's conservative majority that, in his words, "constitutionalizing" the autonomy of certain institutions was simply recognizing that state reformers had gradually created islands of technical competence to insulate core governmental functions from the passions of electoral politics (Castro Vega, 2003: 197–198). Perhaps the most prominent of these were the CCSS and the University of Costa Rica, both founded in 1943. In 1949, the assembly ratified the revolutionary junta's decision to create, among other bodies, an autonomous Central Bank (Facio became its first director) and the ICE. In later years, elected officials created the Mixed Institute of Social Assistance (1971), the National Institute of Housing and Urban Issues (1954), and the National Ward for the Blind (1957).

The PLN was responsible for creating most decentralized institutions. It created 67 percent (or twenty-nine) of the forty-three autonomous institutions established between 1953 and 2004, when most decentralized agencies were created. Put differently, the PLN erected an average of 1.32 autonomous institutions for each of the twenty-nine years it controlled the executive branch during this fifty-one-year period. Its more conservative rivals, in contrast, established 33 percent of these agencies or an average of 0.55 decentralized agencies for every year during the twenty-two years they held the presidency. Programmatic differences between the PLN and its conservative rivals perhaps help explain why the PLN won more elections. Voters, especially lower-income ones, stuck with the party because it delivered on its policy promises to expand the welfare state. That the PLN's opponents did create autonomous institutions (and never closed or underfunded one) makes the point that every party faced incentives to maintain and even expand social policy objectives.

Economic Decline and Regime Decay

The central findings of this chapter – that democratization has been limited and most states continue to ignore citizen demands for more redistribution – raise an important question: Why have half the countries of the isthmus seen authoritarian regressions?

Chapter 4, which discusses the economic wreckage caused by the civil war, suggests an answer, one linking the lack of economic growth with regime breakdown (Bernhard et al., 2001; Bueno de Mesquita et al., 2003; Przeworski et al., 2000). There are, however, at least two reasons to be skeptical of this argument. First, Chapter 2 demonstrates that the economic downturn followed the political crises in the countries that experienced civil war. It was the inability of reactionary despotism to open up that led to civil war and economic recession or collapse, even if the fall in the region's terms of trade, coupled with balance-of-payments crises (and bungled responses to these external shocks), made matters worse and were the principal causes for the lost decade in Costa Rica and Panama. Second, politics in El Salvador has not succumbed to authoritarian temptation. Although the civil war disrupted its prewar economic trajectory, violent conflict liquidated reactionary despotism in this country. Armed conflict led a realignment of political preferences around support for democratic practices.

Perhaps it is sinking deeper into poverty, rather than recession per se, that unravels commitments to open political systems. At the extreme, incomes can become so low that state authority collapses and ushers in a period of ongoing civil war (Bates, 2008). So, even if transitions away from authoritarian rule can occur at any level of per capita income, these political experiments are less likely to consolidate at lower levels of development (Przeworski, 2008). Recent statistics show that this work likely underestimates the rate at which young democracies collapse; democratic or quasi-democratic regimes that have not survived for twenty years are much more likely – approximating a 50-percent risk versus half as much for older systems – to break down than similar regimes that have longer life spans (Svolik, 2008). What are the mechanisms that link poverty and regime decay?

One response is that citizens become disaffected with democracy as their incomes fall. That voter turnout rates are the lowest in Honduras and Guatemala (see Figure 5.8), two of the least functional political systems on the isthmus, is consistent with this line of reasoning. Nicaragua is an exception to this generalization, although its turnout rate has been dropping since 1990. Similarly, Mitchell A. Seligson and John A. Booth (2010: 133), in an ambitious public opinion project on Central America, note that Honduras was, in the years before Zelaya was toppled, the Latin American country "with the highest level of triply dissatisfied citizens, with relatively low support for democracy, and with high support for coups, confrontational political methods, and rebellion." Guatemalan public opinion suffers from a similar syndrome, which Seligson and Booth argue creates an environment in which politicians can play chicken because none fear the costs of holding rivals (and voters) hostage to their demands. If voters blame all politicians for the intransigence of some officials, democratic accountability breaks down. If public opinion does not reward responsible behavior, then citizens unwittingly encourage all politicians, at a minimum, to remain self-interested, if not corrupt and extremist.

Booth and Seligson's (2009) research, however, cautions against concluding that the lack of growth corrodes popular allegiances with democracy. Although recession leads to disaffection and protest activity, this research shows that economic decline does not undermine support for democratic values and institutions. Citizens do not give up on democracy. It is elites who typically undermine democracy. It was the economic elite in each country that benefited from and supported the blatantly autocratic old order. It is members of the political class that have taken the decisions in several Central American republics to prevent the deepening of democracy. Why?

An answer to this question – and another explanation of the relationship between impoverishment and regime decay – focuses on the incentives officeholders face. Becoming just another part of the opposition in economies with few income-generating opportunities is an option inferior to devising (ingenious) ways of staying in power. These are presumably the calculations presidents make, which explains why, in Honduras, the military in association with the supreme court and congress, ousted President Zelaya in 2009 when he began to fidget about running for consecutive reelection. These are among the motives that explain why, in Nicaragua, the Ortega faction of the Sandinistas joined President Alemán and his faction of the liberals to erect barriers to entry for third parties by the late 1990s. On returning to power in 2006, President Ortega later got sympathetic supreme court magistrates to declare the prohibition against consecutive reelection for executives unconstitutional.

It is hard to avoid the conclusion that presidentialism has aggravated political conflict. Systems with executives elected independently of the legislature break down more often than parliamentary or semi-presidential systems, even if there is disagreement about the reasons they are more fragile than their counterparts (Cheibub, 2007). There is little debate that minority presidents face incentives to plan an assault on the other branches of government, especially when their legislative contingents are small and the economy is not growing (Kim and Bahry, 2008). In both Honduras and Nicaragua, Zelaya and Alemán began their terms with parties controlling 48 and 45 percent of legislative seats, respectively; these contingents got smaller as legislators defected from the president's coalition to endorse future presidential contenders. In Guatemala, legislative majorities repeatedly opposed President Serrano's minority government, one with the allegiances of only 16 percent of the legislature, which set the stage for his (failed) attempt to create a dictatorship by closing congress. In these circumstances – and in the context of poor (and stagnating) economies – separation of power systems magnify the losses associated with relinquishing presidential control, losses that erode confidence that incumbents will accept their defeat at the polls.

Conclusion

Optimism about the ability of regime change to transform the region has waned, and not only because reality seldom measures up to expectations about the future. Although elections continue to select political leaders, confrontations between the branches of government have led to breakdowns or the weakening of horizontal accountability. In Guatemala, Honduras, and Nicaragua, authoritarian features have been combined with existing arrangements to halt or reverse democratization.

Electoral competition has done little to diminish income inequality, perhaps the single best measure of the effectiveness of a state, especially of a democratic one. Despite support for public action to narrow the gap between the rich and the poor, governments have been unable to develop policies that increase the relative incomes of the poor, even if the share of the population living in poverty has fallen from 60 to 50 percent between 1990 and 2008. Only three states – Costa Rica, Panama, and Honduras – manage to lessen the burdens of inequality. The first two spend more than the Latin American average on health, education, and pensions. Honduras does not, and still manages to make a dent on inequality, one whereby its effectiveness is slightly above the Central American mean. To a lesser extent, this is the pattern in Nicaragua, which redistributes incomes below this average. The governments of El Salvador and Guatemala have no effect on inequality. The distribution of asset works to maintain the wide gap between rich and poor in what Chapter 4 demonstrated to be two slow-growth societies.

My statistical model indicates that the age of democracy, along with the percentage of the labor force that is unionized, accounts for social spending differences among the Latin American countries, not just Central American ones. Two factors explain why the duration of democracy increases state capacity to ameliorate the injuries of class. First, older democracies, such as Costa Rica's, have party systems that convert citizen demands for social services into spending on education, health, and social security, which labor unions funnel toward their urban-based constituents. Second, older democracies have more effective states, ones that collect a larger share of GDP in the form of taxes and are more organizationally dense. The last explanation contains perhaps the most profound indictment because it argues that, independent of the quality of their democratic procedures, states are primitive. Simply put, they are incapable of becoming an instrument of a democratic majority.

These results help identify the reasons experience improves democracy. Time makes parties in competitive systems more accountable because experience helps voters distinguish credible from irresponsible policy promises (Keefer, 2007). Once campaigning for the support of voters is the only route to power, politicians invest their time in organizing parties, recruiting candidates and policy advisors, and persuading voters to cast ballots in their favor. They often design electoral and party legislation to make democracy more responsive to citizen concerns because politicians attuned to public opinion accumulate votes. Political systems like Costa Rica's also benefit from a vibrant press, free of state harassment, monopolistic control by influential private sector groups, and professionally run (Rockwell and Janus, 2003).

Lack of economic growth has done little to consolidate incipient democratic institutions, though not because it reduces public support for democracy. Citizens back democracy, even if they express dissatisfaction with existing regimes in much of the region. Economic stagnation undermines democracy because it encourages incumbents to manipulate electoral laws and the mechanisms of horizontal accountability to remain in power, a temptation that increases as levels of development fall. Only institutions that defuse power, that ensure that electoral loss is not associated with political and economic marginalization, break the link between underdevelopment and the decay of democracy. This is perhaps the single most important legacy of reactionary despotism; by making civil war the route to modernity, the military regimes of the past imposed a huge burden on future generations.

Conclusion

On the eve of U.S. participation in World War I (1917–8), Dana Munro, an economics graduate student from the University of Pennsylvania traveled, not infrequently by horseback, in Central America. Munro would write *The Five Republics of Central America* (Munro, 1918) and, even later, refashion many of the letters he sent his parents as a traveler's account (Munro, 1983). Both are remarkable, not only for their vivid descriptions of political life in countries dominated by dictatorship, but also for the thesis that political instability contributed to underdevelopment – an argument unfortunately forgotten in subsequent decades, when scholarship assumed that the region's model of economic development made autocracy inevitable.

More than sixty years later, I found myself traveling in the region, although mostly by airplane, bus, and car. Like the young Munro, I too went to Central America in search of answers to basic questions about the nature of political instability. Like my predecessor, I landed in a region very much the target of U.S. foreign policy makers. Although Munro analyzed the consequences of the U.S. decision to prop up a conservative regime in Nicaragua between 1913 and 1933 (that would involve deploying marines), I observed the impact of U.S. foreign policy, based on fighting communists, six decades later. As in Munro's youth, U.S. policy toward the region in the 1980s was controversial and the staple of the daily news.

This chapter begins by discussing the implications raised by this book for central debates in comparative politics and comparative political economy, ones addressing the nature and rhythm of civil war, democratization, and the political dynamics of inequality. I turn the spotlight on the field to ask whether our most rigorous, cross-national findings can make sense of continuity and change in the macropolitics of six societies, most of which belong to what Paul Collier refers to as bottom-billion societies. More progress has been made, I suggest, in understanding the dynamics of income redistribution and why democratization falters than in explaining transitions from democracy and especially the origins of civil war.

I then identify continuities and changes since the decade of revolt and revolution. Several political systems in Central America deliver poor governance; they are fragile and have deteriorated. Yet, as meager as this record is, there has been more change since 1980 than in the long half-century between Munro's initial encounter with the region and my own. By far the biggest change has been the overthrow of reactionary despotism. Key social indicators have continued to improve, even if relative levels of development have barely recovered their prewar high points.

Central Findings and their Implications

The main conclusion of Chapter 2 is that it was a political crisis that led to the descent into violence in Central America. Political systems that resisted change – that is, created obstacles to a genuine rotation of the executive – are what fueled the shift from contesting elections, to street protest, and then to guerrilla warfare. The cross-national, quantitative research that attempts to test for the effects of regime type on political stability, therefore, is in the best position to explain developments on the isthmus.

The cross-national, quantitative research stressing the role of economic and social triggers of violent conflict is of limited use. The first of its two central findings – that countries with larger populations are more likely to experience civil war – adds little to understanding why the microstates of Central America witnessed the loss of so much life. The second of its findings – that poorer countries are more likely to witness the outbreak of violent conflict – sheds a bit more light on the rhythm of politics on the isthmus. The wealthiest pair of countries – Costa Rica and Panama – did remain peaceful. Two of the countries that underwent civil war – El Salvador and Guatemala – were among the poorer countries in GDP per capita terms. The poorest society – Honduras – did not, however, witness an insurgency. Nicaragua, which saw its revolt turn into a social revolution, had a GDP per capita rate remarkably close to Panama's until the mid-1970s. Moreover, none of the countries on the isthmus, at that time, was unusually poor by world standards. GDP per capita levels, with the exceptions of El Salvador and Honduras, placed them slightly below the global mean until the late 1970s. GDP per capita rates had been falling in El Salvador during the post–World War II period and had reached 60 percent of the global average by the late 1970s. Honduras continued its long slide since the late 1920s (Pérez-Brignoli, 2011); by the late 1970s, its GDP per capita rate hovered around half the world average. Broader social conditions, as limited as they were, were better than the developing world's averages (Table 1.3). Illiteracy rates were lower everywhere except in Guatemala, where they were at the developing world's mean. Life expectancy was higher in every country, with the Central American average in 1980 higher – at 66.5 years – than even the Latin American mean. Infant mortality, even at the 1980 high of 67.1 deaths (by age one) per 1,000 live births in Guatemala, was only two-thirds of the way to the developing world average at the time.

The argument that inequality breeds civil war has mixed results, despite the theoretical appeal of the timeless claim that political violence should become pervasive in societies wracked by stark differences between the rich and the poor. Only a handful of the research papers on civil war (Boix, 2008; Muller and Seligson, 1987) find statistically significant results between inequality and civil war. Many other researchers do not even test for inequality because cross-national datasets are of limited quality, especially in the decades before the 1990s. An examination of the available evidence indicates that income inequality was no worse in 1980 than it had been a decade earlier. Only in El Salvador did the income of the wealthiest 10 percent increase between 1970 and 1980. So, to the extent that existing indices accurately measure inequality, the distance between social classes was not worsening in most of Central America.

It is true that an alternative measure of social deterioration – that of working-class wages – reveals that standards of living were declining throughout the 1970s everywhere political polarization spiraled into civil war. Only in Costa Rica, Honduras, and Panama, which did not experience civil war, did wages not fall during this decade. Nevertheless, the rapid decline in the external terms of trade in the late 1970s did produce the recessions that led to declining incomes in the 1980s. Yet, scrutiny of these trends suggests that conflict did not follow the fall in wages; instead, polarization, the increase in urban protest, and rural insurgency preceded the decline in real wages in El Salvador, Guatemala, and Nicaragua. It was a decline in investment in reaction to political uncertainty that led to inflation and therefore to the fall in the purchasing power of wages – a chain of events inconsistent with the claim that deteriorating economic conditions typically precede political conflict. Although the fall of working-class incomes likely contributed to polarization, it was a regime crisis of epic proportions that triggered the economic and social decomposition on the isthmus.

Some of the cross-national, statistical research explores the consequences of regime types on the outbreak of civil war (Goldstone et al., 2010). One of the most well-known studies (Gates et al., 2006) contends that "institutionally inconsistent polities" – systems that have both democratic and autocratic characteristics – are the most likely to experience civil war. My own results agree with the thrust of this research, but suggest that the field must do a better job of conceptualizing and measuring the features of such regimes that lead to breakdown. Contrary to this research, the regimes that began to fight insurgents on the isthmus were not semi-democratic; they were unambiguously authoritarian. Polity IV's classification of the Central American cases, the most commonly cited source on such matters, is inaccurate. In Nicaragua, Somoza ran a police state that restricted press freedoms and held elections where only regime-approved candidates could run for office. In Guatemala, the military not only relied on the security forces and paramilitary squads to exterminate rivals, but also used fraud to engineer presidential elections to bestow high office on favorite generals. In El Salvador, the military regime permitted limited contestation for legislative and municipal offices during the 1960s, but refused to accept the opposition's victory in the 1972 presidential election. Incumbents in both El Salvador and Guatemala reasserted their control in the wake of fraudulent elections in the early 1970s, which signaled that peaceful contestation was pointless. These facts raise doubts about the validity of key cross-national findings and suggest that researchers should be more critical when using regime classification indexes (Bowman, Lehoucq, and Mahoney, 2005).

These findings raise several implications for the study of civil war. On the one hand, political narrowness incites factionalism. Purveyors of violence struggle among each other for dominance and for the principal share of the spoils. It is this factionalism that leads to what I call inconsistent authoritarian regimes: autocracies strong enough to remain in power, but neither capable of institutionalizing rules to regularize the rotation of state offices nor able to exterminate their opponents. Instability within the regime both signals weakness and creates openings for regime opponents to exploit. In the struggle between colonels and generals, one set of officers can establish links with organized civil society to outmaneuver their rivals. Rarely do these openings lead to genuine liberalization and less often to democratization, as the tragic outcome of the Guatemalan Spring (1944–54) best illustrates. More often than not, these strategic moments end with a unification of regime factions around a blatantly authoritarian system. This outcome, which occurred in all three Central American societies that became violent by the late 1970s, set the stage for the civil wars that brought down each regime.

On the other hand, it is political exclusion that creates the wedge between autocrats and their opponents; this is the central characteristic of autocracies that lays the basis for insurgency. Regimes that deploy violence adroitly and manage to incorporate a fair number of opponents – actual or likely – tend to survive. This is the logic behind the finding that one-party dictatorships like the PRI's one-party rule for much of the twentieth century in Mexico tend to be stable (Geddes, 1999). Most tyrannies, however, fail to accomplish these objectives, including those of Central America. In fact, their inability to broaden their base of support forces them to increase violence to stay in power, which further provokes street protest and even guerrilla activity (Brockett, 2005). Once regime factions unified around the strategy of exterminating their opponents, negotiations between pro- and anti-regime moderates become pointless. The deployment of violence then determined the fate of autocracies.

The second major conclusion of this book is that democratization was a product of civil war on the isthmus. It was a coalition of the downtrodden that overthrew dictatorship, one whose members rejected the injustice of political exclusion. It was the lack of the right to voice complaints and to choose their leaders that motivated enough Central Americans to confront tyranny. It was the actions of rebellious peasants, urban street protesters, and guerrillas that ended the rule of oligarchs and officers. Armed struggle forced the wealthy to change their investments, thus leading to the economic diversification conducive for democracy – and to the incorporation of new parties and interests in the political system (Rouquié, 1994; Wood, 2000; Zamora, 1997). It is therefore misleading to claim, as Jeffrey Paige (1997) does or Boix (2003) implies, that the end of landed wealth made democracy possible in the region.

How well insurgents did against these systems shaped the transition as well as the vibrancy of the new regimes. When guerrillas defeated the regime – Nicaragua – their struggle produced more open systems, but systems in which one set of interests played a preponderant role in policy making. The renewal of civil war in Nicaragua – but this time between the Sandinistas and the U.S.-backed "Contras" – forced a broadening of the regime that led to the transition to democracy in 1990, the more conventionally defined start of an open political system in this country. It was a history of periodic confrontations between incumbents and opposition movements that, decades earlier, led to the 1948 civil war that ended fraud and violence in Costa Rica by mid-century. Although the opposition did not overthrow the Noriega dictatorship in Panama, a functional equivalent of armed insurgency – the U.S. invasion – liquidated the military that had been in control of government since 1968. Where insurgents were defeated – as in Guatemala – or did not contest the dictatorship – as in Honduras – transitions were more protracted and preserved the inequities of the old order. Where civil war turned to stalemate, as in El Salvador, incumbents and insurgents negotiated a peace accord that laid the basis for a lasting peace. Where no one won the war, everyone built democracy.

The cross-national, quantitative research on transitions is not that helpful in accounting for the timing of these transitions. Part of the difficulty of assessing this claim is that researchers disagree on the impact economic growth has on democratization, even if an early and pioneering study suggests that the region was approaching an economic threshold by the late 1970s (Seligson, 1987). Four decades of research on this relationship has not, in hindsight, progressed much beyond the claim originally made by Seymour Martin Lipset (1959) that development is associated with democracy. Adam Przeworski and his colleagues (2000) use a database of 135 countries between 1950 and 1990 to conclude that increases in development levels do not boost the probability that a political system will become democratic. Nevertheless, they show that democracy is less likely to collapse at higher levels of development, which, they argue, explains why wealthier countries are more likely to be democratic than poorer countries. Daron Acemoglu and colleagues (2008), who use a database of 120 countries between 1960 and 2000, agree that the relationship between economic development and regime is not linear. They disagree that economic development makes it easier for democracy to persist. Acemoglu and his colleagues (2008) argue that the beneficial effects of development on democracy disappear once statistical models use country fixed effects (that is, statistical models that control for the effects of unexplained or omitted variables in cross-national regression equations). They suggest that the relationship between both factors is a product of how long countries have been independent, how many checks and balances exist on executive authority, and religion. Epstein and his coauthors (2006) are the most supportive of the modernization claim. Their findings, however, are contingent on a threefold classification of democracy: Although development does not encourage autocracies to become democracies, departures from autocracy into partial democracy and transformations from this hybrid regime into democracy are highly contingent on the dynamics of partial democracies.

The Central American cases provide little support for the modernization thesis. Tyrannies collapsed after their economies began to enter prolonged recession caused principally by civil war and secondarily by the fall in the international price of the region's exports by the late 1970s. So, whether Central American economies were beginning to approximate an economic threshold, as Seligson (1987) claims, or not quite there, as the calculations in Przeworski et al. (2000) suggest, democratization began just as the long, post–World War II export boom came to an abrupt halt in the late 1970s. It was, in fact, the combination of civil war and economic crisis that blinded so many analysts in the early 1980s to the transformation that these systems would experience.

The fact that all Central American systems were (briefly) semi-democracies before they became democratic (except Guatemala, which remains semi-democratic) is consistent with the point made by Epstein and his coauthors (2006) that semi-democracies often become full-fledged democracies in countries with positive growth rates, as economies began to recover by the late 1980s in much of Central America. This attempt to salvage the theory, however, strikes me as forced for two reasons. First, politicians and citizens on the isthmus spent only a handful of years competing in what were rapidly liberalizing autocracies (Bowman, Lehoucq, and Mahoney, 2005). Outside of Honduras, which spent more than a decade as a mixed system, all of the other democracies exited swiftly from long-term autocracy to democracy. Second, it ignores the impact of political and institutional changes these (and other) systems were undergoing, which were unleashed by a crisis over control of the state, not of economic development.

The third conclusion of this book is that the comparative research on political economy is the most helpful of the macropolitical research examined in this book. It generates several claims that help explain why some democracies redistribute more income than others and improve social conditions. First, the age of democracy is associated with redistributive spending (Huber, Mustillo, and Stephens, 2008), which helps explain why Costa Rica, which has the oldest democratic state on the isthmus, does the most to lessen the gap between the rich and the poor. One reason time makes democracies increase social spending is that it makes parties in competitive systems more accountable. Experience helps voters distinguish credible from irresponsible policy promises (Keefer, 2007). My analysis of why the newer democracies have not met the aspirations of their citizens to reduce inequality is consistent with this argument. Younger democracies of the isthmus have less stable and programmatic party systems. Voters, in other words, cannot evaluate parties on their redistributive promises: They have not had enough time to form the judgments to hold elected officials accountable for their actions.

A second reason democratic longevity promotes social spending is that it empowers parties of the left to make and act on appeals to lower-income voters. I also find this pattern in Central America, especially in Costa Rica. As the struggle for state power became more institutionalized, parties shifted from being just concerned with sharing the spoils of office to developing platforms that appeal to large numbers of voters. The electoral success of the Party of National Liberation (PLN) in Costa Rica stems from its ability to make commitments of interest to large numbers of voters and act on them every time they return to office. Similarly, a left party in Nicaragua, the more avowedly Marxist Sandinistas, acted on their promises to improve the lot of the poor that economic collapse late forced them to scale back. The struggle for votes, in fact, encourages other parties to furnish a large array of social programs, which is why personalist parties in Honduras and Panama nonetheless support some income redistribution. The absence of a left party in power in El Salvador until 2009 helps explain the inability of this state to redistribute much income; but the threat of a left victory no doubt helps explain why the right did increase social spending since the mid-1990s. An inchoate party system, one without a coherent left party, helps explain why the state does virtually nothing to reduce dramatic income inequality in Guatemala. These results echo the finding from the comparative electoral systems research (e.g., Powell, 2000) and political economy literature (Iversen, 2005) that proportional electoral systems channel competition in a center-left direction that fuels the growth of the welfare state.

My analysis also finds a third reason political systems spend less on social programs than others: Weak states hamper redistributive spending. Collecting little revenue, they spend paltry sums on social programs. They also are less organizationally complex. They possess fewer specialized agencies to design and implement the social programs that lessen the differences between the rich and the poor. Weak states, therefore, are less adept at becoming the instruments of the majority.

My research suggests that sophisticated states deposit these functions of government in nonpartisan institutions, ones that make the Costa Rican state resemble what Bruce Ackerman (2000) calls the "new separation of powers." By separating the political from more technical functions of government, the 1949 constitution created an independent bureaucracy isolated from the partisanship of the elected branches of government, one capable of creating the physical and human capital improvements that fuel economic growth. The postwar political system therefore encouraged public officials to create public policies that are superior by regional standards and impressive by global standards.

The fourth conclusion of this book is that, in the absence of well-designed and inclusive political agreements, economic decline undermines democratic consolidation. That three of the four poorest political systems – Guatemala, Honduras, and Nicaragua – have broken down since the early 1990s suggests that lack of growth is associated with political decay, a long-standing finding in comparative political economy (Bernhard et al., 2001; Bueno de Mesquita et al., 2003; Przeworski et al., 2000). Yet, the Central American experience cautions against echoing a deterministic version of this thesis. First, it was the civil war that was most responsible for the economic slide – and the war was largely a product of the failure of autocrats to reform. Second, it may be poverty more than lack of growth that undermines democracy. The inability of most of Central America to recover from the war-induced carnage has the effect of sinking them further into economic backwardness, a condition in which incomes are low and jobs are scarce. In these conditions, politically active groups are therefore more willing to sacrifice democratization because the stakes of losing office are higher. The range of institutions capable of mediating the demands of politically active groups, as a result, becomes narrower and perhaps explains why breakdown is more likely to occur at lower levels of development (Przeworski, 2008).

Presidentialism has not contributed to democratic consolidation on the isthmus, a result consistent with the large-N research (Cheibub, 2007; Pérez Liñán, 2007). Every case of authoritarian regression in Central America involved a deadlock between the branches of government. Conservative presidents battled Sandinista-dominated Assemblies in Nicaragua until the late 1990s, when the Liberal Party and the FSLN colluded to deactivate the checks on executive authority, strengthen the legislature, and erect barriers to entry to third parties. A minority president in Guatemala tried to close Congress in 1993 before losing and going into exile. An ambitious president in Honduras tried to reform the constitution to run for consecutive election before being deposed in a coup executed by the military and backed by the supreme court and congress. Each confrontation shattered the trust necessary to sustain democratic politics by magnifying the stakes associated with not holding state power.

It takes time to build durable and inclusive agreements to preserve more open political systems. The continuation of non-authoritarian politics in El Salvador stems from, in the first place, broadly representative party systems. Both the right and the left regularly attract the votes of a large number of citizens in El Salvador. Costa Rican politics stabilized once the ex-calderonistas, who had lost the 1948 civil war, were allowed to field candidates in elections a decade later. No major political force has been excluded from organizing electoral campaigns in Panama, even if no left-wing party has developed to contest the hegemony of centrist parties. In the second place, postwar settlements liquidated the military in these countries. Costa Rica, in fact, became the first country to disband its military, a decision that the victors found convenient in the wake of the brief civil war, and one that produced a huge dividend for the country (Bowman, 2002). If civil wars were, in large part, a product of official government repression, eliminating or revamping the security forces went a long way to reducing the grievances that sparked conflict in the first place. Finally, rivalries between the branches of government have not aggravated conflicts because, with the partial exception of Costa Rica, executives in these cases regularly fashion legislative coalitions to enact their programs. It is a striking fact that governments have been either elected with majorities in congress or have fashioned coalitions between a larger, pro-government party and a hand-ful of smaller parties.

The reform of Central American political systems explains why there has not been – nor likely will be – a renewal of armed conflict on the isthmus. Research on the reoccurrence of civil war emphasizes that it happens in polities where governments cannot defeat insurgents or cannot credibly commit to a peace plan (Walter, 2010). Neither of these conditions obtains in Central America. In El Salvador and Nicaragua, incumbents and their armed opponents signed peace agreements that replaced prewar dictatorships with more open com-petitive systems. In Guatemala, the military defeated the URNG by the early 1980s, and then signed an internationally supervised agreement that disarmed the guerrillas by 1996. Although democratic institutions have deteriorated in Guatemala, Honduras, and Nicaragua, states no longer target dissidents for extermination. The political conditions that led to civil war have changed.

Continuities and Changes

The most striking continuity is that relative GDP per capita rates have not gotten better since the 1980s. By the mid-1970s, Costa Rica and Panama had almost 40 percent of the GDP per capita of Western European societies. After the turbulent decade of the 1980s, it took these two countries almost two decades to return to the same level of the development. These two countries, in other words, have not shortened the distance to development in four decades.

The economic growth story is grim elsewhere on the isthmus. The worst case is Nicaragua, which has gone from about a quarter to about a tenth of the Western European average between 1970 and 2010. Honduras's fall is less steep than Nicaragua's, but no less dismal, simply because its growth peak never reached Nicaragua's mid-1970s high. Its relative GDP per capita level is only marginally better in 2010 than it was in 1970. The distance that El Salvador and Guatemala need to make up has gotten larger in forty years. Although El Salvador was 20 percent of the way to Western Europe in 1970, it is now only 15 percent of the way there. Guatemala was close to a third of the way in 1970; by 2010, its GDP per capita rate had fallen by a third, to less than 20 percent of the European average.

The region, however, has experienced some economic and social improve-ments. On the one hand, its GDP per capita rates, in absolute terms, are slightly higher, even if the promised land of development remains distant. Between 1970 and 2006, they increased everywhere, except in Nicaragua, where they have declined to pre-1970 levels. They have barely moved in El Salvador and Honduras; GDP per capita levels have done slightly better than this in Guatemala. They have only doubled in Costa Rica and Panama, which has not only helped them maintain their distance from that of the developed world, but also set them quite apart from their neighbors. On the other hand, some key social indicators have improved. Life expectancy is now 74 years, which is the Latin American average and is within distance of the developed world's mean.

Infant mortality rates, at 17 deaths per 1,000 live births, are slightly lower than the Latin American average, though substantially higher than for a developed country. Rates of illiteracy have fallen to 15 percent of the population by 2010, which still is twice the Latin American average.

Another important continuity is that the region's economies are still small and open. Although openness is often associated with development (Scandinavia's economies are open and support advanced welfare states) smallness has some serious economic as well as political drawbacks. These economies remain price-takers in international markets. As exporters of agricultural products and labor – the region's new export – these economies cannot set the price for their commodities. They exist in abundance; their price is set in global or foreign markets. Their policymakers, and societies more broadly, react rather than spearhead global changes. At their worst, they must adapt to declines in the prices for their commodity exports, which can change swiftly and without warning. This is what happened in the late 1970s, when the international price for coffee – then accounting for the lion's share of the region's exports – fell dramatically, after having reached a postwar high earlier in the decade. The plunge in the value of coffee aggravated (but did not cause) the conflicts brewing into civil war in El Salvador and Guatemala. It placed additional constraints on the revolutionary government of Nicaragua, which had just come to power in 1978. It narrowed policy options for Costa Rica, Honduras, and Panama, especially because global interest rates swiftly began to rise. For small, open economies, these external shocks lead to economic recessions that can be more or less severe, depending upon the reaction of governmental authorities and the depth of the fall in prices. Victor Bulmer-Thomas (1987: 269) estimates that this downswing "wiped out nearly three decades of increases in real GDP per head in El Salvador and Nicaragua, two decades in Honduras, one and one-half in Guatemala and one decade in Costa Rica."

Unskilled workers have become a prominent export from the isthmus. Although the remittances Central Americans laboring in the first world – mostly in the United States – send home have become a new source of foreign exchange for the region, exporting what is, in effect, a new commodity is less new. This "new" export has become a key source of foreign exchange. In every country but Costa Rica and Panama, remittances equaled at least a quarter of all other exports by 2005. In the early 1990s, remittances sent by working-class Salvadorans in the United States basically equaled all exports. Shipping unskilled labor abroad not only demonstrates the underdevelopment of the region's economies, but also signifies that most of the region is specializing in an export possessing low rates of return.

There are two other changes to Central America's exports beyond the export of human beings. On the one hand, Costa Rica and El Salvador sell more manufactured goods than agricultural products in global markets. By the late 1990s, more than 50 percent of exports were factory-made goods. In El Salvador, new exports are mostly textiles and other light consumer goods. Costa Rica's new products include computer micro-chips, a result of Intel setting up an assembly plant in the country. The country's success in promoting nontraditional exports has led one economist to ask whether it is just a matter of time before Costa Rica becomes Ireland, before new exports catapult the country into the first world, the way financial services helped transform the Irish economy. Eva Paus (2005) is doubtful, mostly because there are few backward linkages to the rest of the economy, that is, local suppliers of the inputs needed by microchip manufacturers (also, see Sánchez-Ancochea, 2006). Low levels of public investment, which have only recently returned to pre-1982 crash levels, also thwart rapid gains in educational levels and infrastructure expansion. On the other hand, the weight of coffee and bananas in the region's exports has fallen dramatically, which is the culmination of the gradual shift away from exporting little more than these products to the rest of the world. Along with smaller amounts of cattle and sugar, these products dominated Central America's export profile well into the 1990s. By 2006, these products account for less than 20 percent of each country's exports and, in Costa Rica, substantially less than this amount, even if, for several countries, exports consist of varying bundles of traditional and nontraditional agricultural products (PENR, 2008: 542–552).

The most important change is democratization. The "Third Wave" of democratization swept away the seemingly eternal dictatorships of the isthmus. The fall of the Somoza regime, in particular, electrified Central Americans and the world at large. A broad coalition of Nicaraguans – peasants, the urban poor, middle-class professionals, businessmen, and full-time revolutionaries – toppled the emblematic dictatorship of the region, the dynasty that had gone from father, Anastasio Somoza García (1937–56), to eldest son, Luis Somoza Debayle (1956–63), and then to his other son, Anastasio Somoza Debayle (1967–79). It suggested that anything was possible, perhaps even the eradication of the poverty and underdevelopment. It truly was the best of times, the age of wisdom, the epoch of belief, and the season of light, to cite the memorable start of Charles Dickens's *Tale of Two Cities*.

Salvador Samayoa (2002), an FMLN leader, mentions the surprise of guerrilla commanders returning to El Salvador that, after years of exile, they did not have to get back on an airplane to safeguard life and limb. Signing the peace treaty with ARENA President Alfredo Cristiani (1989–94) on January 16, 1991 meant that they no longer had – or should have – to fear for their lives. They could travel in the country of their birth, a decision that none of them later regretted. None of them were assassinated, their supporters were left in peace, a set of facts that I still find astonishing. Political violence, largely perpetuated by the state security forces, really had ended. Salvadorans have forged a new consensus, one that made politically inspired killings unacceptable.

Suzanne Jonas, a longtime U.S. observer of Guatemala, noted that "December 28, 1996, was the night I could never have imagined. On the eve of the signing of Guatemala's peace accords, the Central Plaza was the scene of unprecedented, previously inconceivable, popular ceremonies and celebrations." It was the last of the Central American conflicts to be settled at the negotiating table, an agreement that many of us found unexpected and superfluous. The formal end of a thirty-six-year conflict, one that cost more than 200,000 individuals their lives and countless others the horrors of a brutal civil war, was no less a moving experience. The relief associated with ending decades of terror was tempered by the enormous loss of life, perhaps becoming more valuable because the carnage was finally over. This may explain the reaction of one of Jonas's friends, who, as "part of the government team, described himself as being in an 'emotional coma,'" which she described as a "combination of exhaustion and delirium" (cited in Kinzer, 2001a: 61).

Some members of the old order had little to celebrate. After stalling for years and months, Somoza decided to flee Nicaragua on July 17, 1979 as civil war and international isolation deprived him of territory and support. Slightly more than a year later, seven Sandinistas gunned him down on the streets of Asunción, Paraguay, where he was living in exile. As Nicaraguans became embroiled in civil war in the ensuing decade, wealthy individuals and other opponents of the Sandinistas lost their property. After defending the privileges of the old order in El Salvador, the army and security forces were dismembered. The size of the army fell by half and many of its officers were cashiered; some, in a courtroom in the State of Florida, were found guilty of the murder and rape of six U.S. nuns. It must have been a bittersweet victory for many Salvadorans; their own government, one led by ARENA, had passed a broad amnesty within days of the signing of the peace accords. Holding murderers accountable for their actions was only possible abroad. The notorious Treasury Police were disbanded. The police were separated from the military. Though a UN-sponsored Truth Commission found the military and its paramilitary allies guilty of most of the war's casualties, few were ever tried, much less convicted in El Salvador (Collins, 2010). Though none of the rich lost their fortunes, landlords did lose property as a result of a half-executed land reform and a civil war that saw the FMLN occupy much of the countryside. This was a pyrrhic victory; vibrant estates were decapitalized and the countryside was emptied of its elite as well as of much of its prewar productivity.

Little more than a decade later, the Sandinistas lost the 1990 election, punished by an electorate fed up with a war that cost an estimated 60,000 lives and a decade of severe economic decline. The hopeful beginning had become a tragedy and, with time, a farce. Some of the heroes and heroines of yesteryear cut a deal with their rivals to insulate themselves from the reach of justice by the late 1990s. The infamous "pact" did not prevent a former president, Arnoldo Alemán (1996–2001) of the ironically named Liberal Constitutionalist Party, from being prosecuted for graft, but helped the first (and only) Sandinista president, Daniel Ortega (1985–90), return to the presidency because the bar for being elected was lowered from more than 50 percent to 40 percent (or 35 percent, if the leading candidate had a majority of 5 percent of the vote). By 2006, the farce had become a travesty. An aging and embittered Daniel Ortega, with a rump faction of the old Frente, finally returned to the presidency. By 2010, he had begun to plot his continuation in power by getting a supreme court to approve his bid to run for reelection in the 2012 elections, which he won by a landslide. Nicaraguan politics had entered an age of foolishness and the epoch of incredulity, the political counterpoint of the opening bars of Dickens's novel.

Democratization, the single most important achievement of the revolutionary decade, has given birth to several low-quality democracies. Democracy has plunged the most in Nicaragua, as this and the preceding chapter point out. Insiders have deactivated the checks and balances of the political system to padlock their grip on power. The 2009 coup against President Manuel Zelaya (2005–10), whose behavior suggests that he too wished to run for consecutive reelection, put on display the institutional shortcomings of the Honduran body politic. They proved unable to prevent skirmishes over political succession from spinning out of control. One reading of these events is that Zelaya's opponents overthrew his regime because they reasoned that a disenchanted citizenry would remain passive as they toppled the president (Seligson and Booth, 2010). The failure to reinstate Zelaya led the international community to boycott the 2009 elections (held in late November, five months after the coup) that the opposition Conservative candidate, Porfirio Lobo Sosa, won with 55.5 percent of the vote (Taylor-Robinson, 2011).

Guatemala arguably has the most dysfunctional democracy on the isthmus. It suffered a near breakdown in 1993, when President Jorge Serrano (1990–3) failed in his attempt to rally the troops to close down congress and the courts. In a campaign with few alternatives, enough citizens gave the former dictator Efraín Ríos Montt's party (1999–2003) control of the presidency and of congress, given his promises to rein in escalating violence and increase social spending. Unable to run for high office because of the constitutional ban on de facto presidents from holding executive office again, Ríos Montt did succeed in getting on the ballot, but failed to win a majority. By the end of this decade, common crime and especially drug related violence was overwhelming the state, one whose primitiveness is best revealed by having the western hemisphere's lowest rate of effective taxation (Azpuru et al., 2007; Seligson, 2005). It was against this backdrop that a former general, Otto Pérez Molina of the Patriotic Party, won the 2011 presidential runoff in a campaign, where he promised to crack down on crime and increase social expenditures (González, forthcoming).

Democracy has gradually become more consolidated in El Salvador and Panama. In El Salvador, often acrimonious campaigns between ARENA and the FMLN have not spiraled into either clashes between the president and congress or, worse yet, politically inspired violence. The respect for civil liberties continues, even as social movements on the left organized marches to block the privatization of the public health care system and make other demands on the system (Almeida, 2008; Smith-Nonini, 2010). Voter turnout rates gradually increased from 54 to 64 percent between 1994 and 2009, even as significant numbers of Salvadorans have abstained from participating in elections that offered options on the left and right, but not in the center (Cruz, 2001). The increasing stability of the country's democracy became unambiguously apparent when the FMLN finally defeated ARENA in the 2009 presidential race. There have been no interruptions of democratic rule in Panama, with civilians gradually asserting their control over the military. In both countries, charges of influence-peddling and unresponsiveness by insiders remain common, and so do demands for governments that take actions to reduce poverty and inequality. Perhaps the inability of outsiders, like the organized and democratic left, to win the presidency permits centrist and right-wing parties to rotate control of key state institutions.

Democratic institutions remain consolidated in Costa Rica, but did undergo some strain by the late 1990s (Lehoucq, 2005; 2006). In a prescient analysis, Mitchell Seligson (2002) warned that citizen support for the political system had been declining since 1983, even if these percentages are high by regional standards. A citizen audit of democracy concluded that the parties had become detached from citizen concerns, a system that increasing number of voters found unresponsive (PEN, 2001; Vargas Cullell, 2004). Voter turnout rates fell from 80 percent to an average of 68 percent in the three general elections between 1998 and 2002 (Raventós Vorst et al., 2005). The center-right United Social Christian Party (PUSC) imploded as a result of having two of its former presidents investigated on charges of bribe-taking and influence-peddling in 2004. Its collapse led to the disintegration of the two-party system, one populated by the PUSC and the center-left PLN that developed in the 1980s. A new party system, one with a new left party, the Citizen Action Party (PAC), and even a libertarian alternative, now is in existence. Party system change has sparked a wide-ranging debate about the strengths and limits of political system design (Arias Ramírez, 2005; Urcuyo, 2003), and its impact on accelerating economic growth (Vargas Cullell, 2006).

The inability of democratization to strengthen states makes them incapable of meeting a new threat: drug trafficking. As the region-wide illegal shipment of drugs shifts from Mexico to the isthmus, Central American states are proving no match for the well-financed and ruthless trade in narcotics. Small states, even relatively high-quality ones like the one in Costa Rica, are largely incapable of stemming the dramatic increase in homicide rates that have made El Salvador, Guatemala, and Honduras the most violent places in Latin America and some of the most violent in the world not experiencing civil war. A recent paper, in fact, quantitatively shows that the dramatic increase in homicide rates is statistically associated with regions favored by the drug trade. The international trade in illegal substances thus not only leads to deaths and an increase in crime, but also contributes to swamping, if not corrupting the region's courts and law enforcement agencies (Demombynes, 2011).

Limited democratization also helps maintain a third continuity: a high degree of inequality. Low-quality democracy restricts the ability of the state to act upon public preferences to narrow the gap between the rich and the poor. At its worst, an archaic and dysfunctional state prevents any reduction in high levels of inequality in Guatemala, and therefore undermines economic competitiveness. This is perhaps the most glaring legacy of a thirty-year civil war, one that saw the military crush both the armed and unarmed left. Nearly fifteen years of neoliberal governments in El Salvador have done little to narrow the difference between high and low income groups. Economic retrogression has largely wiped out the social gains of the revolution so that the redistributive capacity of the Nicaraguan state is smaller than that of its counterpart in Honduras. Panama and Costa Rica, the two countries with the most functional democracies, do the most to breach the divide between the rich and the poor. Democracy helps, and the age of democratic institutions improves their ability to translate citizen preferences into public policy.

Bibliography

Acemoglu, Daron, Simon Johnson, James A. Robinson, and Pierre Yared. 2008. "Income and Democracy." *The American Economic Review* 98.3 (June): 808–842.

Acemoglu, Daron, and James A. Robinson. 2006. *Economic Origins of Dictatorship and Democracy*. Cambridge: Cambridge University Press.

Ackerman, Bruce. 2000. "The New Separation of Powers." *Harvard Law Review* 113.3 (January): 634–727.

Acuña Ortega, Victor Hugo. 1995. "Autoritarismo y democracia en Centroamérica: la larga duración, siglos XIX-XX," in *Ilusiones y dilemas: la democracia en Centroamérica*. ed. Klaus Tangermann. San José, FLACSO, 63–98.

Adams, Richard N. 1970. *Crucifixion by Power: Essays on Guatemalan National Social Structure, 1944–66*. Austin, TX: University of Texas Press.

———. 1988. "Conclusions: What Can We Know About the Harvest of Violence?" In *Harvest of Violence*, ed. Robert M. Carmack. Norman, OK: University of Oklahoma Press, 274–292.

———. 1993. "Etnias y sociedades (1930–79)." In *De la posguerra a la crisis (1945–79)*, ed. Héctor Pérez-Brignoli. Madrid: FLACSO, 165–243.

Agosín, Manuel R., Eduardo Fernández-Arias, and Fidel Jaramillo. 2009. "Binding Constraints to Growth in Latin America: An Overview." In *Growing Pains: Binding Constraints to Productive Investment in Latin America*, eds. Manuel Agosín, Eduardo Fernández-Arias, and Fidel Jaramillo. Washington, DC: Inter-American Development Bank, 1–44.

Agosín, Manuel R., and Roberto Machado. 2006. "Economic Growth in Central America." In *Vanishing Growth in Latin America: The Late Twentieth Century Experience*, ed. Andrés Solimano. Northampton, MA: Edward Elgar Publishing, 101–132.

Aguilera Peralta, Gabriel. 1998. "Realizar un imaginario: La paz en Guatemala." In *Desde el Autoritarismo a la paz*, ed. Edelberto Torres-Rivas. Guatemala: FLACSO, 113–164.

Aguilera Peralta, Gabriel, and Jorge Romero Imery. 1981. *Dialéctica del Terror en Guatemala*. San José, Costa Rica: Editorial Universitaria Centroamericana.

Alesina, Alberto, Arnaud Devleeschauwer, William Easterly, Sergio Kurlat, and Romain Wacziarg. 2003. "Fractionalization." *Journal of Economic Growth* 8.2 (June): 155–194.

Alesina, Alberto, and Edward Glaeser. 2004. *Fighting Poverty in the US and Europe: A World of Difference*. New York: Oxford University Press.

Alfaro Redondo, Ronald. 2004. "Instituciones estatales en Costa Rica: Un balance del período 1990–2003." Working Paper, 10th Informe sobre el Estado de la Nación en Desarrollo Humano Sostenible, http://www.estadonacion.or.cr/Info2004/Ponencias/Fortalecimiento/Alfaro_2004.pdf, accessed January 17, 2010.

2007. "Inconsistencias en el materia electoral del referendum." In PEN (2007): 317–327.

Almeida, Paul D. 2008. *Waves of Protest: Popular Struggle in El Salvador, 1925–2005*. Minneapolis, MN: University of Minnesota Press.

Anderson, Leslie E. 1994. *The Political Ecology of the Modern Peasant: Calculation and Community*. Baltimore, MD: Johns Hopkins University Press.

2006. "The Authoritarian Executive? Horizontal and Vertical Accountability in Nicaragua." *Latin American Politics & Society* 48.2 (Summer): 141–169.

Anderson, Leslie E., and Lawrence C. Dodd. 2005. *Learning Democracy: Citizen Engagement and Electoral Choice in Nicaragua, 1990–2001*. Chicago: University of Chicago Press.

Anderson, Leslie E., and Lawrence C. Dodd. 2009. "Nicaragua: Progress Amid Regress?" *Journal of Democracy* 20.3 (July): 153–167.

Andersson, Krister, Clark C. Gibson, and Fabrice Lehoucq. 2006. "Municipal Politics and Forest Governance: Comparative Analysis of Decentralization in Bolivia and Guatemala." *World Development* 34.3 (March): 576–595.

Archdiocese of Guatemala. 1999. *Guatemala: Never Again*. Maryknoll, NY: Orbis Books. (The 4-volume report is available in Spanish and German for downloading at: http://www.odhag.org.gt/03publicns.htm).

Arias Calderón, Ricardo. 2000. "The Demilitarization of Public Security in Panama." *Small Wars and Insurgencies* 11.1 (Spring): 97–111.

Arias Ramírez, Bernal. 2005. *Ideas sobre reforma política en Costa Rica*. San José, Costa Rica: CEDAL.

Arnson, Cynthia J. 1993. *Crossroads: Congress, the President, and Central America, 1976–1993*. 2nd ed. University Park, PA: Pennsylvania State University Press.

Artana, Daniel, Sebastián Auguste, and Mario Cuevas. 2009. "Tearing Down the Walls: Growth and Inclusion in Guatemala." In *Growing Pains: Binding Constraints to Productive Investment in Latin America*, eds. Manuel Agosín, Eduardo Fernández-Arias, and Fidel Jaramillo. Washington, DC: Inter-American Development Bank, 217–272.

Artiga-González, Álvaro. 2003. "Las elecciones del año 2003 y la 'difícil combinación' institucional." *Estudios Centroamericanos* 653–4 (Marzo-Abril): 213–238.

2004. *Elitismo competitivo: dos décadas de elecciones en El Salvador (1982–2003)*. San Salvador: UCA Editores.

2008. "Gestión de sistemas electorales en Centroamérica y Panamá." Working Paper, III Informe del Estado de la Región. San José, Costa Rica: Estado de la Región, http://www.estadonacion.or.cr/images/stories/informes/ponencias_ca/Aspectos_politicos/Ponencias/INFORME2008/Ponencia_Artiga_elecciones_y_partidos_politicos.pdf, accessed February 27, 2011.

2009. "Las elecciones 2009 en perspectiva." *Estudios Centroamericanos* 64.719 (Enero-Marzo): 11–32.

2010. "Democratización en el acceso al poder en Centroamérica." Working Paper, IV Informe del Estado de la Región. San José, Costa Rica: Estado de la Región.

Atkinson, Anthony B., and Thomas Piketty, eds. 2007. *Top Incomes over the Twentieth Century: A Contrast Between Continental European and English-Speaking Countries*. New York: Oxford University Press.

Azpuru, Dinorah. 2008a. "The 2007 Presidential and Legislative Elections in Guatemala." *Electoral Studies* 27.3 (March): 143–149.

2008b. "The 2007 Presidential and Legislative Elections in Guatemala," *Electoral Studies*, 27.3 (September): 562–566.

2010. "The Salience of Ideology: Fifteen Years of Presidential Elections in El Salvador." *Latin American Politics & Society* 52.2 (Summer): 103–138.

Azpuru, Dinorah, Ligia Blanco, Ricardo Córdova Macías, Nayelly Loya Marín, Carlos G. Ramos, and Adrián Zapata. 2007. *Construyendo la democracia en sociedades posconflicto: Un enfoque comparado entre Guatemala y el Salvador*. Guatemala: F & G Editores.

Ball, Patrick, Paul Kobrak, and Herbert Spirer. 1999. *State Violence in Guatemala, 1960–1996: A Quantitative Reflection*. Washington, DC: American Association for the Advancement of Science.

Baloyra, Enrique A. 1982. *El Salvador in Transition*. Chapel Hill, NC: University of North Carolina Press.

Baloyra-Herp, Enrique A. 1983. "Reactionary Despotism in Central America." *Journal of Latin American Studies* 15.2 (November): 295–319.

Barnes, William A. 1992. "Rereading the Nicaraguan Pre-Election Polls." In *The 1990 Elections in Nicaragua and Their Aftermath*, eds. Vanessa Castro and Gary Prevost. Lanham, MD: Rowman and Littlefield, 42–128.

1998. "Incomplete Democracy in Central America: Polarization and Voter Turnout in Nicaragua and El Salvador." *Journal of Interamerican Studies & World Affairs* 40.3 (April): 63–101.

Barreix, Alberto, Martín Bès, and Jerónimo Roca. 2009. *Equidad Fiscal en Centroamérica, Panamá y la República Dominicana*. Washington, DC: Inter-American Development Bank and Eurosocial (http://www.iadb.org/publications/search.cfm?query=Equidad+Fiscal+en+Centroam%C3%A9rica&context=Title&lang=en&searchLang=all&searchtype=general, accessed May 15, 2011).

Barrios de Chamorro, Violeta. 1996. *Dreams of the Heart: The Autobiography of President Violeta Barrios de Chamorro of Nicaragua*. New York: Simon & Schuster.

Bates, Robert H. 1997. *Open-Economy Politics: The Political Economy of the World Coffee Trade*. Princeton: Princeton University Press.

2008. *When Things Fell Apart: State Failure in Late-Century Africa*. New York: Cambridge University Press.

Benítez Manaut, Raúl. 1989. *La teoría militar y la guerra civil en El Salvador*. San Salvador, El Salvador: UCA Editores.

Bergés, Ame, Valpy FitzGerald, and Rosemary Thorp. 2007. "Oxford Latin American Economic History Database." Latin American Centre, Oxford University, http://oxlad.qeh.ox.ac.uk/

Bernhard, Michael, Timothy Nordstrom, and Christopher Reenock. 2001. "Economic Performance, Institutional Intermediation, and Democratic Survival." *Journal of Politics* 63.3 (August): 775–803.

Bertelsmann Stiftung, ed. 2010. *Bertelsmann Transformation Index 2010: Political Management in International Comparison*. Gütersloh, Germany: Verlag Bertelsmann Stiftung.

Best, Michael H. 1976. "Political Power and Tax Revenues in Central America." *Journal of Development Economics* 3.1 (March): 49–82.

Bethell, Leslie, ed. 1991. *Central America since Independence*. Cambridge: Cambridge University Press.

Bischoping, Katherine, and Howard Schuman. 1992. "Pens and Polls in Nicaragua: An Analysis of the 1990 Preelection Surveys." *American Journal of Political Science* 36.2 (May): 331–350.

Black, George. 1981. *Triumph of the People: The Sandinista Revolution in Nicaragua.* London: Zed Books.

    1984. *Garrison Guatemala*. New York: Monthly Review Press.

    1988. *The Good Neighbor: How the United States Wrote the History of Central America and the Caribbean.* New York: Simon and Schuster.

Blasier, Cole. 1985. *The Hovering Giant: U.S. Responses to Revolutionary Change in Latin America, 1910–1985*, revised edition. Pittsburgh, PA: University of Pittsburgh Press.

    1987. *The Giant's Rival: The USSR and Latin America*. Pittsburgh, PA: University of Pittsburgh Press.

Boix, Carles. 2003. *Democracy and Redistribution*. Cambridge: Cambridge University Press.

    2008. "Economic Roots of Civil Wars and Revolutions in the Contemporary World." *World Politics* 60.3 (April): 390–437.

Bonner, Raymond. 1984. *Weakness and Deceit: U.S. Policy and El Salvador*. New York: Times Books.

Booth, John A. 1982. *The End and the Beginning: The Nicaraguan Revolution.* Boulder, CO: Westview Press.

    1991. "Socioeconomic and Political Roots of National Revolts in Central America." *Latin American Research Review* 26.1: 33–73.

Booth, John A., and Mitchell A. Seligson. 2009. *The Legitimacy Puzzle in Latin America.* Cambridge, NY: Cambridge University Press.

Booth, John A., Christine J. Wade, and Thomas W. Walker. 2010. *Understanding Central America: Global Forces, Rebellion, and Change.* 5th ed. Boulder, CO: Westview Press.

Bowman, Kirk. 2001a. "¿Fue el compromiso o consenso de las elites lo que llevo a la consolidación democrática en Costa Rica? Evidencia de la década de 1950." *Revista de Historia* 41 (January-June): 500–536.

    2001b. "The Public Battles over Militarisation and Democracy in Honduras, 1954–1963." *Journal of Latin American Studies* 33.3 (August): 539–560.

    2002. *Militarization, Democracy and Development: The Perils of Praetorianism in Latin America.* University Park, PA: Penn State University Press.

Bowman, Kirk, Fabrice Lehoucq, and James Mahoney. 2005. "Measuring Political Democracy: Case Expertise, Data Adequacy, and Central America." *Comparative Political Studies* 38.8 (October): 939–970.

Brockett, Charles D. 1992. "Measuring Political Violence and Land Inequality in Central America." *American Political Science Review* 86.1 (March): 169–176.

    1998. *Land, Power, and Poverty: Agrarian Transformation and Political Conflict in Central America.* Boulder, CO: Westview Press.

    2005. *Political Movements and Violence in Central America.* New York: Cambridge University Press.

Brown, Timothy C. 2000. *When the AK-47s Fall Silent: Revolutionaries, Guerillas, and the Dangers of Peace.* Stanford, CA: Hoover Institution Press.

——— 2001. *The Real Contra War: Highlander Peasant Resistance in Nicaragua.* Norman, OK: University of Oklahoma Press.

Brown Araúz, Harry. 2009. *Partidos políticos y elecciones en Panamá: un enfoque institucionalista.* Panamá: Fundación Friedrich Ebert (http://www.fesamerica-central.org/?pbl=23&title=Partidos Políticos y Elecciones en Panamá:Un Enfoque Institucionalista&lang=es, accessed Noviember 1, 2011).

Browning, David. 1971. *El Salvador: Landscape and Society.* Oxford: Clarendon Press.

Buckley, Kevin. 1991. *Panama: The Whole Story.* New York: Simon & Schuster.

Bueno de Mesquita, Bruce, Alastair Smith, Randolph M. Siverson, and James D. Morrow. 2003. *The Logic of Political Survival.* Cambridge, MA: MIT Press.

Bulmer-Thomas, Victor. 1987. *The Political Economy of Central America since 1920.* Cambridge: Cambridge University Press.

——— 1988. *Studies in the Economics of Central America.* New York: St. Martin's Press.

Burke, Melvin. 1976. "El sistema de plantación y la proletarización del trabajo agrícola en El Salvador." *Estudios Centroamericanos* 31.335/336 (September/October): 473–486.

Byrne, Hugh. 1996. *El Salvador's Civil War: A Study in Revolution.* Boulder, CO: Lynne Rienner.

Cabarrús, Carlos Rafael. 1983. *Génesis de una revolución: Análisis del surgimiento y desarrollo de la organización campesina en El Salvador.* México: La Casa Chata.

Cáceres, Luis René. 1990. "Notas sobre la fuga de capital en Centroamérica." *Cuadernos de Economía y Finanzas* 12 (October): Banco Centroamericano de Integración Económica.

Call, Charles T. 2002. "Assessing El Salvador's Transition from Civil War to Peace." In *Ending Civil Wars: The Implementation of Peace Agreements*, eds. Stephen John Stedman, Donald Rothchild, and Elizabeth M. Cousens. Boulder, CO: Lynne Rienner Publishers, 383–420.

Cardoso, Ciro F. S. 1975. "Historia del café en Centroamérica (Siglo XIX): Estudio comparado." *Estudios Sociales Centroamericanos* 10: 9–55.

Carmack, Robert M., ed. 1988. *Harvest of Violence: The Maya Indians and the Guatemalan Crisis.* Norman, OK: University of Oklahoma Press.

Carter, Jimmy. 1992. *Turning Point: A Candidate, a State, and a Nation Come of Age.* New York: Times Books.

Casas-Zamora, Kevin. 2003. *Estudios sobre financiamiento de partidos políticos en Centroamérica y Panama.* Cuadernos de CAPEL, No. 48. San José, Costa Rica: Centro de Asesoría y Promoción Electoral.

——— 2005. *Paying for Democracy: Political Finance and State Funding for Parties.* Colchester, Essex, UK: ECPR Press.

Casas, Kevin, and Daniel Zovatto. 2005. "Political Financing in Central America, Panama, and the Dominican Republic." In *A Challenge for Democracy: Political Parties in Central America, Panama, and the Dominican Republic*, eds. Diego Achard and Luis E. González. Washington, DC: IADB-IDEA-OAS, 219–274.

Casaús Arzú, Marta Elena. 1992. "La metamorfosis de las oligarquías centroamerica-nas." *Revista Mexicana de Sociología* 54.3 (July-September): 69–114.

Castellanos, Miguel. 1991. *The Comandante Speaks: Memoirs of an El Salvadoran Guerrilla Leader*, ed. Courtney E. Prisk. Boulder, CO: Westview Press.

Castro Vega, Oscar. 2003. *Rodrigo Facio en la Constituyente de 1949*. San José, Costa Rica: Editorial de la Universidad Estatal a Distancia.

Caumartin, Corinne. 2007. "'Depoliticisation' in the Reform of the Panamanian Security Apparatus." *Journal of Latin American Studies* 39.1 (February): 107–132.

CEH (Comisión para el Esclarecimiento Histórico). 1999. *Guatemala: Memoria del Silencio*. 12 vols. Guatemala: CEH.

CEPAL (Economic Commission for Latin America and the Caribbean). 2001. "Istmo Centroamericano: Medio siglo de estadísticas macroeconómicas, 1950–2000." CD-Rom.

CEPAL (Economic Commission for Latin America and the Caribbean). 2009. *Anuario Estadístico*. Santiago, Chile: CEPAL.

Cheibub, José Antonio. 2007. *Presidentialism, Parliamentarism and Democracy*. New York: Cambridge University Press.

Child, Jack. 1992. *The Central American Peace Process, 1983–1991: Sheathing Swords, Building Confidence*. Boulder, CO: Lynne Rienner Publishers.

Chong, Alberto, and Florencio López de Silanes, eds. 2005. *Privatization in Latin America: Myths and Reality*. Palo Alto, CA: Stanford University Press.

Christian, Shirley. 1985. *Nicaragua: Revolution in the Family*. New York: Random House.

Clark, Mary A. 2001. *Gradual Economic Reform in Latin America: The Costa Rican Experience*. Albany, NY: State University of New York Press.

Cline, William R., and Enrique Delgado, eds. 1978. *Economic Integration in Central America*. Washington, DC: Brookings Institution Press.

Close, David. 1988. *Nicaragua: Politics, Economics, and Society*. New York: Pinter Publishers.

1994. "President Bolaños Runs a Reverse, or How Arnoldo Alemán Wound Up in Prison." In *Undoing Democracy: The Politics of Electoral Caudillismo*, eds. David Close and Kalowatie Deonandan. Lanham, MD: Lexington Books, 167–182.

1999. *Nicaragua: The Chamorro Years*. Boulder, CO: Lynne Rienner Publishers.

CNDH (National Commission for the Protection of Human Rights in Honduras). 1994. *The Facts Speak for Themselves: Preliminary Report*. New York: Human Rights Watch/Americas, Center for Justice and International Law.

Colburn, Forrest D. 1986. *Post-Revolutionary Nicaragua: State, Class, and the Dilemmas of Agrarian Policy*. Berkeley, CA: University of California Press.

1990. *Managing the Commanding Heights: Nicaragua's State Enterprises*. Berkeley, CA: University of California Press.

Colindres, Eduardo. 1976. "La tenencia de la tierra en El Salvador." *Estudios Centroamericanos* 31. 335/336 (September/October): 463–472.

Colindres, Eduardo. 1978. *Fundamentos económicos de la burguesía salvadoreña*. San Salvador, El Salvador: UCA Editores.

Collier, Paul. 2007. *The Bottom Billion: Why the Poorest Countries Are Failing and What Can Be Done About It*. Oxford: Oxford University Press.

Collier, Paul, Anke Hoeffler, and Måns Söderbom. 2008. "Post-Conflict Risks." *Journal of Peace Research* 45.4 (July): 461–478.

Collins, Cath. 2010. *Post-Transitional Justice: Human Rights Trials in Chile and El Salvador*. University Park: Pennsylvania State University Press.

Cottam, Richard W. 1988. *Iran and the United States: A Cold War Case Study.* Pittsburgh: University of Pittsburgh Press.

Cox, Gary W. 2010. "A Model of Regime Choice." Paper Presented at the Annual Meetings of the American Political Science Association, Toronto, ON (September).

Cruz, José Miguel. 2001. *¿Elecciones para qué? el impacto del ciclo electoral 1999–2000 en la cultura política salvadoreña.* San Salvador: FLACSO.

Cullather, Nick. 2006. *Secret History: The CIA's Classified Account of its Operations in Guatemala, 1952–1954.* 2nd ed. Stanford, CA: Stanford University Press.

CVES (Comisión de la Verdad de El Salvador). 1993. *De la locura a la esperanza: la guerra de 12 años de El Salvador,* http://fundacionpdh.org/lesahumanidad/informes/elsalvador/informe-de-la-locura-a-la-esperanza.htm, accessed August 2, 2011.

Danner, Mark. 1994. *The Massacre at El Mozote: A Parable of the Cold War.* New York: Vintage Books.

Davenport, Christian, and Patrick Ball. 2002. "Views to a Kill: Exploring the Implications of Source Selection in the Case of Guatemalan State Terror, 1977–1995." *Journal of Conflict Resolution* 46.3 (June): 427–450.

Davis, Shelton H., and Julie Hodson. 1983. *Witnesses to Political Violence in Guatemala: The Suppression of a Rural Development Movement.* Boston: Oxfam America.

Demombynes, Gabriel. 2011. "Drug Trafficking and Violence in Central America and Beyond." Background Paper, World Development Report 2011, http://wdr2011.worldbank.org/Trafficking_and_Violence, accessed August 3, 2011.

Devlin, Robert. 1989. *Debt and Crisis in Latin America: The Supply Side of the Story.* Princeton, NJ: Princeton University Press.

Dickey, Christopher. 1985. *With the Contras: A Reporter in the Wilds of Nicaragua.* New York: Simon and Schuster.

Dillon, Sam. 1991. *Comandos: The CIA and Nicaragua's Contra Rebels.* New York: H. Holt.

Dinges, John. 1990. *Our Man in Panama: How General Noriega Used the United States and Made Millions in Drugs and Arms.* New York: Random House.

Dosal, Paul J. 1993. *Doing Business with the Dictators: A Political History of United Fruit in Guatemala, 1899–1944.* Wilmington, DE: Scholarly Resources.

Doyle, Michael W., and Nicholas Sambanis. 2006. *Making War and Building Peace: United Nations Peace Operations.* Princeton, NJ: Princeton University Press.

Duch, Raymond M., and Randolph T. Stevenson. 2008. *The Economic Vote: How Political and Economy Institutions Condition Election Results.* New York: Cambridge University Press.

Dunkerley, James. 1988. *Power in the Isthmus: A Political History of Modern Central America.* New York: Verso.

  1994. *The Pacification of Central America: Political Change in the Isthmus, 1987–1993.* New York: Verso.

Durham, William H. 1979. *Scarcity and Survival in Central America: Ecological Origins of the Soccer War.* Stanford, CA: Stanford University Press.

Dye, David R. 2004. *Democracy Adrift: Caudillo Politics in Nicaragua.* Managua, Nicaragua: Prodeni.

Dye, David R., Jack Spence, and George Vickers. 2000. *Patchwork Democracy: Nicaraguan Politics Ten Years After the Fall.* Brookline, MA: Hemisphere Initiatives.

Dye, David R., Judy Butler, Deena Abu-Lughod, Jack Spence, and George Vickers. 1995. *Contesting Everything, Winning Nothing: The Search for Consensus in Nicaragua, 1990–1995*. Brookline, MA: Hemisphere Initiatives.

Edelman, Marc. 1992. *The Logic of the Latifundio: The Large Estates of Northwestern Costa Rica since the Late Nineteenth Century*. Stanford, CA: Stanford University Press.

    1998. "Transnational Peasant Politics in Central America." *Latin American Research Review* 33.3: 49–86.

    1999. *Peasants Against Globalization: Rural Social Movements in Costa Rica*. Stanford, CA: Stanford University Press.

Edelman, Marc, and Mitchell A. Seligson. 1994. "Land Inequality: A Comparison of Census Data and Property Records in Twentieth-Century Southern Costa Rica." *The Hispanic American Historical Review* 74.3 (August): 445–491.

Edwards, Sebastian. 1995. *Crisis and Reform in Latin America: From Despair to Hope*. New York: Oxford University Press.

Ellis, Frank. 1983. *Las transnacionales del banano en Centroamérica*. San José, Costa Rica: EDUCA.

Epstein, David L., Robert Bates, Jack Goldstone, Ida Kristensen, and Sharon O'Halloran. 2006. "Democratic Transitions." *American Journal of Political Science* 50.3 (July): 551–569.

Escaith, Hubert, and Samuel Morley. 2001. "El efecto de las reformas estructurales en el crecimiento económico de la América Latina y el Caribe. Una estimación empírica." *El Trimestre Económico* 68.4 (Octubre-Diciembre): 469–513.

España Nájera, Annabella. 2009. "Party Systems and Democracy after the Conflicts: El Salvador, Guatemala, and Nicaragua," unpub. Ph.D. Dissertation, University of Notre Dame.

Esquivel, Gerardo. 2001. "Economic Growth in Central America: A Long-Run Perspective." In *Economic Development in Central America*, vol 1., ed. Felipe Larraín B. Cambridge, MA: John F. Kennedy School of Government, 88–117.

Esquivel, Gerardo, and Felipe Larraín B. 2001. "Currency Crises in Central America." In *Economic Development in Central America*. Vol 1, ed. Felipe Larraín B. Cambridge, MA: John F. Kennedy School of Government, 340–374.

Euraque, Darío A. 1996. *Reinterpreting the Banana Republic: Region and State in Honduras, 1870–1972*. Chapel Hill, NC: University of North Carolina Press.

Falla, Ricardo. 1994. *Massacres in the Jungle: Ixcán, Guatemala, 1975–1982*. Boulder, CO: Westview Press.

Fearon, James. D. 2010. "Governance and Civil War Onset," Background Paper, World Development Report 2011, http://wdr2011.worldbank.org/governance-and-civil-war-onset, accessed July 28, 2011.

Fearon, James D., and David D. Laitin. 2003. "Ethnicity, Insurgency, and Civil War." *American Political Science Review* 97.1 (February): 75–90.

Fernández-Arias, Eduardo, and Peter Montiel. 1997. "Reform and Growth in Latin America: All Pain, No Gain?" Working Paper No. 351. Washington, DC: Inter-American Development Bank.

Fernández González, Oscar. 1991. "Costa Rica: Una bipolaridad partidaria hoy apenas cuestionada." *Anuario de Estudios Centroamericanos*. 17.2: 65–74.

Figueroa Ibarra, Carlos. 1991. *El recurso del miedo: ensayo sobre el estado y el terror en Guatemala*. San José, Costa Rica: Programa Centroamericano de Investigaciones.

FitzGerald, Valpy, and Arturo Grigsby. 2001. "Nicaragua: The Political Economy of Social Reform and Armed Conflict." In *War and Underdevelopment: Country Experiences*. Vol. 2, eds. Valpy FitzGerald and Frances Stewart. New York: Oxford University Press, 119–154.

Fortín, Javier. 2010. "Transfuguismo parlamentario en Guatemala: Un caso de altos costos de asociación, monopolio partidario y bajos costos de transacción." *América Latina Hoy* 54: 141–166.

Fuentes, Juan Alberto. 2007. "Aumento de la carga tributaria y retos de la política fiscal en Centroamérica." *Trimestre Fiscal* 84: 649–721.

Fuentes, K., Juan Alberto, and Maynor Cabrera. 2006. "The Fiscal Covenant in Guatemala: Lessons Learned from the Negotiations." *CEPAL Review* 88: 145–157.

Gallagher, Michael. 2010. "Election Indices," http://www.tcd.ie/Political_Science/staff/michael_gallagher/ElSystems/index.php, accessed November 21, 2010.

García-López, Cristina, Felipe Larraín B., and José Tavares. 2001. "Exchange Rate Regimes: Assessing Central America's Options." In *Economic Development in Central America*. Vol. 1, ed. Felipe Larraín B. Cambridge, MA: John F. Kennedy School of Government, 297–339.

García Márquez, Gabriel. 1978. "The Sandinistas Seize the National Palace!" *New Left Review* 1.111 (September-October): 79–88.

García Montero, Mercedes. 2009. *Presidentes y parlamentos: ¿quién controla la actividad legislativa en América Latina?* Madrid: Centro de Investigaciones Sociológicas.

Gardner, John W. 1971. "The Costa Rican Junta of 1948-9," unpub. Ph.D. dissertation. St. John's University.

Garrand-Burnett, Virginia. 2010. *Terror in the Land of the Holy Spirit: Guatemala under General Efraín Ríos Montt, 1982–1983*. New York: Oxford University Press.

Gates, Scott, Håvard Hegre, Mark P. Jones, and Håvard Strand. 2006. "Institutional Inconsistency and Political Instability: Polity Duration, 1800–2000." *American Journal of Political Science* 50.4 (October): 893–908.

Geddes, Barbara. 1999. "What Do We Know About Democratization After Twenty Years?" *Annual Review of Political Science* 2 (June): 115–144.

      2007. "What Causes Democratization?" In *The Oxford Handbook of Comparative Politics*, eds. Carles Boix and Susan C. Stokes. New York: Oxford University Press, 317–339.

Gibson, Bill. 1987. "A Structural Overview of the Nicaraguan Economy." In *The Political Economy of Revolutionary Nicaragua*, ed. Rose J. Spalding. Boston: Allen & Unwin, 15–42.

Gibson, Clark C., and Fabrice Lehoucq. 2003. "The Local Politics of Decentralized Environmental Policy in Guatemala." *Journal of Environment and Development* 12.1 (March): 28–49.

Gleijeses, Piero. 1991. *Shattered Hope: The Guatemalan Revolution and the United States, 1944–1954*. Princeton, NJ: Princeton University Press.

      2006. "Afterward: The Culture of Fear." In *Secret History: The CIA's Classified Account of its Operations in Guatemala, 1952–1954*, by Nick Cullather. 2nd ed. Stanford: Stanford University Press, xxiii–xxxix.

Goldhagen, Daniel J. 2009. *Worse than War: Genocide, Eliminationism, and the Ongoing Assault on Humanity*. New York: Public Affairs.

Goldman, Francisco. 2008. *The Art of Political Murder: Who Killed the Bishop?* New York: Grove Press.

Goldstone, Jack A., Robert H. Bates, David L. Epstein, Ted Robert Gurr, Michael B. Lustik, Monty G. Marshall, Jay Ulfelder, and Mark Woodward. 2010. "A Global Model for Forecasting Political Instability." *American Journal of Political Science* 54.1 (January): 190–208.

González, Secundino. Forthcoming. "Las elecciones guatemaltecas de 2011," *Anuario de Estudios Centroamericanos.*

González Vega, Claudio. 1984. "Fear of Adjusting: The Social Costs of Economic Policies in Costa Rica in the 1970s." In *Revolution and Counterrevolution in Central America and the Caribbean,* eds. Donald E. Schulz and Douglas H. Graham. Boulder, CO: Westview, 351–383.

González Vega, Claudio, and Victor Hugo Céspedes. 1993. "Costa Rica." In *Costa Rica and Uruguay,* ed. Simon Rottenberg. New York: Oxford University Press for the World Bank.

Goodwin, Jeff. 2001. *No Other Way Out: States and Revolutionary Movements, 1945–1991.* Cambridge: Cambridge University Press.

Gorman, Stephen M. 1981. "Power and Consolidation in the Nicaraguan Revolution." *Journal of Latin American Studies* 13.1 (May): 133–149.

Gould, Jeffrey L. 1990. *To Lead as Equals: Rural Protest and Political Consciousness in Chinandega, Nicaragua, 1912–1979.* Chapel Hill, NC: University of North Carolina Press.

   1998. *To Die in This Way: Nicaraguan Indians and the Myth of Mestizaje, 1880–1965.* Durham, NC: Duke University Press.

Gould, Jeffrey L., and Aldo A. Lauria-Santiago. 2008. *To Rise in Darkness: Revolution, Repression, and Memory in El Salvador, 1920–1932.* Durham, NC: Duke University Press.

Gramajo Morales, Héctor Alejandro. 1997. "Political Transition in Guatemala, 1980–1990: A Perspective from Inside Guatemala's Army." In *Democratic Transitions in Central America,* eds. Jorge I. Domínguez and Marc Lindenberg. Gainesville, FL: University Press of Florida, 111–138.

Grandin, Greg. 2004. *The Last Colonial Massacre: Latin America in the Cold War.* Chicago: University of Chicago Press.

Greib, Kenneth J. 1979. *Guatemalan Caudillo: The Regime of Jorge Ubico, Guatemala, 1933–1944.* Athens, OH: Ohio University Press.

Gudmundson, Lowell. 1989. "Peasant, Farmer, Proletarian: Class Formation in a Smallholder Coffee Economy, 1850–1950." *Hispanic American Historical Review* 69.2 (May): 221–257.

   1995. "Lord and Peasant in the Making of Modern Central America." In *Agrarian Structure and Political Power: Landlord and Peasant in the Making of Latin America,* eds. Evelyne Huber and Frank Safford. Pittsburgh: University of Pittsburgh Press, 151–76.

Guidos Vejar, Rafael. 1980. *El ascenso del militarismo en El Salvador.* San Salvador, El Salvador: UCA Editores.

Gurses, Mehmet, and T. David Mason. 2008. "Democracy Out of Anarchy: The Prospects for Post-Civi -War Democracy." *Social Science Quarterly* 89.2 (June): 315–336.

Gutman, Roy. 1988. *Banana Diplomacy: The Making of American Foreign Policy in Nicaragua, 1981–1987.* New York: Simon and Schuster.

Hall, Carolyn, and Héctor Pérez-Brignoli. 2003. *Historical Atlas of Central America*. Norman, OK: University of Oklahoma Press.

Handy, Jim. 1994. *Revolution in the Countryside: Rural Conflict and Agrarian Reform in Guatemala, 1944–1954*. Chapel Hill, NC: University of North Carolina Press.

Hausmann, Ricardo, and Dani Rodrik. 2005. "Self-Discovery in a Development Strategy for El Salvador." *Economía* 6.1 (Fall): 43–101.

Hegre, Håvard, Tanja Ellingsen, Scott Gates, and Nils Petter Gleditsch. 2001. "Toward a Democratic Civil Peace? Democracy, Political Change, and Civil War, 1816–1992." *American Political Science Review* 95.1 (March): 33–48.

Hira, Anil and James W. Dean. 2004. "Distributional Effects of Dollarisation: The Latin American Case," *Third World Quarterly*, 25.3: 461–482.

Holden, Robert H. 2004. *Armies without Nations: Public Violence and State Formation in Central America, 1821–1960*. New York: Oxford University Press.

Honey, Martha S. 1994. *Hostile Acts: U.S. Policy in Costa Rica in the 1980s*. Gainesville, FL: University Press of Florida.

Horton, Lynn. 1998. *Peasants in Arms: War and Peace in the Mountains of Nicaragua, 1979–1994*. Athens, OH: Ohio University Press.

Hoyt, Katherine. 2004. "Parties and Pacts in Contemporary Nicaragua." In *Undoing Democracy: The Politics of Electoral Caudillismo*, eds. David Close and Kalowatie Deonandan. Lanham, MD: Lexington Books, 17–42.

Huber, Evelyne, François Nielsen, Jenny Pribble, and John D. Stephens. 2006. "Politics and Inequality in Latin America and the Caribbean." *American Sociological Review* 71.6 (December): 943–963.

Huber, Evelyne, Thomas Mustillo, and John D. Stephens. 2008. "Politics and Social Spending in Latin America." *Journal of Politics* 70.2 (April): 420–436.

Huntington, Samuel P. 1991. *The Third Wave: Democratization in the Late Twentieth Century*. Norman, OK: University of Oklahoma Press.

ICEFI (Instituto Centroamericano de Estudios Fiscales). 2007. *La política fiscal en la encrucijada: El caso de América Central*. Guatemala: ICEFI (http://www.icefi.org/categories/publicaciones?clas=1&detail=34, accessed December 21, 2010).

IICA-FLACSO. 1991. *Centroamerica en Cifras*. San José, Costa Rica: Instituto Interamericano de Cooperación para la Agricultura: Facultad Latinoamericana de Ciencias Sociales.

Inter-American Indian Institute. 1979. "La población indígena en América en 1978." *América Indígena* 39.2: 217–337.

Iversen, Torben. 2005. *Capitalism, Democracy, and Welfare*. New York: Cambridge University Press.

Jonas, Susanne. 1991. *The Battle for Guatemala: Rebels, Death Squads, and U.S. Power*. Boulder, CO: Westview Press.

  2000. *Of Centaurs and Doves: Guatemala's Peace Process*. Boulder, CO: Westview Press.

Jones, Mark P. 2008. "Political Party Institutionalization in Guatemala: A Policy Dialogue Paper for Guatemala (GU-N1051)." Paper Prepared for the Country Department Central America, Mexico, Panama, and the Dominican Republic of the Inter-American Development Bank.

  2010. "Beyond the Electoral Connection: The Effect of Political Parties on the Policymaking Process." In *How Democracy Works: Political Institutions, Actors, and Arenas in Latin American Policymaking*, eds. Carlos Scartascini, Ernesto

Stein, and Mariano Tommasi. Washington, DC: Inter-American Development Bank, 19–46.

Kagan, Robert. 1996. *A Twilight Struggle: American Power and Nicaragua, 1977–1990*. New York: Free Press.

Kalyvas, Stathis N. 2007. "Civil Wars." In *The Oxford Handbook of Comparative Politics*, eds. Carles Boix and Susan C. Stokes. New York: Oxford University Press, 416–434.

Kapuściński, Ryszard. 1991. *The Soccer War*. New York: Knopf.

Karl, Terry Lynn. 1985. "After La Palma: The Prospects for Democratization in El Salvador." *World Policy Journal* 2.2 (Spring): 305–330.

  1995. "The Hybrid Regimes of Central America." *Journal of Democracy* 6.3 (July): 72–86.

Kaye, Mike. 1997. "The Role of Truth Commissions in the Search for Justice, Reconciliation and Democratisation: The Salvadorean and Honduran Cases." *Journal of Latin American Studies* 29.3 (October): 693–716.

Keefer, Philip. 2007. "Clientelism, Credibility, and the Policy Choices of Young Democracies." *American Journal of Political Science* 51.4 (October): 804–821.

Kim, Young Hun, and Donna Bahry. 2008. "Interrupted Presidencies in Third Wave Democracies." *Journal of Politics* 70.3 (July): 807–822.

Kingstone, Peter. 2011. *The Political Economy of Latin America: Reflections on Neoliberalism and Development*. New York: Routledge.

Kinzer, Stephen. 2001a. "Guatemala: The Unfinished Peace." *The New York Review of Books* 48.10 (June): 61–63.

  2001b. "Country Without Heroes." *The New York Review of Books* 48.12 (July): 31–33.

  2007. *Blood of Brothers: Life and War in Nicaragua*. Boston, MA: David Rockefeller Center for Latin American Studies.

Kirkpatrick, Jeane. 1979. "Dictatorships and Double Standards." *Commentary* 68.5 (November): 34–45.

Korpi, Walter. 1983. *The Democratic Class Struggle*. London: Routledge Kegan & Paul.

Kruijt, Dirk. 2008. *Guerrillas: War and Peace in Central America*. London: Zed Books.

LaFeber, Walter. 1983. *Inevitable Revolutions: The United States in Central America*. New York: Norton.

Lauria-Santiago, Aldo. 1999. *An Agrarian Republic: Commercial Agriculture and the Politics of Peasant Communities in El Salvador, 1823–1914*. Pittsburgh, PA: University of Pittsburgh Press.

Lean, Sharon F. 2007. "The Presidential and Parliamentary Elections in Nicaragua, November 2006." *Electoral Studies* 26.4 (December): 828–832.

Le Bot, Yvon. 1995. *La guerra en tierras mayas: comunidad, violencia y modernidad en Guatemala (1970–1992)*. Mexico: Fondo de Cultura Económica.

Lecayo, Antonio. 2005. *La difícil transición nicaraguense: En el gobierno con Doña Violeta*. Managua, Nicaragua: Fundación Uno.

Lehoucq, Fabrice. 1991. "Class Conflict, Political Crisis, and the Breakdown of Democratic Practices in Costa Rica: Reassessing the Origins of the 1948 Civil War." *Journal of Latin American Studies* 23.1 (February): 37–60.

  1992. "The Origins of Democracy in Costa Rica in Comparative Perspective," unpub. Ph.D. dissertation, Durham, NC: Duke University.

1995a. "Institutional Change and Political Conflict: Evaluating Alternative Explanations of Electoral Reform in Costa Rica." *Electoral Studies* 14.1 (March): 23–45.

1995b. "The Elections of the Century in El Salvador." *Electoral Studies* 14.2 (June): 179–183.

1996. "The Institutional Foundations of Democratic Cooperation in Costa Rica." *Journal of Latin American Studies* 28.2 (May): 329–355.

1998a. *Instituciones democráticas y conflictos políticos en Costa Rica*. San José, Costa Rica: EUNA.

1998b. "Investigando bajo la lluvia." In *Ciencia Social en Costa Rica: experiencias de vida e investigación*, ed. Marc Edelman. San José: EUCR-EUNA, 37–60.

2000. "Institutionalizing Democracy: Constraint and Ambition in the Politics of Electoral Reform." *Comparative Politics* 32.4 (July): 459–477.

2002. "Can Parties Police Themselves? Electoral Governance and Democratization." *International Political Science Review* 23.1 (January): 29–46.

2003. "La economía política de la inestabilidad política: Dana G. Munro y su estudio sobre Centroamérica." In *Las cinco repúblicas de Centroamérica*, by Dana Gardner Munro. San José: Editorial de la Universidad de Costa Rica, 1–22.

2004. "Costa Rica: Modifying Majoritarianism with a 40 Percent Threshold." In *Handbook of Electoral System Choice*, ed. Josep M. Colomer. London: Palgrave Macmillan, 133–144.

2005. "Costa Rica: Paradise in Doubt." *Journal of Democracy* 16.3 (July): 140–154.

2006. "Different Times, Different Demands." *Journal of Democracy* 17.2 (April): 165–167.

2008. "Proceso de políticas, partidos e instituciones en la Costa Rica Democrática." In *Democracia estable, ¿alcanza? Análisis de la gobernabilidad en Costa Rica*, eds. Miguel Gutiérrez Saxe and Fernando Straface. Washington, DC: Banco Interamericano de Desarrollo, Estado de la Nación, 165–202 (http://www.iadb.org/publications/search.cfm?query=democracia+estable&context=Title&lang=en&searchLang=all&searchtype=general, accessed January 30, 2008).

2010. "Political Competition, Constitutional Arrangements, and the Quality of Public Policies in Costa Rica." *Latin American Politics and Society* 52.4 (Winter): 53–77.

2011. "The Third and Fourth Waves of Democracy." In *Routledge Handbook of Democratization*, ed. by Jeffrey Haynes. London: Routledge, 273–286.

Lehoucq, Fabrice, and Iván Molina. 2002. *Stuffing the Ballot Box: Fraud, Electoral Reform, and Democratization in Costa Rica*. New York: Cambridge University Press.

Lehoucq, Fabrice, and Aníbal Pérez-Liñán. 2009. "Regimes, Competition, and Military Coups in Latin America, Paper Presented at the Annual Meetings of the American Political Association, Toronto, Ontario, Canada (3–6 September).

Lehoucq, Fabrice, and Harold Sims. 1982. "Reform with Repression: The Land Reform in El Salvador." *ISHI Occasional Papers in Social Change*, No. 6. Philadelphia: Institute for the Study of Human Issues.

Lehoucq, Fabrice, and David L. Wall. 2004. "Explaining Voter Turnout Rates in New Democracies: Guatemala." *Electoral Studies* 23.3 (September): 485–500.

Leiby, Michele L. 2009. "Wartime Sexual Violence in Guatemala and Peru." *International Studies Quarterly* 53.2 (June): 445–468.

LeoGrande, William M. 1979. "The Revolution in Nicaragua: Another Cuba?" *Foreign Affairs* 58.1 (Fall): 28–50.

1998. *Our Own Backyard: The United States in Central America, 1977–1992.* Chapel Hill, NC: University of North Carolina Press.

Leogrande, William M., and Philip Brenner. 1993. "The House Divided: Ideological Polarization over Aid to the Nicaraguan 'Contras'," *Legislative Studies Quarterly* 18.1 (February): 105–136.

Leogrande, William M., and Carla Anne Robbins. 1980. "Oligarchs and Officers: The Crisis in El Salvador." *Foreign Affairs* 58.5 (Summer): 1084–1103.

Leonard, Thomas M. 1991. *Central America and the United States: The Search for Stability.* Athens, GA: University of Georgia Press.

Levenson-Estrada, Deborah. 1994. *Trade Unionists against Terror: Guatemala City, 1954–1985.* Chapel Hill, NC: University of North Carolina Press.

Levitsky, Steven and Lucan Way. 2010. *Competitive Authoritarianism: Hybrid Regimes After the Cold War.* New York: Cambridge University Press.

Lindenberg, Marc. 1990. "World Economic Cycles and Central American Political Instability." *World Politics* 42.3 (April): 397–421.

Lindert, Kathy, Emmanuel Skoufias, and Joseph Shapiro. 2006. "Redistributing Income to the Poor and the Rich: Public Transfers in Latin America and the Caribbean." World Bank Institute. SP Discussion Paper No. 0605 (August).

Lipset, Seymour Martin. 1959. "Some Social Requisites of Democracy: Economic Development and Political Legitimacy." *American Political Science Review* 53.1 (March): 69–105.

Lizano, Eduardo. 1999. *Ajuste y crecimiento en la economía de Costa Rica, 1982–1994.* San José, Costa Rica: Academia de Centroamérica.

Loayza, Norman, Pablo Fajnzylber, and César Calderón. 2005. *Economic Growth in Latin America and the Caribbean: Stylized Facts, Explanations, and Forecasts.* Washington, DC: World Bank.

López, José Roberto. 1986. *La economía del banano en Centroamérica.* San José, Costa Rica: DEI.

1986. "Los orígenes económicos de la crises en Centroamérica." In *Centroamérica: política económica y crisis,* ed. Eugenio Rivera Urrutia et al. Costa Rica: DEI, ICADIS, UNA, 115–201.

Lora, Eduardo. 2001. "Structural Reforms in Latin America: What Has Been Reformed and How to Measure It?" Research Department Working Paper No. 466. Washington, DC: Inter-American Development Bank (December).

Lora, Eduardo, and Felipe Barrera. 1997. "Una década de reformas estructurales en América Latina: El crecimiento, la productividad y la inversión, ya no son como antes." Research Department Working Paper No. 350. Washington, DC: Inter-American Development Bank.

Luciak, Ilja A. 1995. *The Sandinista Legacy: Lessons from a Political Economy in Transition.* Gainesville, FL: University Press of Florida.

Lungo Uclés, Mario. 1996. *El Salvador in the Eighties: Counterinsurgency and Revolution.* Philadelphia: Temple University Press.

McClearly, Rachel M. 1999. *Dictating Democracy: Guatemala and the End of Violent Revolution.* Gainesville, FL: University Press of Florida.

McClintock, Cynthia. 1998. *Revolutionary Movements in Latin America: El Salvador's FMLN and Peru's Shining Path.* Washington, DC: United States Institute of Peace Press.

McCreery, David. 1994. *Rural Guatemala, 1760–1940.* Stanford, CA: Stanford University Press.

McGuire, James W. 2010. *Wealth, Health, and Democracy in East Asia and Latin America*. New York: Cambridge University Press.

Maddison, Angus. 2010. "Statistics on World Population, GDP and Per Capita GDP, 1–2008 AD (Horizontal file)," http://www.ggdc.net/MADDISON/oriindex.htm, accessed February 15, 2011.

Madrid, Raul L. 2003. *Retiring the State: The Politics of Pension Privatization in Latin America and Beyond*. Stanford, CA: Stanford University Press.

Mahoney, James. 2001. *The Legacies of Liberalism: Path Dependence and Political Regimes in Central America*. Baltimore: Johns Hopkins University Press.

Mainwaring, Scott P., Daniel Brinks, and Aníbal Pérez-Liñán. 2008. "Political Regimes in Latin America, 1900–2007," http://kellogg.nd.edu/scottmainwaring/Political_Regimes.pdf, accessed October 12, 2010.

Mainwaring, Scott P., Timothy R. Scully, and Jorge Vargas Cullell. 2010. "Measuring Success in Democratic Governance." In *Democratic Governance in Latin America*, eds. Scott Mainwaring and Timothy Scully. Stanford, CA: Stanford University Press, 11–51.

Manwaring, Max G., and Court E. Prisk, eds. 1988. *El Salvador at War: An Oral History of Conflict from the 1979 Insurrection to the Present*. Washington, DC: National Defense University Press.

Manz, Beatrice. 1988. *Refugees of a Hidden War: The Aftermath of the Counterinsurgency in Guatemala*. Albany, NY: SUNY Press.

2005. *Paradise in Ashes: A Guatemalan Journey of Courage, Terror, and Hope*. Berkeley: University of California Press.

Markoff, John. 1996a. *The Abolition of Feudalism: Peasants, Lords, and Legislators in the French Revolution*. University Park, PA: Pennsylvania State University Press.

1996b. *Waves of Democracy: Social Movements and Political Change*. Thousand Oaks, CA: Pine Forge Press.

Martí i Puig, Salvador. 2004. *Tiranías, rebeliones y democracia: Itinerarios políticos comparados en Centroamérica*. Barcelona: Edicions Bellaterra.

2008 "El regreso del FSLN al poder: ¿Es posible hablar de realineamiento electoral en Nicaragua?" *Política y Gobierno* 15.1 (1 semestre): 75–112.

2010. "The Adaptation of the FSLN: Daniel Ortega's Leadership and Democracy in Nicaragua." *Latin American Politics and Society* 52.4 (Winter): 79–106.

Martín-Baró, Ignacio. 1994. *Writings for a Liberation Psychology*, ed. by Adrianne Aron and Shawn Corne. Cambridge, MA: Harvard University Press.

Martín-Baró, Ignacio, and Victor Antonio Orellana. 1984. "La necesidad de votar: actitudes del pueblo salvadoreño ante el proceso electoral de 1984." *Estudios Centroamericanos* 39 (April-May): 253–264.

Martínez Franzoni, Juliana. 2008a. "Welfare Regimes in Latin America: Capturing Constellations of Markets, Families, and Policies." *Latin American Politics and Society* 50.2 (Summer): 67–100.

2008b. "Costa Rica's Pension Reform: A Decade of Negotiated Incremental Change." In *Lessons from Pension Reform in the Americas*, eds. Stephen J. Kay and Tapen Sinha. Oxford: Oxford University Press, 317–339.

Maurer, Noel, and Carlos Yu. 2010. *The Big Ditch: How America Took, Built, Ran, and Ultimately Gave Away the Panama Canal*. Princeton, NJ: Princeton University Press.

Meléndez, Dennis, and Mauricio Meza Ramírez. 1993. *Codesa: Origen y consecuencias*. San José, Costa Rica: Litografía e Imprenta Lil.

Meltzer, Allan H., and Scott F. Richard. 1981. "A Rational Theory of the Size of Government." *Journal of Political Economy* 89.5 (January): 914–927.

Mesa-Lago, Carmelo. 2000. *Market, Socialist, and Mixed Economies: Comparative Policy and Performance: Chile, Cuba, and Costa Rica*. Baltimore: Johns Hopkins University Press.

Midlarsky, Manus I., and Kenneth Roberts. 1985. "Class, State, and Revolution in Central America: Nicaragua and El Salvador Compared." *The Journal of Conflict Resolution* 29.2 (June): 163–193.

Miller, Peter V. 1991. "Which Side Are You On? The 1990 Nicaraguan Poll Debacle." *Public Opinion Quarterly* 55.2 (Summer): 281–302.

Millet, Richard. 1977. *Guardians of the Dynasty*. New York: Orbis Books.

Molina, Iván, and Steven Palmer. 2004. "Popular Literacy in a Tropical Democracy: Costa Rica 1850–1950." *Past & Present* 184.1 (August): 169–207.

Montejo, Victor. 1995. *Testimony: Death of a Guatemalan Village*. Willimantic, CT: Curbstone Press.

Montgomery, Tommie Sue. 1995. *Revolution in El Salvador: From Civil Strife to Civil Peace*. Boulder, CO: Westview Press.

Morris, J. A., and M. F. Sánchez Soler. 1977. "Factores de poder en la evolución política del campesinado Hondureño." *Estudios Sociales Centroamericanos* 6.16 (Enero): 85–103.

Muller, Edward N., and Mitchell A. Seligson. 1987. "Inequality and Insurgency." *American Political Science Review* 81.2 (June): 425–452.

Munro, Dana G. 1918. *The Five Republics of Central America*. New York: Oxford University Press.

   1983. *A Student in Central America, 1914–1916*. New Orleans: Tulane University Middle American Research Institute.

Naím, Moisés. 1994. "Latin America: The Second Stage of Reform." *Journal of Democracy* 5.4 (October): 32–48.

Negretto, Gabriel. 2006. "Minority Presidents and Democratic Performance in Latin America." *Latin American Politics and Society* 48.3 (September): 63–89.

Negretto, Gabriel. 2008. "Political Parties and Institutional Design: Explaining Constitutional Choice in Latin America." *British Journal of Political Science* 39.1 (January): 117–139.

O'Campo, José Antonio. 1991. "Collapse and (Incomplete) Stabilization of the Nicaraguan Economy." In *The Macroeconomics of Populism in Latin America*, eds. Rudiger Dornbusch and Sebastian Edwards. Chicago: University of Chicago Press, 331–368.

OECD (Organisation for Economic Co-operation and Development). 2007. *Revenue Statistics, 1965–2006*. Paris: OECD.

OECD (Organisation for Economic Co-operation and Development). 2010. "OECD Stat Extracts," http://stats.oecd.org/index.aspx, accessed October 10, 2010.

Offerdal, Erik. 2004. "Fiscal Sustainability." In *The Macroeconomy of Central America*, eds. Robert Rennhack and Erik Offerdal. Houndmills, Basingstoke, Hampshire: Palgrave Macmillan, 1–40.

Orozco, Manuel. 2007. "Central America: Remittances and the Macroeconomic Variable." Inter-American Dialogue (September).

Ortega Hegg, Manuel. 2007. "Nicaragua 2006: El regreso del FSLN al poder." *Revista de Ciencia Política* 27: 205–219.

Paige, Jeffery M. 1983. "Social Theory and Peasant Revolution in Vietnam and Guatemala." *Theory & Society* 12.6 (November): 699–737.

   1997. *Coffee and Power: Revolution and the Rise of Democracy in Central America*. Cambridge, MA: Harvard University Press.

Parker, Franklin. 1964. *The Central American Republics*. NewYork: Oxford University Press.

Parkman, Patricia. 1988. *Nonviolent Insurrection in El Salvador: The Fall of Maximiliano Hernández-Martínez*. Tucson, AZ: University of Arizona Press.

Pásara, Luis. 2003. *Paz, ilusión y cambio en Guatemala: El proceso de paz, sus actores, logros y límites*. Guatemala: Instituto de Investigaciones Jurídicas.

Pastor, Robert A. 2002. *Not Condemned to Repetition: The United States and Nicaragua*. Boulder, CO: Westview Press.

Paus, Eva. 2005. *Foreign Investment, Development, and Globalization: Can Costa Rica Become Ireland?* New York: Palgrave Macmillan.

Payne, J. Mark. 2007. "Legislative Electoral Systems and Democratic Governability." In *Democracies in Development: Politics and Reform in Latin America*, ed. J. Mark Payne. Rev. ed. Washington, DC: Inter-American Development Bank and the International Institute for Democracy and Electoral Assistance, 37–80.

Pearce, Jenny. 1986. *Promised Land: Peasant Rebellion in Chalatenango, El Salvador*. New York: Monthly Review Press.

Peceny, Mark, and William D. Stanley. 2001. "Liberal Social Reconstruction and the Resolution of Civil Wars in Central America." *International Organization* 55.1 (Winter): 149–183.

———. 2010. "Counterinsurgency in El Salvador." *Politics and Society* 38.1 (March): 67–94.

Pelupessy, Wim. 1997. *The Limits of Economic Reform in El Salvador*. New York: St. Martin's Press.

Pelupessy, Wim, and John Weeks, eds. 1993. *Economic Maladjustment in Central America*. New York: St. Martin's Press.

PEN (Proyecto del Estado de la Nación). 2001. *Auditoría Ciudadana sobre la Calidad de la Democracia*. San José, Costa Rica: Programa del Estado de la Nación.

PEN (Programa del Estado de la Nación). 2003. *Estado de la Nación en Desarrollo Humano Sostenible, X Aniversario*. San José, Costa Rica: Programa del Estado de la Nación.

———. 2004. *Estado de la Nación en Desarrollo Humano Sostenible*. San José, Costa Rica: Programa del Estado de la Nación.

PENR (Programa del Estado de la Nación – Región). 2008. *Estado de la región en desarrollo humano sostenible 2008*. San José, Costa Rica: Proyecto Estado de la Nación – Región.

———. 2011. *Estado de la región en desarrollo humano sostenible 2011*. San José, Costa Rica: Proyecto Estado de la Nación – Región.

PER (Proyecto del Estado de la Región). 2003. *Estado de la región en desarrollo humano sostenible 2003*. San José, Costa Rica: Proyecto Estado de la Nación.

———. 2006. *Estado de la región en desarrollo humano sostenible 2006*. San José, Costa Rica: Proyecto Estado de la Nación.

Perera, Victor. 1993. *Unfinished Conquest: The Guatemalan Tragedy*. Berkeley, CA: University of California Press.

Pérez-Brignoli, Héctor. 1989. *A Brief History of Central America*. Berkeley, CA: University of California Press.

———. 1994. "Crecimiento agroexportador y regímenes políticos en Centroamérica: un ensayo de historia comparada." In *Tierra, café y sociedad: ensayos sobre la historia agraria centroamericana*, eds. Héctor Pérez-Brignoli and Mario Samper. San José, Costa Rica: FLACSO, 25–54.

2011. "Las economías centroamericanas, 1810–2010," In *Institucionalidad y desarrollo económico en América Latina* eds. Luis Bértola and Pablo Gerchunoff. Santiago de Chile: CEPAL, 93–134.

Pérez-Liñán, Aníbal. 2007. *Presidential Impeachment and the New Political Instability in Latin America.* New York: Cambridge University Press.

Pérez Sáinz, Juan Pablo. 1994. *El dilema del nahual: Globalización, exclusión y trabajo en Centroamérica.* San José, Costa Rica: FLACSO.

Pérez Sáinz, Juan Pablo, and Minor Mora Salas. 2007. *La persistencia de la miseria en Centroamérica: Una mirada desde la exclusión social.* San José, Costa Rica: FLACSO.

Pezzullo, Lawrence, and Ralph Pezzullo. 1993. *At the Fall of Somoza.* Pittsburgh, PA: University of Pittsburgh Press.

PITF (Political Instability Task Force). 2010. Replication Data for "A Global Model for Forecasting Political Instability," http://globalpolicy.gmu.edu/pitf/AJPSmat.htm, accessed July 7, 2011.

Posas, Mario. 1981. *Luchas del movimiento obrero Hondureño.* San José, Costa Rica: EDUCA.

   1989. *Modalidades del proceso de democratización en Honduras.* Tegucigalpa, Honduras: Editorial Universitaria.

Powell, G. Bingham, Jr. 2000. *Elections as Instruments of Democracy: Majoritarian and Proportional Visions.* New Haven, CT: Yale University Press.

Przeworski, Adam. 1991. *Democracy and the Market: Political and Economic Reforms in Eastern Europe and Latin America.* Cambridge: Cambridge University Press.

   2005. "Democracy as an Equilibrium." *Public Choice* 123.3–4 (June): 253–273.

   2008. "Self-Enforcing Democracy." In *The Oxford Handbook of Political Economy,* eds. Barry R. Weingast and Donald A. Wittman. New York: Oxford University Press, 312–328.

   2010. *Democracy and the Limits of Self-Government.* New York: Cambridge University Press.

Przeworski, Adam, Michael E. Alvarez, José Antonio Cheibub, and Fernando Limongi. 2000. *Democracy and Development: Political Institutions and Well-Being in the World, 1950–1990.* New York: Cambridge University Press.

Ramírez, Sergio. 1999. *Adiós muchachos: Una memoria de la revolución Sandinista.* Mexico, DF: Aguilar.

Ramírez Cover, Alonso. 2011. "Institucionalidad Pública en Centroamérica." working paper, IV Informe del Estado de la Región. San José, Costa Rica: Estado de la Región.

Raventós, Ciska. 1986. "Desarrollo económico, estructura y contradicciones sociales en la producción de café." *Revista de Historia* 14: 179–195.

Raventós Vorst, Ciska, Marco Vinicio Fournier Facio, Olman Ramírez Moreira, Ana Lucía Gutiérrez Espeleta, and Jorge Raúl García Fernández. 2005. *El abstencionismo en Costa Rica ¿Quiénes y por qué no votan los ciudadanos en las elecciones nacionales?* San José, Costa Rica: Editorial de la Universidad de Costa Rica.

Remijnse, Simone. 2002. *Memories of Violence: Civil Patrols and the Legacy of Conflict in Joyabaj, Guatemala.* Amsterdam, Netherlands: Rozenberg.

Reynolds, Clark. 1978. "Employment Problems of Export Economies in a Common Market: The Case of Central America." In *Economic Integration in Central America,* eds. William R. Cline and Enrique Delgado. Washington, DC: Brookings Institution Press, 181–266.

Ricord, Humberto E. 1991. *Noriega y Panamá: orgía y aplastamiento de la narcodictadura*. México, D.F.: n.p.

Robinson, James A. 2006. "Economic Development and Democracy." *Annual Review of Political Science* 9 (June): 503–527.

Robinson, William I. 1992. *A Faustian Bargain: U.S. Intervention in the Nicaraguan Elections and American Foreign Policy in the Post-Cold War Era*. Boulder, CO: Westview Press.

2003. *Transnational Conflicts: Central America, Social Change and Globalization*. New York: Verso.

Rockwell, Rick, and Noreene Janus. 2003. *Media Power in Central America*. Urbana, IL: University of Illinois Press.

Rodríguez-Clare, Andrés, Manrique Sáenz, and Alberto Trejos. 2004. "Análisis del crecimiento en Costa Rica 1950–2000." In *Pequeñas economías, grandes desafíos: Políticas económicas para el desarrollo en Centroamérica*, eds. Manuel R. Agosín, Roberto Machado, and Paulina Nazal. Washington, DC: Inter-American Development Bank, 111–178.

Roemer, John E., Woojin Lee, and Karine van der Straeten. 2007. *Racism, Xenophobia, and Distribution: Multi-Issue Politics in Advanced Democracies*. New York: Russell Sage Foundation.

Romer, Thomas. 1975. "Individual Welfare, Majority Voting, and the Properties of a Linear Income Tax." *Journal of Public Economics* 4.1 (February): 163–185.

Ropp, S. C. 1992. "Explaining the Long-Term Maintenance of a Military Regime: Panama before the U.S. Invasion." *World Politics* 44.2 (January): 210–234.

Ros, Jamie. 2005. "Divergence and Growth Collapses: Theory and Empirical Evidence." In *Beyond Reforms: Structural Dynamics and Macroeconomic Vulnerability*, ed. José Antonio O'Campo. Palo Alto, CA: Stanford University Press, 211–232.

2006. "Changing Growth Constraints in Latin America." In *Vanishing Growth in Latin America: The Late Twentieth Century Experience*, ed. Andrés Solimano. Northampton, MA: Edward Elgar Publishing, 133–160.

Rosas, Guillermo. 2010. "Trust in Elections and the Institutional Design of Electoral Authorities: Evidence from Latin America." *Electoral Studies* 29.1 (March): 74–90.

Rouquié, Alain. 1994. *Guerras y paz en América Central*. México, DF: Fondo de Cultura Económica.

Rovira Mas, Jorge. 1982. *Estado y política económica en Costa Rica, 1948–70*. San José, Costa Rica: Editorial Porvenir.

2001. "¿Se debilita el bipartidismo?" In *La democracia de Costa Rica ante el Siglo XXI*, ed. Jorge Rovira Mas. San José, Costa Rica: Editorial de la Universidad de Costa Rica, 195–232.

Ruccio, David F. 1987. "The State, Planning and Transition in Nicaragua." *Development and Change* 18.1 (January): 5–27.

1988. "State, Class, and Transition in Nicaragua." *Latin American Perspectives* 15.2 (Spring): 50–71.

Rueda, David. 2005. "Insider–Outsider Politics in Industrialized Democracies: The Challenge to Social Democratic Parties." *American Political Science Review* 99.1 (February): 61–74.

Rueschemeyer, Dietrich, Evelyne Huber Stephens, and John D. Stephens. 1992. *Capitalist Development and Democracy*. Chicago: University of Chicago Press.

Ruhl, J. Mark. 1984. "Agrarian Structure and Political Stability in Honduras." *Journal of Interamerican Studies and World Affairs* 26.1 (February): 33–68.

    1996. "Redefining Civil-Military Relations in Honduras." *Journal of Interamerican Studies and World Affairs* 38.1 (Spring): 33–66.

    2003. "Civil-Military Relations in Post-Sandinista Nicaragua." *Armed Forces & Society* 30.1 (Fall): 117–139.

    2005. "The Guatemalan Military since the Peace Accords: The Fate of Reform Under Arzú and Portillo." *Latin American Politics & Society* 47.1 (Spring): 55–85.

    2010. "Honduras Unravels." *Journal of Democracy* 21.2 (April): 93–107.

Rustow, Dankwart A. 1970. "Transitions to Democracy: Toward a Dynamic Model." *Comparative Politics* 2.3 (April): 337–363.

Saiegh, Sebastian M. 2011. *Ruling by Statute: How Uncertainty and Vote Buying Shape Lawmaking.* Cambridge: Cambridge University Press.

SALA. 1984. *Statistical Abstract of Latin America.* Los Angeles: UCLA Latin American Center Publications.

Salomón, Leticia. 1982. *Militarismo y reformismo en Honduras.* Tegucigalpa, Honduras: Editorial Guaymuras.

    1992. *Política y militares en Honduras.* Tegucigalpa, Honduras: Centro de Documentación de Honduras, 1992.

Samayoa, Salvador. 2002. *El Salvador: La reforma pactada.* San Salvador, El Salvador: UCA Editores.

Sambanis, Nicholas. 2004. "What Is Civil War? Conceptual and Empirical Complexities of an Operational Definition." *Journal of Conflict Resolution* 48.6 (December): 814–858.

Samper K., Mario. 1990. *Generations of Settlers: Rural Households and Markets on the Costa Rican Frontier, 1850–1935.* Boulder, CO: Westview Press.

    1998. *Producción cafetalera y poder político en Centroamérica.* San José, Costa Rica: EDUCA.

Sánchez, Fernando F. 2007. *Partidos políticos, elecciones y lealtades partidarias en Costa Rica: Erosión y cambio.* Salamanca: Ediciones Universidad de Salamanca.

Sánchez, Omar. 2008. "Guatemala's Party Universe: A Case Study in Underinstitutionalization." *Latin American Politics & Society* 50.1 (Spring): 123–151.

Sánchez-Ancochea, Diego. 2006. "Development Trajectories and New Comparative Advantages: Costa Rica and the Dominican Republic under Globalization." *World Development* 34.6 (June): 996–1015.

Sandbrook, Richard, Marc Edelman, Patrick Heller, and Judith Teichman. 2007. *Social Democracy in the Global Periphery: Origins, Challenges, Prospects.* New York: Cambridge University Press.

Sanford, Victoria. 2003. *Buried Secrets: Truth and Human Rights in Guatemala.* New York: Palgrave Macmillan.

Schirmer, Jennifer G. 1998. *The Guatemalan Military Project: A Violence Called Democracy.* Philadelphia: University of Pennsylvania Press.

Schlesinger, Stephen, and Stephen Kinzer. 2005. *Bitter Fruit: The Story of the American Coup In Guatemala.* Cambridge, MA: Harvard University Press.

Schulz, Donald E., and Deborah S. Schulz. 1994. *The United States, Honduras, and the Crisis in Central America.* Boulder, CO: Westview Press.

Scranton, Margaret E. 1991. *The Noriega Years: U.S.-Panamanian Relations, 1981–1990.* Boulder, CO: Lynne Rienner Publishers.

2000. "Electoral Reform and the Institutionalization of the Electoral Tribunal in Post-Invasion Panama." In *Post-Invasion Panama: The Challenges of Democratization in the New World Order*, ed. Orlando J. Pérez. Landham, MD: Lexington Books, 101–124.

Segovia, Alexander. 2002. *Transformación estructural y reforma económica en El Salvador*. Guatemala: F & G Editores.

2004. "Centroamérica después del café: El fin del modelo agroexportador tradicional y el surgimiento de un nuevo modelo." *Revista Centroamericana de Ciencias Sociales* 2.1 (Diciembre): 5–38.

Seligson, Mitchell A. 1987. "Development, Democratization, and Decay: Central America at the Crossroads," In *Authoritarians and Democrats: Regime Transition in Latin America*, eds. James M. Malloy and Mitchell A. Seligson. Pittsburgh, PA: University of Pittsburgh Press, 167–192.

2002. "Trouble in Paradise? The Erosion of System Support in Costa Rica, 1978–1999." *Latin American Research Review* 37.1: 160–185.

2005. "Democracy on Ice: The Multiple Challenges of Guatemala's Peace Process." In *The Third Wave of Democratization in Latin America: Advances and Setbacks*, eds. Frances Hagopian and Scott P. Mainwaring. New York: Cambridge University Press, 202–234.

Seligison, Mitchell A., and Miguel Gómez B. 1989. "Ordinary Elections in Extraordinary Times: The Political Economy of Voting in Costa Rica," In *Elections and Democracy in Central America*, eds. John A. Booth and Mitchell A. Seligson. Chapel Hill, NC: University of North Carolina Press, 158–84.

Seligson, Mitchell A., and John A. Booth. 2010. "Crime, Hard Times, and Discontent." *Journal of Democracy* 21.2 (April): 123–135.

Seligson, Mitchell A., and John Kelley. 1986. "Tierra y trabajo en Guatemala: La ecuación desequilibrada." *Anuario de Estudios Centroamericanos* 12.2: 5–34.

Seligson, Mitchell A., and Vincent McElhinny. 1996. "Low-Intensity Warfare, High-Intensity Death: The Demographic Impact of the Wars in El Salvador and Nicaragua." *Canadian Journal of Latin American and Caribbean Studies* 12.42: 211–241.

Skocpol, Theda. 1979. *States and Social Revolutions: A Comparative Analysis of France, Russia, and China*. Cambridge: Cambridge University Press.

1994. *Social Revolutions in the Modern World*. New York: Cambridge University Press.

Smith, Carol A. 1988. "Destruction of the Material Bases for Indian Culture: Economic Changes in Totonicapán." In *Harvest of Violence: The Maya Indians and the Guatemalan Crisis*, ed. Robert M. Carmack. Norman, OK: University of Oklahoma Press, 206–231.

1990. "The Militarization of Civil Society in Guatemala: Economic Reorganisation as a Continuation of War." *Latin American Perspectives* 17.4 (Fall): 8–41.

Smith, Carol A. and Jeff Boyer. 1987. "Central America since 1979: Part I," *Annual Review of Anthropology*, 16: 197–221.

Smith, Carol. A., Jefferson Boyer, and Martin Diskin. 1988. "Central America since 1979: Part II," *Annual Review of Anthropology*, 17: 331–364.

Smith-Nonini, Sandy. 2010. *Healing the Body Politic: El Salvador's Popular Struggle for Health Rights – From Civil War to Neoliberal Peace*. New Brunswick, NJ: Rutgers University Press.

Sobrado González, Luis Antonio. 2010. "Financiamiento de los partidos políticos en Costa Rica." *Revista de Derecho Electoral* 9.1: 1–44.

Spalding, Rose J. 1994. *Capitalists and Revolution in Nicaragua: Opposition and Accommodation, 1979–1993.* Chapel Hill, NC: University of North Carolina Press.

——— 1999. "From Low-Intensity War to Low-Intensity Peace: The Nicaraguan Peace Process." In *Comparative Peace Processes in Latin America*, ed. Cynthia J. Arnson. Washington, DC: Woodrow Wilson Center Press, 31–64.

Spence, Jack. 2004. *War and Peace in Central America: Comparing Transitions Toward Democracy and Social Equity in Guatemala, El Salvador, and Nicaragua.* Brookline, MA: Hemisphere Initiatives.

Spence, Jack, David Dye, George Vickers, Garth David Cheff, Carol Lynne D'Arcangelis, and Ken Ward. 1994. *El Salvador's Elections of the Century: Results, Recommendations, Analysis.* Brookline, MA: Hemisphere Initiatives.

Spence, Jack, Mike Lanchin, and Geoff Thale. 2001. *From Elections to Earthquakes: Reform and Participation in Post-War El Salvador.* Cambridge, MA: Hemisphere Initiatives.

Stahler-Sholk, Richard. 1997. "Structural Adjustment and Resistance: The Political Economy of Nicaragua under Chamorro." In *The Undermining of the Sandinista Revolution*, eds. Gary Prevost and Harry E. Vanden. New York: St. Martin's Press, 74–113.

Stanley, William. 1996. *The Protection Racket State: Elite Politics, Military Extortion, and the Origins of El Salvador's Civil War.* Philadelphia: Temple University Press.

Stanley, William, and David Holiday. 2002. "Broad Participation, Diffuse Responsibility: Peace Implementation in Guatemala." In *Ending Civil Wars: The Implementation of Peace Agreements*, eds. Stephen John Stedman, Donald Rothchild, and Elizabeth M. Cousens. Boulder, CO: Lynne Rienner Publishers, 421–462.

Stoll, David. 1993. *Between Two Armies in the Ixil Towns of Guatemala.* New York: Columbia University Press.

Straface, Fernando, and Jorge Vargas Cullell. 2008. "Gestión pública." In *Democracia estable, ¿alcanza? Análisis de la gobernabilidad en Costa Rica*, eds. Miguel Gutiérrez Saxe and Fernando Straface. Washington, DC: Banco Interamericano de Desarrollo, Estado de la Nación, 97–130.

Svolik, Milan. 2008. "Authoritarian Reversals and Democratic Consolidation." *American Political Science Review* 102.2 (May): 153–168.

Taracena Arriola, Arturo. 1993. "Liberalismo y poder político en Centroamérica (1870–1929)." In *Historia general de Centroamérica: las repúblicas agroexportadoras*, ed. Victor Hugo Acuña Ortega. Madrid: FLACSO, 167–253.

Taylor, Michelle M. 1996. "When Electoral and Party Institutions Interact to Produce Caudillo Politics: The Case of Honduras." *Electoral Studies* 15.3 (August): 327–337.

Taylor-Robinson, Michelle M. 2007. "Presidential and Congressional Elections in Honduras, November 2005." *Electoral Studies* 26.2 (June): 521–524.

——— 2010. *Do the Poor Count? Democratic Institutions and Accountability in a Context of Poverty.* University Park, PA: Penn State University Press.

——— 2011. "The Honduran General Elections of 2009," *Electoral Studies*, 30.2 (June): 369–372.

Tilly, Charles. 2004. *Contention and Democracy in Europe, 1650–2000.* New York: Cambridge University Press.

Toft, Monica Duffy. 2010. *Securing the Peace: The Durable Settlement of Civil Wars.* Princeton, NJ: Princeton University Press.

Torres-Rivas, Edelberto. 1993. *History and Society in Central America*. Austin, TX: University of Texas Press.

    1998. "Construyendo la paz y la democracia: el fin del poder contrainsurgente." In *Del autoritarismo a la paz*, eds. Edelberto Torres-Rivas and Gabriel Aguilera. Guatemala City: FLACSO.

Towers, Marcia, and Silvia Borzutzky. 2004. "The Socioeconomic Implications of Dollarization in El Salvador." *Latin American Politics & Society* 46.3 (September): 29–54.

Trudeau, Robert H. 1993. *Guatemalan Politics: The Popular Struggle for Democracy*. Boulder, CO: Lynne Rienner Publishers.

Urcuyo, Constantino. 2003. *Reforma política y gobernabilidad*. San José, Costa Rica: Editorial Juricentro.

Vanden, Harry E., and Gary Prevost. 1993. *Democracy and Socialism in Sandinista Nicaragua*. Boulder, CO: Lynne Rienner Publishers.

Vargas Cullell, Jorge. 2004. "Democracy and the Quality of Democracy: Empirical Findings and Methodological and Theoretical Issues Drawn from the Citizen Audit of the Quality of Democracy in Costa Rica." In *The Quality of Democracy: Theory and Applications*, eds. by Guillermo O'Donnell, Jorge Vargas Cullell, and Osvaldo M. Iazzetta. Notre Dame, Ind.: University of Notre Dame Press.

    2006. "Del estancamiento económico al desarrollo acelerado." In *Tribuna Pública: Una visión de Costa Rica para los próximos 10 años*, ed. Yanancy Noguera Calderón. San José, Costa Rica: El Financiero, 166–86.

    2008. "Costa Rica: una decisión estratégica en tiempos inciertos." *Revista de Ciencia Política* 28.1: 147–169.

Vela, Castañeda, Manolo E. 2007. "Guatemala 1982: El corazón del orden burgués contemporáneo." *Foro Internacional* 47 (April-June): 369–407.

Viales Hurtado, Ronny José. 1998. *Después del enclave: Un estudio de la Región Atlántica Costarricense*. San José, Costa Rica: Editorial de la Universidad de Costa Rica.

Vilas, Carlos M. 1983. "Nicaragua: una transición diferente." *Revista Mexicana de Sociología* 45.3 (July-September): 935–979.

    1986. *The Sandinista Revolution: National Liberation and Social Transformation in Central America*. New York: Monthly Review Press.

    1990a. "Especulaciones sobre una sorpresa: Las elecciones en Nicaragua." *Desarrollo Económico* 30.118 (July-September): 255–276.

    1990b. "La contribución de la política económica y la negociación internacional a la caída del gobierno sandinista." *Revista Mexicana de Sociología* 52.4 (October-December): 329–351.

    1995. *Between Earthquakes and Volcanoes: Market, State, and the Revolutions in Central America*. New York: Monthly Review Press.

    1996. "Prospects for Democratisation in a Post-Revolutionary Setting: Central America." *Journal of Latin American Studies* 28.2 (May): 461–503.

Villagrán Kramer, Francisco. 2004. *Biografía política de Guatemala. Vol. 2, Años de guerra y años de paz*. Guatemala: FLASCO.

    2009. *Biografía política de Guatemala: Los pactos políticos de 1944 a 1970*. Guatemala: Editorial de Ciencias Sociales.

Viterna, Jocelyn S. 2006. "Pulled, Pushed, and Persuaded: Explaining Women's Mobilization into the Salvadoran Guerrilla Army." *American Journal of Sociology* 112.1 (July): 1–45.

Walker, Thomas W. 2003. *Nicaragua: Living in the Shadow of the Eagle*. Boulder, CO: Westview Press.

Walter, Barbara F. 2010. "Conflict Relapse and the Sustainability of Post-Conflict Peace." Background Paper, World Development Report 2011, http://wdr2011. worldbank.org/conflict-relapse-and-sustainability-of-post-conflict-peace, accessed July 18, 2011.

Walter, Knut. 1993. *The Regime of Anastasio Somoza, 1936–1956*. Chapel Hill, NC: University of North Carolina Press.

Wantchekon, Leonard. 2004. "The Paradox of 'Warlord' Democracy: A Theoretical Investigation." *American Political Science Review* 98.1 (February): 17–33.

Weaver, Frederick S. 1994. *Inside the Volcano: The History and Political Economy of Central America*. Boulder, CO: Westview Press.

Webre, Stephen A. 1979. *José Napoleón Duarte and the Christian Democratic Party in San Salvadoran Politics (1960–72)*. Baton Rouge, LA: Louisiana State University Press.

Weeks, John. 1985. *The Economies of Central America*. New York: Holmes & Meier.

Whitfield, Teresa. 1994. *Paying the Price: Ignacio Ellacuría and the Murdered Jesuits of El Salvador*. Philadelphia, PA: Temple University Press.

Wickham-Crowley, Timothy P. 1992. *Guerrillas and Revolution in Latin America: A Comparative Study of Insurgents and Regimes since 1956*. Princeton, NJ: Princeton University Press.

Wilkie, James W. 1974. "Recentralization: The Budgetary Dilemma in the Economic Development of Mexico, Bolivia, and Costa Rica." In *Statistics and National Policy*, ed. James W. Wilkie. Los Angeles, CA: UCLA Latin American Center Publication.

Wilkinson, Daniel. 2002. *Silence on the Mountain: Stories of Terror, Betrayal, and Forgetting in Guatemala*. Boston: Houghton Mifflin.

Williams, Phillip J., and Knut Walter. 1997. *Militarization and Demilitarization in El Salvador's Transition to Democracy*. Pittsburgh, PA: University of Pittsburgh Press.

Williams, Robert G. 1986. *Export Agriculture and the Crisis in Central America*. Chapel Hill, NC: University of North Carolina Press.

   1994. *States and Social Evolution: Coffee and the Rise of National Governments in Central America*. Chapel Hill, NC: University of North Carolina Press.

Williamson, John. 1990. "What Washington Means by Policy Reform." In *Latin American Adjustment: How Much Has Happened?* ed. John Williamson. Washington, DC: Institute for International Economics, 5–20.

Wilson, Bruce M. 1994. "When Social Democrats Choose Neoliberal Economic Policies: The Case of Costa Rica." *Comparative Politics* 26.2 (January): 149–168.

   1998. *Costa Rica: Politics, Economics and Democracy*. Boulder, CO: Lynne Rienner Publishers.

Wilson, Bruce M., and Juan Carlos Rodríguez-Cordero. 2006. "Legal Opportunity Structures and Social Movements: The Effects of Institutional Change on Costa Rican Politics." *Comparative Political Studies* 39.3 (April): 325–351.

Wilson, Bruce M., Juan Carlos Rodríguez-Cordero, and Roger Handberg. 2004. "The Best Schemes… Gang Aft A-Gley: Judicial Reform in Latin America – Evidence from Costa Rica." *Journal of Latin American Studies* 36.3: 507–531.

Winson, Anthony. 1989. *Coffee and Democracy in Modern Costa Rica*. New York: St. Martin's Press.

Wolf, Sonja. 2009. "Subverting Democracy: Elite Rule and the Limits to Political Participation in Post-War El Salvador." *Journal of Latin American Studies* 41.3 (August): 429–465.

Wood, Elisabeth J. 2000. *Forging Democracy from Below: Insurgent Transitions in South Africa and El Salvador*. Cambridge: Cambridge University Press.

    2003. *Insurgent Collective Action and Civil War in El Salvador*. Cambridge: Cambridge University Press.

Woodward, Ralph Lee, Jr. 1999. *Central America: A Nation Divided*. New York: Oxford University Press.

World Bank. 1983. *World Bank Tables. Vol. 2, Social Data*. 3rd ed. Washington, DC: World Bank.

    2001. *World Development Indicators*. Washington, DC: The World Bank, http://data.worldbank.org.libproxy.uncg.edu/data-catalog/world-development-indicators, accessed September 1, 2011.

Yashar, Deborah. 1997. *Demanding Democracy: Reform and Reaction in Costa Rica and Guatemala, 1870's – 1950's*. Stanford, CA: Stanford University Press.

Zamora, Rubén. 1997. "Democratic Transition or Modernization? The Case of El Salvador since 1979." In *Democratic Transitions in Central America*, eds. Jorge I. Dominguez and Marc Lindenberg. Gainesville: University Press of Florida, 165–179.

Zegarra, Luis Felipe, Martha Rodríguez, and Carlos Acevedo. 2007. "Competitiveness and Growth in Latin America: Country Case, El Salvador," unpublished Paper, Inter-American Development Bank.

Zimbalist, Andrew S., and John Weeks. 1991. *Panama at the Crossroads: Economic Development and Political Change in the Twentieth Century*. Berkeley, CA: University of California Press.

Zoco, Edurne. 2006. "Legislators' Positions and Party System Competition in Central America: A Comparative Analysis." *Party Politics* 12.2 (March): 257–280.

Zuvanic, Laura, Mercedes Iacoviello, and Ana Laura Rodríguez Gusta. 2010. "The Weakest Link: The Bureaucracy and Civil Service Systems in Latin America." In *How Democracy Works: Political Institutions, Actors, and Arenas in Latin American Policymaking*, eds. Carlos Scartascini, Ernesto Stein, and Mariano Tommasi. Washington, DC: Inter-American Development Bank, 147–176.

Index